DATE DUE

THE GREAT WAR OF WORDS

The Propaganda of Peer Pressure

THE GREAT WAR
OF WORDS

BRITISH, AMERICAN, AND CANADIAN
PROPAGANDA AND FICTION, 1914-1933

Peter Buitenhuis

UNIVERSITY OF BRITISH COLUMBIA PRESS
VANCOUVER 1987

The Great War of Words: British, American, and Canadian
Propaganda and Fiction, 1914-1933

©The University of British Columbia Press 1987

This book has been published with the help of a grant from the
Canadian Federation for the Humanities, using funds provided
by the Social Sciences and Humanities Research Council of
Canada.

Canadian Cataloguing in Publication Data

Buitenhuis, Peter, 1925-
The Great War of Words

Bibliography: p.
ISBN 0-7748-0270-7

1. World War, 1914-1918—Progaganda.   2. World War, 1914-
1918—Literature and the war.   3. War and literature.   I. Title.
D639.P6B84 1987   940.4'886   C87-091088-4

International Standard Book Number 0-7748-0270-7
Printed in Canada

For Ann, Adrian, Juliana

CONTENTS

ILLUSTRATIONS

PREFACE

The genesis of this study was in some reading I was doing years ago in the late writings of Henry James. I came across a collection of pamphlets that he wrote in support of the Allied cause in the Great War and was surprised at the passion, as well as the loss of that famous detachment and objectivity, that they displayed. I looked further into the subject in the work of James's contemporaries, Edith Wharton, Ford Madox Ford, Owen Wister and others. The story of the younger writers—the so-called Lost Generation—and the war has been told often enough; I had blundered upon an untold story, or one only partly told in scattered sources—the efforts made by many older British, American, and Canadian writers to promote and publicize the efforts made by their nations against the Central Powers in the war. The sequel to this story lies in the fiction that they wrote about the war.

With the generous help of the American Council of Learned Societies, the Social Sciences and Humanities Research Council of Canada, and the President's Research Fund of Simon Fraser University, I pursued my research in the British Library, the Public Record Office, the House of Lords Library, the Imperial War Museum, the Library of Congress, the National Archives of the United States, the Public Archives of Canada, and other archives and libraries.

I had dropped my stone into the great current of history and found that the ripples kept on spreading infinitely outwards. The ripples had to be stopped somewhere, but the problem was to find the logical place. In the end, I decided to focus on those writers from Britain, the United States, and Canada who wrote not only propaganda articles and books, but who also wrote about the war, or their reactions to it, in fictional form. Consequently, I excluded from the study the work of many writers I had looked at as well as many other promising areas of research, particularly of writers in other combatant countries. Even so, of necessity, my work took me into military and political history, private letters and public documents, biography and literary criticism. The most absorbing and difficult problem that I have had to face has been how to organize all this disparate material into a narrative that would make sense and avoid repetition. I could in the end find no ideal form, and, in the present version, I am still uneasily aware of the division between "life" and "works" that haunts this study. The fact remains, however, that many of the writers concerned did lead wartime lives which took them far from the workroom and into public roles and tasks. I had to fit these lives into the complex social, political, and military environments of the time. These environments have had to be recreated, as they gave rise in the first place to the enthusiasm with which many writers greeted the outbreak of war and later to the doubts which assailed them. James M. Barrie articulated these doubts in a short story in which a mother tells her son about to leave for the front: "I wouldn't have had one of you stay at home, though I had a dozen sons. That is, if it is the noble war they all say it is. I'm not clever, Rogie, I have to take it on trust. Surely they wouldn't deceive mothers." The disillusion which became so pervasive after the end of the war is implicit in the doubts of the older writers during the conflict.

Writing a book of this nature leaves the writer with many debts of gratitude. I have space to acknowledge only a few of these. The first is Claude Bissell who first encouraged me to make a book after I had given a lecture on this subject at the University of Toronto. Thanks are due in particular to the staffs of the libraries and archives I have worked in, especially those manning the hub of the great wheel of the British Library, with whom I have had many encounters in person and by mail, and the reference librarians at Simon Fraser. I want to thank Reg and Betty Ford for the quiet place they found for me to work in their farmhouse near Cambridge, and Peter Clarke of St. John's College Cambridge, Tom Vincent of the Royal Military College, Kingston, and Maria Tippett for their advice. I am grateful for the editorial advice of Dona Sturmanis at an early stage of revision, for the canny suggestions of the anonymous readers for the Canadian Federation for the Humanities, and for the insights gained from my students. Barbara Barnett and Anita Mahoney of the Dean of Arts Office of Simon Fraser admirably word-processed successive drafts of the manuscript, and Jane Fredeman, my editor at the UBC Press, has been an unfailing source of help.

For permission to publish from manuscripts I wish to thank the Rt. Hon. Lord Tweedsmuir and the Queen's University Archives, Kingston for the John Buchan material; the National Trust and the House of Lords Record Office for the Rudyard Kipling and Lord Beaverbrook material, Mary de Rachewiltz, Quentin Keynes, New Directions, and Faber & Faber for the Ezra Pound letter first published in AGENDA, Autumn-Winter 1985/86, and A. P. Watt Ltd. for the Arnold Bennett letter in the Beaverbrook archive in the House of Lords Record Office.

For permission to reproduce photographs and other illustrations, I am particularly grateful to the Imperial War Museum, an unfailing source of help. For permission to reprint other illustrations, I am grateful to André Deutsch, Frank Cass & Co. Ltd., Weidenfeld & Nicolson, Borealis Press Ltd., Author's Edition Inc., The Bodley Head, and Princeton University Press.

West Vancouver, B.C.,
April, 1987

INTRODUCTION

In the afternoon of 2 September 1914 a yellow sun poured through the windows onto the great blue conference table of Wellington House in Buckingham Gate, London, the home of the National Health Insurance Commission. The group gathered round the table had not come, however, to discuss insurance. This was a secret meeting of Britain's most famous authors, convened by the head of the commission, C. F. G. Masterman, a cabinet minister who had recently been appointed chief of Britain's war propaganda bureau. The twenty-five authors around the table had gathered to discuss ways and means by which they could contribute to the Allied war effort.

How this group came to be there and what they did in consequence is the main subject of this study, which sets out to show that seldom in recorded history have a nation's writers so unreservedly rallied round a national cause. Why did they join up in such numbers and what were the results?

Although Wells, Conan Doyle, and Kipling had had previsions of the coming of the Great War and the young writers of the *Blast* group anticipated it in the violent imagery of their work, the majority of British writers maintained their belief in a stable, even progressive world until August 1914. They were immeasurably surprised and shocked by the fiery consequences of the shots at Sarajevo and joined in the wave of hysterical patriotism that swept all Europe.

As soon as Masterman had been installed in his hastily improvised propaganda department in Wellington House, he convened the meeting noted above. The writers pledged themselves to England's cause with the same zeal as their younger brethren who rushed to join the armed forces. Traditionally, writers have often been in opposition both to the state and to war. As a contemporary writer, S. K. Ratcliffe, pointed out, there had never been such a demonstration of loyalty as this one of 1914. "They have nearly all undergone a spiritual conversion," he wrote. With the exception of George Bernard Shaw, Bertrand Russell, and a few lesser-known authors, British writers of all persuasions were at this time uncritically united behind the Allied cause.

Pre-war German militarist writings and the invasion of Belgium provided British propaganda writers with their first opportunities to speak out. The

Bryce *Report on Alleged German Outrages*, which was published by Wellington House early in 1915, highlighted the Belgian issue. Lord Bryce's great
moral authority gave this report, based on lurid, largely undocumented and
unsworn evidence, an immense authority among the Allied and neutral
nations. It became the fodder for much of the pamphlet and book material
that British writers turned out.

Authors were soon used in a different capacity. Since Allied military
leaders at the outset of the war prevented newspaper reporters from visiting
the front and exercised a powerful censorship of whatever was published
about the fighting, they starved the public of news. Later on, as a remedy,
Wellington House and the War Office organized visits for a few British
writers, under close supervision, to the war zones. Among them were Bennett,
Conan Doyle, and Kipling. They wrote reports about their experiences
"over there" which were full of praise for the Allied soldiers and their
generals and which carefully concealed the real conditions of trench warfare.
Other writers in uniform, like John Buchan and John Masefield, were also
employed to write accounts of the fighting. Masefield did a whitewash of the
disaster at Gallipoli, and Buchan wrote an account of the Battle of the
Somme which turned that defeat into a glowing victory. Alone among
propagandists, Sir Max Aitken (later Lord Beaverbrook) was able to exert
his power to give some detail and reality to his accounts of the Canadian
forces in Flanders. Official censors suppressed all specifics and colour from
other reports from the front. To counteract this dullness, Conan Doyle,
Kipling, Arthur Machen, and Ian Hay created colourful fantasies in the form
of novels and short stories which emphasized the glorious exploits of the
Allies and the vileness of the Germans.

In fact, British authors soon created a propaganda myth which prevailed,
in spite of all evidence to the contrary, until the end of the war. The Allies,
they wrote, particularly Britain, had no responsibility for starting the war,
which was a product of German militarism and lust for conquest. The
Germans, Huns of ancient memory, left behind them in invaded territories a
trail of ruins, blood and terror, murder and rapine. The French, on the other
hand, the most urbane and civilized people in the history of the world, were
defending their ancient homeland from enslavement. The plucky British
army was filled with loyal and cheerful soldiers, enduring their rounds of
trench duty without complaint. These common soldiers, drawn from all over
the Empire, were led by incisive and efficient generals. All were united in the
belief that it was necessary to fight the war to victory, regardless of cost, so
that German militarism could be finished forever.

Writers promulgated this view of history and current events in countless
newspaper articles, pamphlets, and books that were sponsored by Wellington House. Private publishing houses were used for the publication of books

and pamphlets to make it seem that British propaganda was solely the creation of private citizens.

Authors enshrined this myth in language full of sonorous platitudes and romantic clichés. They spoke of gallant soldiers laying down their lives on the fields of honour, of bronzed warriors running with fixed bayonets at the foe, of victorious assaults on enemy ramparts, of sacrifices not made in vain, even of waves of troops whose numbers melted away in successful attacks, of resolute and resourceful commanders, and of the need for total victory over the bestial Hun. This language distanced and falsified the sordid reality of trench warfare, the inept staff-work and poor leadership, and the wastage of men and material. Wellington House also used its writers to ridicule and discredit the voices of protest, like Shaw and Russell and the statesman Lord Lansdowne, so that any realistic attempt to assess the cost of the war in human terms or any discussions of peace through negotiation were stifled before they could be properly aired.

The United States became the prime target for British propaganda. Wellington House distributed hundreds of thousands of books and pamphlets there. The American press was subtly used to promote the British case, and American authors were enlisted to write for the Allies. Expatriate American authors like Henry James and Edith Wharton were influential catalysts of American opinion, and Theodore Roosevelt became a powerful advocate of American intervention. President Woodrow Wilson's efforts to act as a peacemaker in the conflict were increasingly undermined by growing pro-Allied sentiment, which was also fed by clumsy German propaganda and infringements upon American neutrality. When the United States declared war in 1917, the Committee on Public Information, under the direction of the newspaper publisher George Creel, used many of the stereotypes of British propaganda for its literature, although Creel was unable to employ authors secretly as the British had.

The enthusiasm and loyalty of the British authors were sufficient to carry them through until late 1916 when it became evident that the war was going to be a long-drawn-out and costly affair. Although they continued to write propaganda, some of them began to think sceptically about British leadership and the alleged bestiality of the Germans. Such doubt appears in the ironic fiction of H. G. Wells (*Mr. Britling Sees It Through*), Arnold Bennett (*The Pretty Lady*), John Galsworthy (*Saint's Progress*), and Ford Madox Hueffer (*Zeppelin Nights*). The last named eventually gave up writing propaganda and joined the army.

When the Asquith government fell in December 1916, the direction of British propaganda rapidly changed. Masterman was demoted and literary propaganda was de-emphasized in favour of the press and film. Newspapermen became more evident in the production and direction of propaganda.

From the beginning, propaganda had been a hotbed of political intrigue and infighting as various departments of state fought over its control. Lloyd George hoped that by creating a Ministry of Information under Beaverbrook's direction he could ensure a more unified and effective propaganda machine. However, internal squabbles and conflicts with other departments persisted. Beaverbrook resigned in September 1918, and the ministry came under the direction of Arnold Bennett until the end of hostilities. When the ministry was abolished soon after the end of the war, many of its files were lost or destroyed. The same fate overtook the American Committee on Public Information. This has made accurate research on propaganda in the two countries difficult.

After the war, many of the writers who had been used by the state to write propaganda took a sober second look at their activities. Edith Wharton and the Canadian writer, Beckles Willson, though critical of the Allied conduct of the war, reaffirmed their idealism about the conflict. Many British writers, including Kipling, Wells, Ford, Galsworthy, and Bennett, expressed their disillusionment with many aspects of Allied military and political leadership and raised some bitter questions in their novels and short stories about the conduct and effect of the Great War. They came to believe that in subscribing to and propagating Allied myths, and in some cases in helping direct the propaganda organizations of the state, they had sacrificed the traditional and all-important detachment and integrity of the writer.

These authors' propaganda activities had profound consequences for postwar literature. The younger writers, many of whom had served in the trenches, lost confidence in the authority of the written word and turned against their elders. The reading public no longer had the trust in important authors that they had in the days before the Great War. The prestige and power of authorship dwindled significantly. The old rhetoric based on a widely held set of common values and aspirations collapsed to be replaced by a laconic, ironic, and often understated language. Writers resumed their more traditional role as critics of the state.

1

SIGNS AND PORTENTS OF WAR

We are uncertain whether civilization is about to blossom into flowers, or wither in a tangle of dead leaves and faded gold.
C. F. G. MASTERMAN, 1909

In the early years of the twentieth century, famous writers were often influential in forming or changing public opinion. In Britain, H. G. Wells, Arnold Bennett, Rudyard Kipling, Conan Doyle, John Galsworthy, Bernard Shaw, James M. Barrie, G. K. Chesterton; in America, W. D. Howells, Mark Twain, Henry James, Booth Tarkington, Upton Sinclair; in Canada, Ralph Connor and Charles G. D. Roberts were all names to conjure with. In the heyday of the book, they helped to shape the views and mores of the time. As the power of the mass press increased, their publishers sought authors' views on current affairs.

European international relations began to deteriorate at the end of the nineteenth century. In particular, the fellow-feeling between Britain and Germany dissolved after the Kaiser sent his provocative telegram in support of Paul Kruger, president of the Transvaal, who had repulsed a British attack early in the Boer War. German naval, imperial, and commercial enterprise increasingly intruded on what Britain believed to be her prerogatives. Harold Innes has claimed that in the views advocated in his newspapers, Lord Northcliffe "played an important role in shifting the interest of Great Britain from Germany to France and in policy leading to the First World War."[1] Authors also played their part in creating the atmosphere which led up to L'Entente Cordiale of 1910. Led by James, Anglo-American authors as diverse as Bennett, Kipling, Ford Madox Hueffer, Joseph Conrad, Conan Doyle, Wharton, and Owen Wister expressed their admiration for the life and culture of France.

British authors, too, had played their part in creating the imperial idea which led to increasing strains in international relations. In his Rectorial Address at Glasgow University in 1910, Lord Rosebery painted the ideal of Empire in glowing colours: "Human and yet not wholly human, for the most heedless and the most cynical must see the finger of the Divine. Growing as trees grow, while others slept; fed by the faults of others; reaching with the ripple of resistless tide over tracts and islands and continents, until our little Britain woke up to find herself the foster-mother of nations and the source of united empires."[2] Kipling, Rider Haggard, Conrad, and John Buchan, while more critical and ambiguous about the idea of Empire than Rosebery,[3] helped create in the public mind the image of imperial power and glory. This image was taken by the popular press of Harmsworth and Northcliffe and given mass popularity and appeal.

Such dreams of glory may have been a necessary distraction for many in Edwardian England, in which the rich and well-to-do, comprising about five million people, shared a total income of £830,000,000, while the rest of the population of thirty-eight million shared the remaining £880,000,000 of the national income.[4] H. G. Wells deplored the extravagance of the rich in *Tono-Bungay* (1909), and C. F. G. Masterman, social historian as well as politician, analysed the waste and the maldistribution of wealth in *The Condition of England* (1909). Masterman compared the growth of expenditure by the rich to the competition between Germany and Britain to build ever bigger battleships. Naturally, he was led to speculate on the future: "We are uncertain," he wrote, "whether civilization is about to blossom into flowers, or wither in a tangle of dead leaves and faded gold . . . whether we are about to plunge into a new period of tumult and upheaval or whether a door is to be suddenly opened, revealing unimaginable glories."[5]

Many were convinced of a glorious future, among them David Lloyd George, who in a speech as late as 17 July 1914, declared to an audience of London businessmen that "although you never get a perfectly blue sky in foreign affairs," he was sure that the few clouds were clearing. He was confident that European problems would soon be solved.[6]

Yet, there were clouds on the literary and social horizons that not only foretold the coming disaster but also in subtle ways prepared writers for Armageddon. There was in fact a profound ambivalence in the minds of many authors: they anticipated catastrophe but did not really believe that it could happen—just as many now realize the terrible possibility of nuclear war but would be incredulous if it should suddenly break out.

Writers of the avant-garde showed their anger at the complacencies of Edwardian life and art by advocating a revolutionary programme based on exploding old myths and pieties, cleansing the word from worn-out associations, and recognizing the function and power of the machine. Wyndham Lewis's magazine *Blast* led the way, and Pound's Vorticist movement showed an equal iconoclastic energy. In his article, "Before 1914: Writers and the Threat of War," Bernard Bergonzi cites several writers, including E. M. Forster and G. K. Chesterton,[7] who in one way or another hinted at coming disaster. Science fiction writers were busy with works of doom, including Saki's ingenious *When William Came* (1913) and William Le Queux's *The Invasion of 1910* (1906). In his study, *Voices Prophesying War*, I. F. Clarke shows how Le Queux's work was promoted by Lord Harmsworth in a big publicity campaign in the *Daily Mail*, which serialized it. Harmsworth was backing Lord Roberts's plan to re-arm Britain in the face of Germany's growing military might. Le Queux's sensational account of a Britain invaded and overrun by German troops made the *Daily Mail* a bestseller on the newstands. *The Invasion of 1910* later sold over a million copies in book form.[8]

Sir Arthur Conan Doyle was one of the few major authors of the time who clearly foresaw the impending dangers. Now known mainly for his Sherlock Holmes stories, he was also an expert in military affairs, bluff, and outspoken in his criticism of the government. Ever since the Boer War he had been warning his countrymen about the inadequacies of the armed services. In 1912, he wrote an article called "Great Britain and the Next War," a response to General Friedrich von Bernhardi's book *Germany and the Next War*. Among other things he advocated the immediate building of a channel tunnel in order to supply an expeditionary force from a Britain blockaded by enemy submarines and the creation of a territorial army.[9] In a story called "Danger" (1914), Conan Doyle made more explicit his fear of the submarine menace. In his scenario, Britain is brought to her knees in a few months by a blockade. The seven experts who replied to Conan Doyle's idea in the same issue of *The Strand Magazine* all poured scorn on the story. Some of them even doubted whether a civilized nation would use such a barbarous weapon as unrestricted submarine warfare.

H. G. Wells, too, had in abundance what Henry James called the imagination of disaster. In a series of books and essays beginning in 1898 he saw with a terrible insight the kinds of assault that could be unleashed on the fragile body of man by the growing power of technology. *The War of the Worlds* often anticipated with precision the developments of weapons like poison gas in the Great War. "A Dream of Armageddon" (1911) has an even more explicit picture of a war fought with aircraft as well as artillery and infantry. A character in the story says, "No one could imagine, with all these new inventions, what horror war might bring. I believe most people still believed it would be a matter of bright uniforms and shouting charges and triumphs and flags and bands—in a time when half the world drew its food-supply from regions ten thousand miles away."[10]

In *The World Set Free: A Story of Mankind* (1914), Wells outlines the coming conflict more clearly, though he delays its outbreak to 1956, which he predicts will be the age of atomic energy. France and Britain fight against the central powers, and the battle-line runs entrenched from Holland to the Alps. Paris, London, and Berlin are devastated by atomic bombs dropped by aircraft. Even more remarkable than Wells's prediction of events was his forecast of war psychology. When war breaks out, there is a tremendous outbreak of patriotic fervour and exhilaration after the long expectation of vague dangers. Many feel relief after years of threats and preparation for war.

But the last part of the novel is not convincing. After the devastation of the capital cities of the rest of the world, peace is declared and society is reconstructed under a world government, led by a king who abandons his crown. But this sanguine side of Wells is often overcome by nightmares in these prewar fictions, and the sleeper has to struggle harder with each book to awake from his dream of Armageddon.

The smooth and elegant surface of Edwardian life in the years before 1914 was, after all, an illusion, and the deepening abyss yawned below. Currents of unrest and fear prepared the way to war as George Dangerfield has discerningly pointed out in *The Strange Death of Liberal England*. Dangerfield writes of the profound changes that were going on in British political and social life, most significantly in the rising agitation over women's suffrage. Such agitation was, he contends, the most visible sign of a rising passion and energy in public and private life. There were violent confrontations in Ireland, in which even the British Army practised civil disobedience, storms in Parliament over the question of the power of the Lords, and strident militancy in the trade unions. All the Victorian and Edwardian verities were challenged: the place of women, the class structure, the political order were placed under the most severe strain. It may well be that the writers who represented and defended this order—sometimes aptly known as the Genteel Tradition—were among the most threatened by its imminent collapse. Dangerfield, with a touch of hyperbole sums up: "Given the time, [England] might have destroyed itself—in civil war, in revolution, in the raptures of martyrdom. But it was not given the time. War, when it came, was nothing more than a necessary focus: political furies, sex hatreds, class hatreds were forgotten; with all the simulations of patriotic fervor, the united energy of England hurled itself against Germany."[11] Thus, while the summer of 1914 appeared to be serene, the currents of hysteria ran deep. As Bergonzi observed: "It is not hard to see why the country should have found in the outbreak of war, that apparent thunderbolt from a cloudless sky, something very like an act both of fulfilment and deliverance."

2

THE REASONS WHY:
SETTING UP THE PROPAGANDA MACHINE

It would have been impossible to essay the great task of enlightening foreign countries as to the justice of the Allied cause and the magnitude of the British effort without the co-operation of our leading writers, and we have been most fortunate in receiving that co-operation in full and ungrudged measure.

JOHN BUCHAN TO MRS. HUMPHREY WARD,
DECEMBER 1918

At least since the age of Virgil, poets have occasionally been useful to the state in writing propaganda. In Britain, such service has been sporadic. Milton wrote on behalf of Cromwell's regime, and Wordsworth strove to keep up England's spirits during the latter years of the Napoleonic Wars in his "Sonnets on Liberty." As these extracts from Sonnets XII and XV show, Wordsworth fell easily into the abstractions common to the genre:

> We know the arduous strife, the eternal laws
> To which the triumph of all good is given,
> High sacrifice and labour without praise,
> Even to death:—else wherefore should the eye
> Of man converse with immortality?
>
>   What lawless violence
> A kingdom doth assault, and in the scale
> Of perilous war her weightiest Armies fail.
> Honour is hopeful elevation—whence
> Glory and Triumph.[1]

Tennyson's "The Charge of the Light Brigade" did more to glorify and thus in part to justify the blunders of the Crimean War than any other piece of writing:

Their's not to reason why,
Their's but to do or die.

Rudyard Kipling's staunch defence of Britain's imperial mission led naturally to his propaganda work in South Africa during the Boer War. The
stocky, fiery writer and the lanky pugnacious General Kitchener made a
formidable pair working together, as a contemporary cartoon shows (plate
2). Conan Doyle also volunteered as a propagandist for the British in the
Boer War after writing a series of articles about the conflict for the press. In
1902, he published *The War in South Africa: Its Cause and Conduct*. In
words which echo other famous propaganda pieces, such as Jefferson's
"Declaration of Independence" and Tom Paine's "Common Sense," he
justifies the writing of this apologia: "For some reason, which may be either
arrogance or apathy, the British are very slow to state their case to the
world. . . . In view of the persistent slanders to which our politicians and
our soldiers have been equally exposed, it becomes a duty which we owe our
national honour to lay the facts before the world." He then defends criticized
aspects of British policy such as the concentration camps and farm-burning.
Throughout the war, Conan Doyle asserts, British soldiers, in Lord Roberts's
words, "behaved like gentlemen." The Boers and others have, of course, told
a different story.[2]
Given such rare forays by writers into propaganda, no one could have
foreseen the willingness of novelists, poets, and dramatists to write on behalf
of the government in the Great War. Even a contemporary observer of this
phenomenon expressed surprise. In an article that appeared in *Century
Magazine* in October 1917, called "The English Intellectuals in War-Time,"
S. K. Ratcliffe notes that few could have foreseen how literary craftsmen could
have been drawn in such numbers into the public service, as correspondents,
translators, censors, and pamphleteers in the Foreign Office, the press
bureau, and the propaganda agencies. He also comments that Oxford men
rallied enthusiastically to the cause, while the resisters appeared mostly to
have come from Cambridge. Ratcliffe names Bertrand Russell and G. Lowes-
Dickinson as two of this small band. Ratcliffe observes that in the past
England at war had "always meant an educated public bitterly divided, with
the intellectuals mostly in opposition. Even during the Napoleonic wars
some of the greatest writers of the age were openly admiring of their
country's arch-enemy." In the current war, he believes, apart from the
Cambridge group, Bernard Shaw, and a few others, the rest "have nearly all
undergone a spiritual conversion."[3]
At the outbreak of the Great War, the general confusion caused an abrupt
break in the usual flow of publication and a disruption of royalty and other

Men of different trades and sizes
Here you see before your eyeses;
Lanky sword and stumpy pen,
Doing useful things for men;
When the Empire wants a stitch in her
Send for Kipling and for Kitchener.

Plate 1   Kipling satirized as a propagandist during the Boer War.

payments to writers. The demand for works of the imagination also temporarily slackened. There was thus an economic motive for writers to turn towards propaganda; it paid, and often paid quite well, the writer whose prestige carried weight in public opinion. No doubt, also, the writers were flattered by being asked by the government to lend a hand in the great cause and, for a time at least, leave the isolation of the work-room to identify themselves with the war effort of the nation. Many felt that it was one way in which they could assuage their vague guilt for being too old to serve on the fighting front.

There can be no doubt, however, that patriotic fervour was the chief motivation that caused writers to be carried away by the tide of dedication and ardour that marked England's early war effort. They apparently felt the same sense of escape, of liberation and purification, that was felt and expressed by young soldiers like Rupert Brooke and Julian Grenfell. All the grey complexities and ambiguities of the prewar period fell away, and in the subsequent grand simplification, the Germans became the enemy of whom any barbarism could be believed, the French became the noble saviours of an ancient civilization, and the British and imperial troops became as knights of old, riding out of the west to the succour of a beleaguered ally. James, Wharton, Conrad, Bennett, Wells, Kipling, Conan Doyle, Hueffer, and many others genuinely believed that the cause of civilization itself was at stake in this conflict, which thus justified their greatest and most passionate efforts to help. The rhetoric of romance and of the Victorian genteel tradition lay ready at their hands to express these sentiments.

It is commonplace to note that language conditions response and that culture controls perceptions. It did not require much effort of imagination on the part of these writers to transform the platitudes of the British imperial idea, the worship of French culture, and the dislike of German militarism into a propaganda rhetoric embodying unconscious prejudices and stereotypes. They were willing to believe the worst about the enemy and accepted that worst unhesitatingly when it came in the form of rumours and reports of atrocities. Moreover, the German invasion of Belgium and France broke into a placid dream of peace—a dream which had held sway in Europe for nearly fifty years.

The imagination of these writers invested the events of that summer of 1914 with a vast and apocalyptic importance. Over and over again, writers used the image of the abyss into which the nations of the West seemed to be irrevocably falling. The prewar years were retrospectively transformed into a paradisal state which was succeeded by the fall into that abyss. In a poignant section of her autobiography, *A Backward Glance*, the patrician American author Edith Wharton, who had lived for some years in France, recalled the summer of 1914. "An exceptionally gay season was drawing to its close," she writes. "The air was full of new literary and artistic emotions, and that dust of ideas with which the atmosphere of Paris is always laden sparkled like motes in the sun." Although the incident at Sarajevo struck an ominous note, she proceeded with her plans for a quick dash to Spain and the Balearic Islands before going to England for the summer. But rumours of war made her change her plans while she was still in Spain, and she decided to return to Paris. She travelled through thickening crisis to reach the French capital. "Everything seemed strange, ominous and unreal," she reports, "like the yellow glare which precedes a storm. There were moments when I felt as if I had died, and waked up in an unknown world. And so I had. Two days later war was declared."[4]

Henry James, who had lived in England for nearly forty years, proudly retaining his American citizenship, was surprised and devastated by the outbreak of war. In a well-known letter to Howard Sturgis, written on 5 August 1914, James observes that civilization had been plunged into an abyss of "blood and darkness." What the "treacherous years" had been all along *really* meaning was this descent into war—a situation that is "too tragic for any words."[5] Leon Edel notes that James inscribed in the copy of *Notes on Novelists* he sent to Edmund Gosse shortly after the outbreak of war the phrase "Over the Abyss."[6]

Even Wells, for all his prevision, was overcome by shock and hysteria when war came. He dashed off a letter to George Bernard Shaw: "The Germans are frightfully efficient and will invade us too. . . . We must get out our shot guns and man the hedges and ditches, but it will be the end of civilization."[7] Even before England declared war on Germany, Wells entered the propaganda battle with an article in the *New York Times* with a call to arms: "The defeat of Germany," he writes, "may open the way to disarmament and peace throughout the earth. To those who love peace there can be no other hope in the present conflict than her defeat, the utter discrediting of the German legend—ending it for good and all—of blood and iron, the superstition of Krupp, flag-waving, Teutonic Kiplingism, and all that criminal sham of efficiency that centres in Berlin." Already his words are charged with the moral earnestness which was to sustain him through the whole war. "Never was war so righteous," he goes on, "as is this war against Germany now." He asserts that England has to enter the war at once, otherwise it "will cease to be a country to be proud of and we shall have a dirt bath to escape from."[8]

In the letters and articles of the period, images of apocalypse vied with those of excitement and euphoria. Writers joined eagerly in what the psychohistorian Eric J. Leed has called "the community of August," which affected all the combatant nations.[9] The emotional charge of the time was so strong that it temporarily broke down traditional reserves, class barriers, and regional differences. The young men of the European nations marched off, bands playing, to war. Cheering them on, the civilian populations united behind them with overpowering feelings of national pride. The stage was set for a war which involved civilians as never before in history. So it was imperative that the population should be hardened in their resolve by the publication of war aims, statements of principles, and endeavours to excite their antagonism against the enemy.

But, as L. C. F. Turner has discerningly written in *Origins of the First World War*, "Whatever aims they proclaimed during the conflict, none of the rulers of the Great Powers really knew what they were fighting about in August, 1914."[10] After the Austrian ultimatum to Serbia, events moved so fast, emotions rose so quickly, and the demands of mobilization and railway schedules and the Schlieffen plan to invade through Belgium were so pressing that circumstances overtook the statesmen trying desperately to find a way out of war. All belligerent governments had at once to invent their war aims and to search for ways to justify their actions.

The Allies were fortunate in having a ready-made subject for their propaganda efforts, the German invasion of Belgium. By this move the army commanders hoped to surprise the French, roll up the defence, capture the Channel ports and Paris, and thus quickly end the war. However, once the German army had been stopped short of its goals, a quick victory was no longer possible. The propaganda advantage Germany had provided the Allies by the invasion ensured her ultimate defeat. "Remember Belgium" became the clarion call uniting the Allies and persuading neutral nations to join their cause (plate 2).

Plate 2   Particularly after the publication of the Bryce Report, such posters were very common.

In the cold light of history, it should have been obvious to France and Britain that the German army could drive through a weakly defended Belgium. It was an invasion carried out in defiance of treaties and international law, but it was done with great efficiency and speed and, viewed in the light of earlier and later wars, with comparatively little loss of civilian life or damage to civilian property.

Richard Harding Davis, the dashing, ubiquitous American novelist and war-correspondent, was in Brussels when the German army came through. He stood on the sidewalk lost in wonder as the endless columns swept through the city. "No longer was it regiments of men marching, but something uncanny, inhuman, a force of nature like a landslide, a tidal wave, or lava sweeping down a mountain. It was not of this earth, but mysterious, ghostlike." He marvelled at the splendour of their equipment, their organization, and their precision. "The German army," he continues, "moved into Brussels as smoothly and as compactly as an Empire State Express." Their singing of "Fatherland, my Fatherland" seemed to him like "blows from giant pile-drivers"; their grey columns of infantry and cavalry, their transport wagons and ammunition carts, ambulances and cannon cut Brussels in two "like a river of steel."[11]

The metaphors of this rhetorical piece are significant. Many are drawn from nature—a nature transformed and mechanized, but somehow allied to the inevitable forces of the universe. The metaphor, as Eric J. Leed points out, was a common one at the time, implying a release of pent-up social energies. Davis later went through Louvain shortly after the destruction of much of the city and had ample opportunity to observe the German army of occupation among the Belgian people. He mentions the shootings of some civilians whom the Germans claimed were snipers, but he says nothing about atrocities. The Germans suspended civil rights and seized private property. In retaliation, some civilians took to provocative acts and sniping, and there were arrests and some summary executions. It does not seem, however, that the German treatment of the civilian population was excessively violent. Apparently there were comparatively few unprovoked atrocities.

On the other hand, wild rumours and reports of countless atrocities pervaded the Allied nations. Knowing this, the German government appealed to American journalists in Belgium to clarify the situation. A group of them sent a wire to the Associated Press on 7 September 1914 denying the reports of German atrocities. They wrote: "In spirit we unite in rendering the reports of German atrocities groundless, as far as we are able to. After spending two weeks with and accompanying the troops upward of 100 miles we are unable to report a single instance unprovoked. . . . Refugees with stories of atrocities were unable to supply direct evidence. . . . To the truth of these statements we pledge our professional and personal word." The statement was signed by Irvin S. Cobb of the *Saturday Evening Post*, Roger Lewis of the Associated Press, and four other well-known American journalists.[12]

In the hysteria of the time, this report seems to have had no effect. As Belgian refugees streamed into England, they spread tales of atrocities as apparent eyewitness reports. Very soon the invasion of Belgium became in the popular mind a chronicle of murder, rapine, pillage, arson, and wanton destruction. The image used throughout is unmistakable. In poster and report and appeal, Belgium is the raped and mutilated maiden, left to die. Pent-up sexual fantasies in a Britain just emerging from the Victorian era of restraint seemed to concentrate on her hapless head. The jack-booted and steel-helmeted Germans at one stroke became the ancient Huns, leaving behind them a trail of blood, ruin, and sorrow.

The Liberal government led by Herbert Asquith was, with the notable exceptions of Lord Haldane and Winston Churchill, totally unprepared for the outbreak of war.[13] The German government, on the other hand, had not only anticipated the need for armies and supplies, but also prepared for psychological warfare. There was a German propaganda agency in place in the United States that began to distribute leaflets in many cities and to passengers arriving on transatlantic liners at the outbreak of war.

Lloyd George was told about this activity after an August Sunday luncheon at a golf club (where so many matters of the Asquith government seem to have been decided). He realized at once that German actions had to be countered and that the United States and other neutral nations had to be persuaded to share Britain's view of the war. He turned to his cabinet colleague, C. F. G. Masterman, and said: "Will you look into it, Charlie, and see what can be done."[14] In this casual manner, he launched one of England's most significant war efforts.

Charles Masterman was a brilliant and remarkable individual who has not yet been accorded his proper place in history (plate 3). In 1903 he had been appointed the literary editor of the *Daily Chronicle* and in that capacity had come to know many of England's leading literary men. He attracted many of them as contributors and appointed Hilaire Belloc and John Masefield to his staff. He entered Parliament in 1906 at the age of thirty-one and immediately embarked on a successful career, exciting attention as a prospect for the premiership. Shortly before the war, Prime Minister Asquith appointed him Chancellor of the Duchy of Lancaster. At that time, newly appointed cabinet ministers had to resign their seats in the House of Commons and run for re-election before they could take up their cabinet posts. When he did so, Masterman narrowly lost his seat, and so in February 1915, he had to resign from the government. Before then he had done much of the gruelling work of formulating and putting into effect Britain's first national health insurance scheme. In view of this, he was appointed to head the National Health

Insurance Commission. Although not the most effective politician, he was a fine administrator, a devoted public servant, a successful author, and a widely read man. These qualities made a strong appeal to his long-time friend, Ford Madox Hueffer, who may have used some of these elements of character in Tietjens of *Parade's End*. Late in August 1914, the cabinet sanctioned Masterman's job as head of the War Propaganda Bureau. Because his work was to be kept highly secret, it made sense to place it in Masterman's existing office at Wellington House, Buckingham Gate. In *British Propaganda during the First World War, 1914-1918*, M. L. Sanders and Philip M. Taylor have described in detail how Masterman organized the work there. Wellington House was used as a cover until the Bureau became the Department and later on the Ministry of Information and had to find more spacious quarters.[15]

Plate 3   C. F. G. Masterman.

Plate 4   Sir Gilbert Parker.

Masterman's first instinct was to turn to the writers of England for help. He sent out a call for many of England's major writers to attend a secret meeting. On the afternoon of 2 September 1914, they gathered in the conference room. Around the table sat William Archer, Sir James M. Barrie, Arnold Bennett, A. C. Benson, R. H. Benson, Robert Bridges, Hall Caine, G. K. Chesterton, Sir Arthur Conan Doyle, John Galsworthy, Thomas Hardy, Anthony Hope Hawkins, Maurice Hewlett, W. J. Locke, E. V. Lucas, J. W. Mackail, John Masefield, A. E. W. Mason, Gilbert Murray, Sir Henry Newbolt, Sir Gilbert Parker, Sir Owen Seaman, George Trevelyan, H. G. Wells, Israel Zangwill, and assorted government officials. Rudyard Kipling and Sir Arthur Quiller Couch were unable to come but sent messages offering their services.[16] Even without them it was probably the most important gathering of creative and academic writers ever assembled for an official purpose in the history of English letters.

They were all well-known writers at the time, but the passing years have dimmed the reputation of some of them. William Archer was probably the best-known London drama critic of the period, the man most responsible for introducing the plays of Ibsen to the English stage. A. C. Benson was a famous Eton master, novelist, critic, and biographer of his father, the Arch-bishop of Canterbury. R. H. Benson, another son of the archbishop, became a noted Catholic author and a monsignor as well as a novelist. Robert Bridges was the current poet laureate and also a critic of some note. Sir Hall Caine, former secretary to D. G. Rossetti, wrote a large number of enor-mously popular novels and was perhaps the leading romanticist of the day. Maurice Hewlett, the historical novelist, was best known for his *The Forest Lovers*, but he was also a poet and essayist. W. J. Locke was secretary of the Royal Institute of British Architects and a popular novelist. E. V. Lucas, assistant editor of *Punch*, was the author of many books of satire, humour, and travel and wrote a fine biography of Charles Lamb. J. W. Mackail, classicist and literary critic, was Professor of Poetry at Oxford from 1906 to 1911. Sir Henry Newbolt was popularly known for his patriotic and imperial-istic poems, and he was also a naval historian. Sir Owen Seaman, the editor of *Punch*, was a literary parodist and poet. George Trevelyan was one of the most famous historians of the period, and Israel Zangwill, probably the best-known Zionist of his time, a journalist and dramatist.

Unfortunately, no minutes have survived of that Wellington House meeting, if any were kept. All we have are glimpses from writers' letters and journals; Thomas Hardy recalled in a letter written much later to Anthony Hope "that memorable afternoon in September, 1914, the yellow sun shining in upon our confused deliberations in a melancholy manner that I shall never forget."[17] And Arnold Bennett laconically noted in his diary: "Masterman in the chair. Zangwill talked a great deal too much. The sense was talked by Wells and

Chesterton. Rather disappointed in Gilbert Murray, but I like the look of little R. H. Benson. Masterman directed pretty well, and Claud Schuster and the Foreign Office representative were not bad. Thomas Hardy was all right. Barrie introduced himself to me. Scotch accent; sardonic canniness."[18] Whatever was said, the writers all pledged themselves to assist the war effort in any way they could, and the recruiting parade was over.

It was a remarkable success and began the march of writers to join the government service that continued throughout the war. William Archer, Anthony Hope, Sir Gilbert Parker, G. H. Mair, and Gilbert Murray joined the staff at Wellington House at the outset; Arnold Toynbee, Lewis Namier, John Masefield, John Buchan, Ian Hay, and Hugh Walpole joined later on. Arnold Bennett and H. G. Wells signed up in 1918. Most of the others, wrote propaganda pieces at the direct request of the government. One of those who did not was Thomas Hardy.[19]

All the writers present at the conference readily agreed to the utmost secrecy, and it was not until J. D. Squires published his story of British propaganda in the First World War in 1935 that it became known that many writers had been used by the government. Unfortunately, it is not easy to reconstruct exactly how the writers were used, since most of the records of Wellington House and the successive Department and Ministry of Information were scattered and destroyed at war's end. A commentator on British official propaganda, Ivor Nicholson, wrote in 1931 that an authoritative history of the subject could never be provided because the three men who could have written it, Masterman himself, G. H. Mair, the journalist and literary critic, and Sir James Headlam-Morley of the Foreign Office, were by that time already dead.[20] This is a great pity since this untold story would have been one of the most significant in the multifarious history of the Great War. But from Nicholson's own account, from references to the subject in other books and articles,[21] and from the files of Wellington House and the successive Department and Ministry of Information that were declassified by the Foreign Office (some as late as 1972), at least part of the story can be pieced together. In one of those files released to the Public Record Office in 1972 is a short history of British propaganda during the 1914-18 war made for the Foreign Office by H. O. Lee when it became necessary to re-institute propaganda at the outbreak of the Second World War. Lee related how the existence of a publishing operation at Wellington House was kept secret and how the work was distributed under the imprint of commercial publishing houses.[22]

In a parliamentary enquiry into the activities of Wellington House in November 1917, H. T. Sherringham, in charge of publications, testified that the agency got commercial houses to print their material in England and paid five guineas for the use of their imprint. He added that some authors received royalties for books published and distributed free by Wellington House. During the same enquiry Masterman testified that Wellington House guaranteed the purchase of a number of copies of pamphlets and books from publishers at a previously agreed price. It became clear to the parliamentary committee, somewhat to their surprise, that the books were used for propaganda purposes at home as well as abroad.[23] Some of the publishing houses used most often by Wellington House were Hodder and Stoughton, Methuen, Blackwood and Sons, John Murray, T. Fisher Unwin, Darling and Son, Macmillan, and Thomas Nelson and Sons.

For a time, unofficial organizations also swelled the chorus of Allied propaganda. Cate Haste has described some of them in *Keep the Home Fires Burning*. The first in the field was the Central Committee for National Patriotic Associations, formed in the latter part of August 1914. The prime minister, H. H. Asquith, became the honorary president, and the vice-presidents were the Earl of Rosebery and Arthur Balfour. It organized the efforts of some writers, journalists, and politicians to lecture and write pamphlets upon the causes of the war and to justify England's role in the struggle. The committee organized patriotic clubs and rallies throughout Britain and set up subcommittees for various parts of the Empire and for neutral nations. The central committee co-ordinated the activities of groups such as "The Fight for Right Movement," founded by Sir Francis Younghusband, which numbered in its ranks such writers as Sir Edmund Gosse, John Buchan, Thomas Hardy, Sir Henry Newbolt, and Gilbert Murray. The Oxford Faculty of Modern History organized a group of historians to write pamphlets, published by the university press, which were also distributed by the central committee.[24]

The invasion of Belgium and the consequent flood of refugees into England was a direct cause of the founding of other patriotic and charity organizations, including the Belgian Relief Fund and the National Relief Committee in Belgium. Many of these groups converted the cause of charity into propaganda work. A favourite method of raising money for these funds was to publish literary anthologies selling for high prices to which many noted writers donated articles, poems, or stories.

The Allies and their enemies, the Central Powers, both recognized that the United States, the richest and most powerful of the neutral nations, had the power to tip the balance of the war, and both concentrated their propaganda efforts there. Great Britain had an enormous advantage in this respect from the start since a common heritage and a common language provided a firm ground for persuasion. But there was a large number of German immigrants and descendants in the United States and a strong reservoir of sympathy for that country, especially among the academics, many of whom had received their graduate training in Germany. However, most German propaganda was crude and inept, and it soon alienated potential support.

Even though many people in the United States were predisposed towards the Allied cause, the task of the Allied propagandists called for discretion and subtlety. It was important not to appear to infringe upon American neutrality; it was equally important not to give ammunition to the strong isolationist element, let alone the pro-German groups. For some time, no attempt was made to bring the United States into the war on the side of the Allies. The major goal of British propaganda in the first two years was to maintain a benevolent neutrality on the part of the United States to ensure the availability of loans and the shipment of foodstuffs and, later, war material. The first, and probably the most effective, of the agents in charge of this work was Sir Gilbert Parker, who was appointed in November 1914 and remained in charge until late in 1916. One of his chief assistants was Arnold Toynbee. Parker was a Canadian by birth and a popular romantic novelist by profession. As a young writer, he had travelled extensively in the United States before marrying a rich New Yorker. He then moved to England, where he became domiciled in 1890. Following one of his own major fictional themes, the young man from the provinces made good in the capital of the empire. He was elected to Parliament in 1900 and knighted in 1902 for his services to Canada as a writer. He served as M.P. for Gravesend from 1900 to 1919 (plate 4).[25]

Although his romantic imagination was an undoubted asset for his work as a writer of propaganda, Parker's main task was to ensure proper distribution of propaganda material in the United States. In a secret report to the cabinet dated June 1915, Parker described how he set about the work. He made a careful analysis of American press opinion and of the temper of the universities. Then, with the help of *Who's Who*, he prepared a gigantic, categorized mailing list of people in the professions, the church, the press, and the universities who were in the best position to influence public opinion.[26] By December 1914, Wellington House had received from Parker a complete file on the people to whom propaganda should be sent and some indication of what kind of information they should receive. Parker's own connection with propaganda was concealed. Books and pamphlets were sent out not under the name of Wellington House but ostensibly by "friends" or interested parties to their opposite numbers in the United States. This material, it was claimed in a later enquiry, "fans out . . . in the shape of editorials, reviews, lectures, addresses, speeches, sermons, and so forth to audiences all over the States. . . . It is quite undisputable that it has had a powerful shaping influence upon the American mind in regard to all the issues of the war."[27]

In his part of the report to cabinet, Masterman claimed that Parker had built up an informal organization of thirteen thousand influential people in the United States who were distributing British propaganda. The Carnegie Fund for International Peace, headed by Nicholas Murray Butler, was a particularly useful source of assistance. American presses were also commissioned to publish books and pamphlets from Wellington House, and Parker's lists were made available to them. Parker had excellent working relationships with the senior reporters of the *New York Times* and the *Chicago Daily News*, and he used them for the dissemination of advantageous news and the suppression of bad. British authors, at the instigation of Masterman, had already announced their support of the war in an Authors' Manifesto which appeared in the *New York Times* on 18 September 1914. This was signed by all those present at the Wellington House meeting of 4 September, plus Granville Barker, A. C. Bradley, Laurence Binyon, Rider Haggard, Jerome K. Jerome, Henry Arthur Jones, Eden Philpots, Arthur Pinero, May Sinclair, Sir Gilbert Parker, and others—a total of fifty-four authors. This manifesto was reprinted on a full page of the Sunday supplement of the *New York Times* on 18 October, with the authors' signatures in facsimile—an impressive and apparently spontaneous demonstration of British authors' solidarity (plate 5). Parker followed this up by arranging a series of interviews and articles by prominent authors in the American press. These included Thomas Hardy, who, although he refused to write any propaganda, did consent to an interview, Arthur Conan Doyle, Henry James, Arnold Bennett, H. G. Wells, G. K. Chesterton, George Trevelyan, Mrs. Humphry Ward, and Israel Zangwill.

A considerable number of American professors volunteered to aid British propaganda efforts. The chief of these was Dr. Charles W. Eliot, former president of Harvard, who became one of the most active and zealous in the Allied cause. Other public figures, like Theodore Roosevelt and Joseph Choate, former ambassador to the Court of St. James, were subtly integrated into the British propaganda effort. "In fact," Parker concludes in his secret 1915 report to the cabinet, "we have an organisation extraordinarily widespread in the United States, but which does not know it is an organisation. It is worked entirely by personal association and inspired by voluntary effort, which has grown more enthusiastic and pronounced with the passage of time. . . . Finally, it should be noticed that no attack has been made upon us in any quarter of the United States, and that in the eyes of the American people the quiet and subterranean nature of our work has the appearance of a purely private patriotism and enterprise."[28] Parker recapitulates some of this material in his next report to the cabinet in February 1916 and adds, tantalizingly, "By these and other ways (some of a too confidential nature to be placed on paper) we are endeavouring by every various channel to make the two peoples understand each other's point of view . . . and to stimulate and thank [*sic*] a large body of people upon a course favourable to the Allies."[29]

FAMOUS BRITISH AUTHORS DEFEND ENGLAND'S WAR

Fifty-three of the Best-Known Writers of the Empire Sign a Vigorous Document Saying That Great Britain Could Not Have Refused to Join the War Without Dishonor.

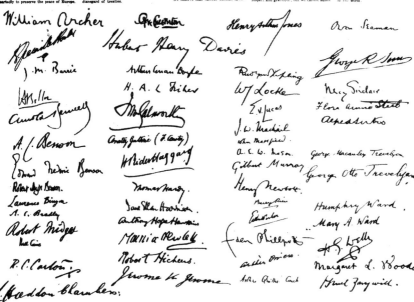

WHO'S WHO AMONG THE SIGNERS

Plate 5   The Authors' Manifesto. *The New York Times.* 18 October 1914.

Given the total lack of preparation for psychological war in Britain, it is remarkable how quickly and effectively the propaganda efforts were organized. Starting from scratch, Masterman had put together an office, engaged staff, and set out the main lines of propaganda production and distribution by the end of 1914. There is no doubt that the main reasons why he was so successful in this complex task was that he had the complete support of the British writing establishment. Without their skills and their quick action, he would have had little to show by the year's end. It is the object of succeeding chapters to show how these skills were put to the task of winning the war.

3

THE PAMPHLET WAR

*The ultimate purpose of this war is propaganda, the destruc-
tion of certain beliefs, and the creation of others. It is to this
propaganda that reasonable men must address themselves.*
H. G. WELLS, 1914

Many of those who wrote propaganda for war were men skilled in bringing
language to a high pitch of emotional effect, such as Rudyard Kipling,
Conan Doyle, Anthony Hope, and Sir Gilbert Parker. They turned initially
to the pamphlet as a means of rapidly disseminating their views. Only a few
voices, most notably Bernard Shaw, challenged them.

The pamphlet, which is usually an ephemeral literary form, had its origins
in Britain in the sixteenth and seventeenth century controversies between
religious sects, and it has often displayed the evangelical fervour and excess
of its origins. Usually published in paper covers, the pamphlet is cheap and
easy to reproduce and simple to distribute. In the confidential *Schedule of
Wellington House Literature* (n.d.: last entry, 26 November 1918)—the only
copy of which appears to be in The Imperial War Museum, London—there
are 1162 items, most of them pamphlets. In addition to persuading the
neutral nations of the virtues and efficiency of the Allies, attacking German
militarism, urging recruitment, and documenting atrocities, pamphlets were
written to counter the arguments of the few men in Britain who tried to
present opposing views of the causes and effects of the war or who wished to
advance the cause of peace through negotiation. Some of the biggest literary
guns in Britain were rolled out to fight battles against the "pro-Prussian
apologists," as they were called.

The evangelical tradition of the pamphlet was often reinforced by a moral
schema drawn directly from John Bunyan's *Pilgrim's Progress*—surely one of
the most influential books of the Great War. In this schema, the British

soldier becomes identified with Christian, the City of Destruction becomes the ruins of devastated towns in Flanders, Apollyon is the German enemy, and the Celestial City, the victory towards which the soldiers strive. Also, in the pamphlets Darwinian evolutionary theory is integrated into the evangelical idea of spiritual progress to form a compelling argument for the liberal march of civilization. In such a schema, the Germans, of course, become identified with beasts far down the evolutionary ladder. Racist ideas of the primitive Hun did not so much contradict as somehow confirm this typology. Another strain of rhetoric was drawn from the school story (the archetype of which was Kipling's *Stalky and Co.*), which had been given mass popular distribution through such organs as the *Boy's Own Paper*. These stories promulgate the code of the public-school devotion to games and the spirit of sportsmanship (which was somehow shared by the other ranks, who had never been to public school). It was axiomatic that God was on the side of the good sportsman.

The Great War propagandist could thus rely on a powerful set of stock responses to his appeals for recruits, to his depiction of the lure of glory, and to his assertion of the need for sacrifice. He could justify his attacks on the Germans with the rationale that they were stopping the march of progress. At the same time, the propagandist could point to the beneficial effects of war which, like sport carried out on a larger scale, would raise the moral tone of society and help reduce the conflict between the classes. The language in which these pamphlets are written, as Paul Fussell has ably shown in Chapter One of *The Great War and Modern Memory*, is elevated, formulaic, and clichéd.[1]

Urged on not only by Wellington House but also by the Foreign Office, the War Office, and the Admiralty and fired with their sense of mission, many novelists rushed into print with pamphlets on all kinds of subjects in support of the war. One writer in the *New Statesman* had the temerity to question the competence of the eminent novelists who set themselves up as authorities on "all matters of Foreign policy and military strategy." Arnold Bennett was quick to respond to this attack. In a letter to the *New Statesman* on 1 September 1914, he says: "As war is preeminently an affair of human nature, a triumph of instinct over reason, it seems to me not improper that serious novelists (who are supposed to know a little about human nature and to be able to observe accurately and to write) should be permitted to express themselves concerning the phenomenon of a nation at war without being insulted."[2]

So fortified, the novelists wrote on an astonishing number of military and civilian concerns on behalf of the government. At the outset and until conscription became law, recruiting was a paramount concern for propagandists. Although he was fifty-five when war began, Conan Doyle volunteered for the

Plate 6   Private Arthur Conan Doyle as "Ole Bill," 1914.

army and, when rejected, served for the rest of the war as a private in a volunteer defence force which he himself helped to organize (plate 6). His son Kingsley and his brother Innes both joined the army, and Conan Doyle envied them their opportunity. However, he was equally effective in his own way. A strong opponent of conscription, his aim was to encourage enough volunteers to continue to fill the needs of the army. To that end he wrote one of the earliest recruiting pamphlets, *To Arms!*, which has a stirring preface by F. E. Smith. Patriotism, honour, and sacrifice are the keynotes of *To Arms!* "Happy the man," he argues fervently, "who can die with the thought that in this greatest crisis of all he had served his country to the uttermost, but who could bear the thoughts of him who lives with the memory that he had shirked his duty and failed his country at the moment of her need?"[3] *To*

Plate 7   The most Famous Recruiting Poster of the War—perhaps inspired by
Conan Doyle's *To Arms!*

Arms! concludes with a rhetorical flourish reminiscent of William Blake's
"Jerusalem." Neutrals and other nations might doubt the issue of the war, he
writes, "But fear not, for our sword will not be broken, nor shall it ever drop
from our hands until this matter is for ever in order." It still seemed appropriate in 1914 to write of swords. *To Arms!* was the verbal equivalent of the
famous poster showing Kitchener pointing at the viewer, which bears the
legend, "Your Country Needs You!" (plate 7).

   Another writer who was ready when the time came was Kipling. Ever
since the Boer War, his name had become in the minds of many synonymous
with militarism and imperialism. In 1906 he had become the foremost
advocate of General Roberts's National Defence League, which had as its
chief aims a rearmed Britain and a national military service scheme. From

then up to the outbreak of the European war, Kipling was a caustic critic of the Liberal party's pacifism, as well as of its imperial and Ulster policies. To many writers of the liberal or socialist persuasion, Kipling was no better than the German Junkers—an advocate of a hierarchical society at the apex of which was a military caste. In his defence, it can be pointed out that Kipling detected the menace of rising German might and imperial ambitions before most of his contemporaries and was simply trying to prepare England for the inevitable struggle.

When it came, he gave his services unstintingly. To his immense pride, his seventeen-year-old son, John, gained a commission in the crack Irish Guards. John's death at the Battle of Loos in October 1915 was, however, a blow from which he never fully recovered, and it changed the current of his propaganda work and his fiction. Until that time, he was an indefatigable speechmaker at recruiting rallies and writer of recruiting pamphlets. The War Office sent him out on a tour of the camps of the New Army, which was being rapidly trained in late 1914 and early 1915 to replace the first British Expeditionary Force, the regular army detachment decimated in the early months of the war.[4] This tour resulted in pamphlets on infantry, gunners, Canadians, Indian troops, and Territorials all collected under the title *The New Army*. The Canadians came in for particular praise. They were camped on Salisbury Plain, and Kipling goes into raptures over their bearing: "They were all supple, free and intelligent; and they moved with a lift and a drive that made one sing for joy." He came across a group of Engineer privates digging a trench in the chalk. All were former undergraduates at McGill, Queen's, or Toronto. "They were young," Kipling writes, "they were beautifully fit, and they were all truly thankful that they lived in these high days." He goes on at length on this note and concludes: "It was their rigid humility that impressed one as most significant—and, perhaps, most menacing for such as may have to deal with this vanguard of an armed Nation."[5] The Indian troops brought out a burst of nostalgia in Kipling, but it is obvious, even from his breezily optimistic account, that they were having a grim time in the English winter. Needless to say, however, they were all devoted and disciplined. Kipling sums up their sentiments: "It is a war of *our Raj*—'everybody's war,' as they say in the bazaars."[6]

The New Army is about an ideal, not a real, fighting force. All the men are brave, fit, disciplined, loyal, and true. There is no grousing, no crime. All the troops are itching to get at the enemy. Kipling ignored the real conditions, the inevitable frustrations, sicknesses, annoyances, eruptions that all men, especially new recruits, endure in training. He wanted to see this war as a crusade and so managed to endow every soldier and sailor whom he saw with his own spirit. Their only differences lay in their accents: cockney, Scots, West Country, Canadian. The inevitable lesson that he drew from all this was

"The Real Question" with which the pamphlet concludes: "What will be the position in years to come of the young man who has deliberately elected to outcast himself from this all-embracing brotherhood? What of his family and, above all, what of his descendants, when the books have been closed and the last balance struck of sacrifice and sorrow throughout every hamlet, village, parish, suburb, city, shire, district, province, and Dominion throughout the Empire?"[7] The reader is reminded of the poster "Daddy, what did YOU do in the Great War?" (plate 8).

Plate 8   The appeal to conscience—the theme of Kipling's recruiting speeches and pamphlets.

But as the real war continued, Belgian refugees poured into England, and the air was thick with reports and rumours about merciless atrocities. In order to investigate and establish the truth or falsehood of these rumours, the government set up the Committee to Investigate Alleged German Outrages under the distinguished chairmanship of Lord Bryce in December 1914. Bryce was a man of impeccable credentials, a noted historian, author of *The American Commonwealth*, former ambassador to the United States, a man whose word was trusted at home and abroad. He headed a committee of eminent historians and lawyers who set to work to take testimony from witnesses and to read reports. The committee's report was published by Wellington House early in 1915. It is presented in the format and with the apparent precision of a legal brief. In his book on propaganda, H. C. Peterson quotes the Wellington House press report that observes, with triumph, "Even in papers hostile to the Allies, there is not the slightest attempt to impugn the correctness of the facts alleged. Lord Bryce's prestige in America put scepticism out of the question, and many leading articles begin on this note."

The Bryce Report continued to exert a powerful influence on American public opinion throughout the war. And yet the report, as is now generally acknowledged, was largely a tissue of invention, unsubstantiated observations by unnamed witnesses, and second-hand eyewitness reports, depending far more on imagination than any other factor. The witnesses were not put on oath, nor were they cross-examined. There was no attempt at scholarly investigation and evaluation of this evidence. Most significant of all, the documents and testimony of the witnesses disappeared from British records at the end of the war, so it has been impossible to make a subsequent check of the evidence.

The Bryce Report was the origin of most of the gruesome stories which had such effective currency throughout the war—stories of mass rapes, the spitting of babies on bayonets, the cutting off of children's hands and women's breasts, hostage murders, Germans excreting on private possessions, and so on. How could an honourable man like Lord Bryce affix his signature to such a document? Probably the American journalist, Frederick Palmer, came as close to an explanation as is possible: "We may look back on Lord Bryce's signing of the atrocity report as a venerable statesman's 'bit' when in the name of its beloved dead and wounded, every combatant nation realised that its future was to be signed and sealed by victory or defeat at arms." With some justice, H. C. Peterson calls the Bryce Report "one of the worst atrocities of the war."[8]

When the Bryce Report came out, Wellington House was getting into top gear. It provided material for many books, pamphlets, posters, and cartoons. The great Dutch cartoonist, Louis Raemakers, often cited the Bryce Report as the source for his extraordinarily powerful and repellent cartoons about the German invasion of Belgium. Some of these cartoons were published and circulated by Wellington House (plates 9 and 10). The Bryce Report remained the source of atrocity propaganda for the British throughout the war and was extensively used by American propaganda writers and cartoonists when the United States entered the fray.

When a German submarine torpedoed the *Lusitania* coincidentally with the publication of the Bryce Report, there was more fuel for the flames of righteous indignation. As the Germans claimed at the time, the ship was carrying contraband, including rifles and munitions, and therefore could be regarded as a legitimate target. The British strongly denied the German

Plate 9   The caption to this Raemaker's cartoon entitled "The Shields of Rosselaere" read: "It is proved that the rules and usages of war were broken, particularly by the using of civilians, including women and children, as a shield for advancing forces exposed to fire."

allegations and played up to the full the slaughter of over a thousand civilian passengers, including 124 Americans. Wellington House exploited the horrors of this marine disaster in articles, photographs, and pamphlets which had a profound effect on opinion in the United States.[9]

Another *cause celèbre* was the case of Edith Cavell. Nurse Cavell was head of the nursing staff in a hospital in Brussels when the city was captured by the Germans. Early in 1915 she was arrested by the occupation forces on a charge of helping Allied prisoners escape across the Dutch frontier. She pleaded guilty and was sentenced to death by a German tribunal. Technically, the Germans had some justification for the sentence, but Allied and neutral opinion was greatly stirred up by the case. The American minister to

Plate 10   Raemaker's Cartoon "We find many well-established cases of the slaughter of . . . quite small children."   *Report of Lord Bryce's Committee on German Atrocities.*

Belgium, Brand Whitlock, appealed for clemency. But it was denied, and Nurse Cavell was executed by firing squad on 11 October 1915. Wellington House fully exploited this German blunder and made a martyr of Edith Cavell in many pamplets.

Wellington House staff were encouraged to write propaganda along with the authors they enlisted. Masterman himself set an example by writing several pamphlets, mostly of a political nature, and Sir Gilbert Parker, in addition to his duties as director of the American operation, turned out an astonishing volume.

Parker's first piece came in response to a question that was often being asked in the United States during the early part of 1915, after the stalemate in Flanders had set in: "What Is the Matter with England?" His pamphlet took that title and supplied the answer that there was nothing wrong with the nation. He rapidly explains away the drink problem, strikes in the mines, alleged ammunition shortages, and the lack of action at sea. In the second part of the pamphlet, Parker goes on the offensive. Britain is confident of victory, he writes. Income tax has been doubled without complaint; the second war loan has been fully suscribed. The German navy is powerless: "a fleet of submarines, steadily diminishing, and preying upon a peaceful merchant marine was taking its place." Britain, he concludes, "will save European civilization and the civilization of the world from that German Kultur which makes of Belgium a charnel-house and an abattoir."[10]

One of his favourite themes is the moral benefits to be derived from the war. In *Is England Apathetic?*, Sir Gilbert comments on how class tensions had been reduced by the war—even his own footman had been immeasurably improved by his army service. The discipline of the Army is a joy to all: "All were playing the game of the eleven." He concludes cheerily, "We can truthfully say that the nation has profited by its sacrifice, its effort, its bereavement. National character has been made, inherent goodness has become magnificent merit."[11]

Parker also wrote a long propaganda book aimed specifically at Americans: *The World in the Crucible: An Account of the Origins and Conduct of the Great War*, published in New York in 1915 and widely distributed in the United States. It fully exploits the Bryce Report and attacks the German militarists. Its racism can be deduced from this remark: "Physically and morally . . . the German of today is the same as the German who strove and conquered in the Teutoberger forest in the dawn of our era. He is still in most essentials a primitive man."[12] Parker carefully and cleverly builds up a case to show Germany's disregard for the Monroe doctrine of American hegemony in the Western hemisphere and her consequent interference in the Caribbean, and Central and South America. He also endeavours to establish that the German government deliberately cultivated disloyalty to the United States among the German-American population and that that group and the German Press Bureau had tried to influence elections and issues. From there he moves to demonstrating German perfidy in the Balkans and her violation of all the Geneva and Hague conventions and winds up with a catalogue of Belgian atrocities. *The World in a Crucible* is a book that has all the apparatus of scholarship and the appearance of objectivity, but on examination it proves to be full of large and unsubstantiated claims and inferences.

Another assiduous Wellington House pamphleteer was Anthony Hope Hawkins, who had achieved his fame under the name of Anthony Hope, author of *The Prisoner of Zenda* and many other romances. It was surprising that Hawkins found time for writing since he was kept busy at Wellington House as the chief literary adviser. Masterman described his role during a secret parliamentary enquiry: "Every book that we wish to produce on every subject, or any book that any of us think might be useful for our purposes is submitted to Mr. Hawkins. They number many thousands. Mr. Hawkins reads the book and writes, often at some length, his review of that book, with a view to seeing whether it is desirable to use it for publicity purposes."[13]

Four of Hawkins' pamphlets were published under the title *The New (German) Testament, Some Texts and a Commentary*. All of them attack the favourite whipping boy of British propaganda, General Friedrich von Bernhardi. The first essay ironically assesses Bernhardi's work under the title of "The Blessings of — War." The second, aimed at the American market, makes useful capital out of Bernhardi's view that Britain blundered in not aiding the South in the American Civil War. The fourth and final round with Bernhardi takes up his view that the German people were unfit to govern themselves and that they must be ruled by "Powerful Personalities." What is sauce for the conquering gander, Hawkins argues, must also be sauce for the conquered goose. States falling to German militarism must expect to have Powerful Personalities put over them. The conquered would live then in some Alice-in-Wonderland political faith in which "everything is turned upside down, all values changed, all standards reversed."[14]

From reading Hawkins and many other British pamphleteers, one would be led to believe that Bernhardi was a major influence on German policy before the war. He was instead a heaven-sent opportunity for Allied propagandists. His worth to them was out of all proportion to his influence on German policy. As Gerhard Ritter points out in his authoritative study of German militarism, *The Sword and the Sceptre: The Problem of Militarism in Germany*, the Bernhardi book always quoted by Allied propagandists, *Germany and the Next War*, is in fact extracted from a much longer treatise on war by a publisher with his eye on the main chance. Ritter points out that this little book was "a best seller and a political disaster." He adds, "The fact that it was written in a purely private capacity by an outsider not in the General Staff's good graces was completely ignored. It was cited on count-less occasions as proof that the German General Staff was systematically fostering war, with the aim of making Germany the principal power in the world." His work never had the gospel effect that the Allies claimed. Helmuth von Moltke, Chief of the German General Staff, called Bernhardi "a perfect dreamer."[15]

Anthony Hope Hawkins wrote little propaganda after 1915, although he did edit a Wellington House publication destined for South America on the question "Which do you consider to be the worst act committed in the War?" Jumping aboard this bandwagon of German atrocities were H. G. Wells, Rudyard Kipling, G. K. Chesterton, John Masefield, and Hawkins himself. For the most part, however, he stuck to his desk, doing the less glamorous jobs of the professional propagandist, serving a succession of masters through-out the war. He got his reward of a knighthood in the New Year's Honours' List of 1919.

But the output of Wellington House was not received without dissent. Its most famous opponent in the pamphlet war was George Bernard Shaw, in 1914 at the peak of his playwriting career. He was skilled in controversy and had honed a polemical style that could cut the arguments of opponents to pieces with a few well-chosen epigrams (plate 11). As early as 11 August 1914, he contributed an article on the war to the London *Daily News and Leader* in which he states that, in spite of all the current patriotic and pugnacious slogans, the war was really about the Balance of Power. England's first business was to fight the war, for its power at the peace table depended upon the country's part in the conflict.

Shaw's old opponent, H. G. Wells, would have no part of this view (plate 12). In a reply, Wells asserts that this was a war to end Prussian militarism. With the naiveté characteristic of much of his writing about the war, Wells goes on: "This war is not going to end in diplomacy. It is going to end diplomacy."[16]

Before replying to Wells, Shaw decided to try to get to the root of the whole question. He collected all the diplomatic documents he could, retired to a hotel at Torquay on the south shore of England, sunned himself on the roof, and wrote his famous essay, *Common Sense about the War*.

The pamphlet, which was first published as a supplement to the *New Statesman* on 14 November, and the next day in the *New York Times*, is written in Shaw's most aggressively buccaneering manner. It is full of the hyperbole, paradox, and perversity that fill his plays and which partly mask the common sense and underlying seriousness. Shaw wrote it to be read: to amuse, anger, and instruct, and surely not to be swallowed whole. It is clear from the responses that most of his readers were in no mood to be amused. The most famous remark in the essay—that the soldiers at the front on both

Plate 11   George Bernard Shaw. Hilaire Belloc and G. K. Chesterton in a moment of bonhomie.

Plate 12   H. G. Wells.

sides should shoot their officers and return home—was greeted with a howl
of rage. The readers did not think about the premise of the remark—that the
English officer caste was the same as the Prussian Junkers—but treated it as
an incitement to riot.

Shaw did not exempt British writers from responsibility for the war.
Rudyard Kipling in his imperialist and jingoistic poems, H. G. Wells in his
War in the Air, and General Chesney's *The Battle of Dorking* had done as
much as the Navy League and the Dreadnought builders to encourage
England to go to war. "Therefore let us have no more nonsense," he says,
"about the Prussian Wolf and the British Lamb."[17]

He blames the Liberal foreign secretary, Sir Edward Grey, for missing
opportunities to prevent the war, insinuating that he was really a tool of "the
British Junkers" who were opposed to peaceful solutions. Shaw claims that
the invasion of Belgium was a mere excuse for Britain to go to war, since the
treaty of 1839 guaranteeing Belgian neutrality was obsolete. He pours scorn
on British hypocrisy over the destruction of Rheims, which was the inevitable
result of the destructive power of modern artillery, and denigrates the
evidence of German atrocities in Belgium. In dwelling on the consequences
of the outbreak of war, Shaw foresees serious threats to civil liberties and
suspensions of the democratic process.

Common Sense seems designed to outrage most people in one or more of
its details. Its main strength lay in its blistering attacks on British hypocrisy.
Shaw wanted to set the record straight. He thought that if he could explain
the reasons for the war and make the British understand their responsibility
for it, there would be less cant in the propaganda and more clarity about war
aims. This attitude constituted an attack on the whole official position as it
had developed until the end of 1914 with its emphasis on the innocence of
the British and the barbarism of the Hun. Shaw wanted to introduce something saner: an understanding of the nature of war and the need to end it
quickly, without emotional maundering. This would, in his eyes, lay the
ground for a just peace, without vindictiveness towards the defeated and
with the hope of a strong international order.

Common Sense about the War was repeatedly reprinted and provoked
many responses. Arnold Bennett issued a rebuttal in the *New York Times* on
18 November 1914, just three days after it had appeared in that journal. He
attacked Shaw where he was particularly vulnerable: on the issue of British
Junkerism. There was really little evidence that Britain had anything remotely
resembling the warlike German caste. He asserted that Shaw had made a
travesty out of the diplomatic documents of the war. Significantly, however,
he does not address Shaw's specific point that Grey could have prevented the
war by openly standing by Russia and France. Bennett also catches another
weak point in Shaw's argument: it was true that the treaty guaranteeing

Belgian neutrality was ratified as long ago as 1839; but that fact did not render it obsolete.

By attacking Shaw where he was vulnerable, Bennett was able to avoid some of the central issues: British hypocrisy, threats to civil liberties, and allegations about atrocities. Bennett concentrated on generalities: Shaw's flippancy, perversity, and "downright inexactitude."[18] In fact, throughout the debate on *Common Sense about the War*, the main issues were repeatedly dodged, for Shaw's shotgun tactics allowed everyone to attack peripheral questions.

Shaw's incurable wittiness made him the butt of all the patriotic solemnity and humbug with which propaganda was conducted. There is, too, at the heart of *Common Sense* an ambivalence which made Shaw a much less dangerous opponent to the conduct of the war than he might have been — and which kept him out of serious trouble with the authorities. Perhaps he had another value. An American of German descent, George Sylvester Viereck, claimed after the war that Shaw had been part of British propaganda. "The British cleverly exploited the fact that you were permitted to speak with so much candour," he observes in a letter to Shaw. "This induced the illusion that freedom of speech was safe only in England."[19] This may well have been the case.

None of the other articles that Shaw wrote about the war had the same impact. They were usually ambivalent, although always witty. For example, as if to prove his loyalty, he contributed an article to the *New York Times* on 16 April 1916 called "The German Case against Germany," in which he lists all the ways in which that country condemned itself: in corruption in government, authoritarianism in the universities, duelling, autocratic rule by the Kaiser, and military blundering. Then, three months later, in another article in the same journal, he turned round and had another crack at Sir Edward Grey to even the score. He accuses Grey of continuing to misunderstand the nature of the war. The issue, which apparently Grey failed to see, was to guarantee the independence of Belgium so that a peace could be negotiated. Shaw believes that none of the belligerent powers was in a position to make that guarantee. Accordingly, he asks President Wilson to intervene in the war by guaranteeing the independence of Belgium and thus providing both sides with the opportunity to stop fighting without losing face. Shaw could see no end to the stalemate in Flanders otherwise, with both sides "feeding in fresh drafts of men to be slaughtered every year."[20] Ironically, this appeal was published eight days after the Battle of the Somme had begun.

Though hardly a popular position in England at the time, it was far from the swashbuckling statements that Shaw had made earlier. Shaw had become more respectable, so much so that, in January 1917, an imaginative staff

officer at British G.H.Q. organized an invitation from Sir Douglas Haig for
him to visit the front. It was a safe move, since each tour of the kind was
cleverly conducted to give the guest a taste of danger and a view of only the
right things. In any event, anything written about visits to the front had to be
submitted to the censor. Shaw was no less susceptible to flattery than other
men. He was given the royal treatment at Haig's chateau, fed a carefully
prepared vegetarian lunch, and granted a long interview with the field
marshall. An M.P. complained later that a man who had recommended
soldiers shoot their officers should not have been allowed such a privilege. A
War Office spokesman replied, "I have always found that when any gentleman visits the front in France he comes back with a salient desire to help the
British Army and is proud of it." As Stanley Weintraub comments, "If
permitting the nation's leading gadfly to have a first-hand look at the war had
been a calculated risk, it had paid off."[21] Shaw was thenceforth a fairly
effectively chained tiger. His real feelings about the war are to be found in
Heartbreak House, which he wrote during 1916 and '17. In that play, he
poignantly expresses the plight of a civilization which, through its aimless
and trivial materialism, comes to look upon the war as a glorious release
from boredom and exults in the coming of violence. It is tantamount to
Shaw's confession of the uselessness of all his rational arguments. Ironically
enough, Shaw himself had felt such exaltation during a Zeppelin raid that he
found himself hoping for another. His emotion is echoed in the play by Mrs.
Hushabye's exclamation after a raid: "But what a glorious experience. I hope
they'll come again."

4

MASTERMAN'S MOTLEY ARMY— AND TWO OUTSIDERS

I wish Germany did not exist, and I hope that it will not exist much longer. Burke said that you cannot indict a whole nation. But you can.

FORD MADOX HUEFFER, 1915

The most remarkable aspect of Masterman's pamphlet and book campaign was his ability to recruit to his ranks writers of all political, social, and intellectual persuasions. He thus ensured that a variety of views favourable to the war could be expressed and at the same time reinforced the case that England's writers were united behind the war effort as they had declared in the Authors' Manifesto of 18 September 1914. This chapter includes a survey of the early propaganda work of six of these writers and of two men who did not work with Masterman, one a pacifist and the other a belligerent supporter of the war.

The six writers are Arnold Bennett, the great chronicler of working class and bourgeois life in the Midlands, G. K. Chesterton, the master of paradox, Hilaire Belloc, the conservative Roman Catholic, John Galsworthy, chronicler of the lives of the rich and also a social critic, Ford Madox Hueffer, maverick Tory and leader of the avant-garde, and Gilbert Murray, the famous classical scholar and former pacifist. Sir Edmund Gosse, the biographer and critic, did not write for Wellington House, and his propaganda work had a hysterical tone that Masterman would surely not have permitted. Against the array of yea-sayers stood Bertrand Russell, mathematician, philosopher, and resolute opponent of the war.

Chesterton was not only a skilled novelist, but also a fine journalist, humourist, and mythologist. In his two early propaganda pamphlets, *The Barbarism in Berlin* and the ironically titled *The Crimes of England*, he shows all of his myth-making skill. In both booklets the reader is treated to

Plate 13   St. George and the Dragon: England versus Germany. Ironically,
German propagandists also used the icon, with roles reversed.

some typically quirky Chestertonian history and the evocation of the spirits of St. George and Joan of Arc leading the knighthood of Christendom against the Prussian barbarians. After the defeat of the German thrust on Paris in 1914, Chesterton, in his chivalric vision of the war in the west, sonorously writes: "The empire of blood and iron rolled slowly back towards the darkness of the northern forests; and the great nations of the West went forward; where side by side as after a long lovers' quarrel, went the ensigns of St. Denys and St. George."[1] Chesterton would doubtless have produced much more propaganda for Masterman had he not been stricken by a long illness that curtailed his work in 1915 and early 1916.

Hilaire Belloc was born in France, and, though he became a British subject in 1902, he remained a passionate francophile and had a close and detailed knowledge of the terrain over which the fighting in France took place. When the journal *Land and Water* was established in order to deal almost exclusively with war matters, Belloc became the military correspondent. He turned out weekly reports on the fighting which were later periodically issued in book form. These reports were not only jaunty but sunny; his estimates of German casualties were invariably inflated, and his prophecies of future developments wildly optimistic.

In a rare moment of frankness, he defended the government's policy of concealing the truth from the public in time of war. "It is . . . wise," he says, "to keep the mass of people in ignorance of disasters that may be immediately repaired, or of follies or even vices in government which may be repressed before they become dangerous."[2] The trouble with this policy was that it could all too easily lead to a permanent suppression of news of disasters and follies. A letter that Belloc wrote to Chesterton on 12 December 1917 reveals how far Belloc was prepared to go to suppress the truth: "It is sometimes necessary to lie damnably in the interests of the nation . . . it wasn't only numbers that lost us Cambrai; it was very bad staff work on the south side. Things like that oughtn't to happen."[3] But events like Cambrai, and worse disasters, went on happening in large part because Belloc and the other propagandists continued to lie about them. Throughout 1916, Belloc was one of the most vociferous voices against peace negotiations. He went on proclaiming British triumphs and calling for total victory.

By no means all of Belloc's readers believed his propaganda. In 1915 someone published a notebook entitled *What I Know about the War* by Blare Hilloc. On opening it, the reader finds only blank pages. Even Northcliffe's *Daily Mail* published an article condemning what the writer called "Belloc's Fables." Undaunted, Belloc continued to write his weekly column and to turn out propaganda books, obviously finding enough readers to make these publishing ventures worthwhile.

Though his enthusiasm for the war was as fervent as anyone else's, the workman-like and practical Arnold Bennett also needed money at the outbreak of war since revenues from his novels and plays dropped off (plate 14). He soon became one of Masterman's most productive and effective writers. In the course of the war, he wrote no fewer than three hundred propaganda articles. His wide acquaintance in the London literary world brought him in touch with the whole spectrum of opinion about the war. He was even asked if he would edit Shaw's *Common Sense about the War* for book publication. He indignantly refused. His agent, J. B. Pinker, also kept him up on the gossip. He heard how Henry James was often closeted with the American ambassador, Walter Hines Page, and how James's pro-Allied emotions and his frustrations with American neutrality often brought him to the weeping point. Bennett's service as director of the left-wing journal *The New Statesman* brought him in contact with the pacifists. At the same time, he was an active member of several war charities' committees.

His first major propaganda effort was published in the *Saturday Evening Post* on 17 October 1914 and called "Liberty: A Statement of the British Case." Wellington House rapidly brought out an expanded version of this article in book form before the end of 1914, following its usual practice of using a commercial publisher to conceal its official origin. The book was richly set up and bound even though it was only fifty-eight pages in length. In a letter to his American publisher, George Doran, Bennett confided that he had written the pamphlet because he feared that "pacifist and financial influences" in the United States and England might "force a peace too soon." If common sense prevailed, he thought that "Germany's activities in the war department" could be finished "for at least fifty years." "You know that I am not a Kiplingian patriot," he continues, "but rather the reverse; nevertheless I have the greatest confidence in the handling of affairs here and in the general spirit of the nation I have been really surprised."[4]

Liberty is a characteristic tract of the time, devoted largely to proving that the war was the culmination of an extended German plot, with the usual ritual references to Bismarck and General Bernhardi. A section specifically aimed at American opinion deals with a memorandum by General von Edlesheim on how to defeat the United States: "Thus in New York, the new City Hall, the Metropolitan Museum, and the Pennsylvania Railway Station, not to mention the Metropolitan Tower, would go the way of Louvain, while New York business men would gather in Wall Street humbly to hand over the dollars amid the delightful strains of 'The Watch on the Rhine' and the applause of Professor Munsterburg."[5] Bennett's major concern is to attack Germany's conception of war, a conception "which added all the resources of science to the thievishness and the sanguinary cruelty of primeval man." Germany has changed the meaning of war. "She began the vast altercation

Plate 14   Arnold Bennett.

Plate 15   John Galsworthy.

Plate 16   Ford Madox Hueffer, 1915.

Plate 17   Bertrand Russell.

by a cynical and overwhelming wickedness garnished with the most nauseating hypocrisy." She has broken all the Hague conventions, flouted treaties, and committed a long list of atrocities. A description of some of these outrages takes up most of the rest of his space. Bennett concludes by stating that the German military caste planned to conquer the earth and institute slavery. "For," argues Bennett, with curious logic, "under the German ideal every male citizen is a private soldier, and every private soldier is an abject slave." We won't have it, declares Bennett roundly. "It is for liberty we are fighting. We have lived in alarm, and liberty has been jeopardized, too long."[6]

Most of these charges against Germany are not completely false. But Bennett's strategy was to ignore all the problems that the country faced before the war, to whitewash the policies of the Allies, to blacken German acts, exaggerate her atrocities, and distort her objectives.

Others who participated in the war of words were less certain about the adversaries. An imaginatively compassionate man, John Galsworthy felt loathing and abhorrence for the war, which took him quite by surprise. Although his only propaganda work so far had been on behalf of dumb animals, he felt duty-bound to volunteer his services after the writers' meeting at Wellington House; he resolved to give whatever he made from such work to war charities (plate 15).

A letter written by Arnold Bennett to Masterman on 17 March 1916 reveals how Wellington House continued to direct the propaganda efforts of their writers. "All my work," Bennett writes, "and all the work of John Galsworthy which appears in the United States is handled by our agent, Mr. James B. Pinker. . . . Mr. Pinker has placed for me considerably over £2000 worth of stuff as to the war in the best journalistic mediums, and the greater part of this stuff has been written at the suggestion of either yourself or G. H. Mair."[7] The letter was a plea to Masterman to save one of Pinker's staff from being "combed out" for war service. Masterman intervened and kept the man from being conscripted.

As S. K. Ratcliffe pointed out in 1917, the war "transformed John Galsworthy out of recognition." On the basis of his former career, it seemed inevitable that he would become a dissident, yet, as Ratcliffe went on: "He lined himself up with the multitude of his countrymen; he can write expositions of the war policy or exhortations to America which appear without incongruity in the popular prints. . . . But—and here is the odd contradiction—in his propagandist writing he reveals himself as a typical Englishman of the class to which in his novels and plays he has offered a merciless and persistent challenge."[8]

Galsworthy's propaganda pieces, through Pinker's efforts, were widely published in the United States, in the *New York Times*, the *Tribune*, *Scribner's* and *The Literary Digest* as well as in British and European papers and magazines. Galsworthy later collected some of these works and published them in two volumes, *A Sheaf* and *Another Sheaf*. Typically, Galsworthy wrapped up his propaganda in titles with strong overtones of peace and harvest.

Galsworthy's propaganda tends to be more independent and humane than that of most of his fellow writers. He attacks those who think of the war as a cleanser, the notion of the glory of war, and the Christians who call on God to support the Allies. There is little glory for him in the battles in Flanders, only a sense that the war was a long nightmare from which there would be no quick awakening. On the other hand, Galsworthy fully supports the prosecution of the war to victory and calls to his aid the usual clichés about the German military machine and the British "playing the game." France he depicts in an article as a "Woman with a caress in your eyes, and your floating robe; with mystery in your clear woman's smile . . . Great and touching comrade! Clear invincible France!"[9]

Many of Galsworthy's propaganda pieces are pleas for help for wounded and disabled soldiers for whom he did a great deal of work, for the fight against poverty and social injustice after the war, and for support for a league of nations. His was on the whole a voice of sanity and moderation amid a din of exaggeration.

The same could hardly be said of the propaganda of Ford Madox Hueffer, one of Masterman's closest friends in the literary world (plate 16). In the summer of 1913, Mr. and Mrs. Masterman, Hueffer, and Hueffer's mistress, Violet Hunt, had made a tour of Germany. Hunt's and Hueffer's affair was then the scandal of London. They uninhibitedly carried on together even though Hueffer was still married. The scandal was exacerbated by the lawsuit that Mrs. Hueffer brought against Ford and Violet after he claimed that he had obtained a divorce in Germany. No doubt Ford and Violet made a colourful, even fantastic, couple, strange companions for a junior minister of the government and his wife. They travelled up the Rhine, through Bavaria, Metz, and Treves, and then spent some time at Spa. Hueffer later alleged that on this trip, on 2 August 1913, Masterman said: " 'By this date next year we shall be at war with Germany.' " The reason was that Germany was bankrupt. "As for me," Hueffer claimed, "I screamed with laughter." In a public speech at a dinner of one of the City Corporations not long before, Hueffer had said that nothing would ever make the German people go to war. He said to Masterman as late as 3 August 1914, " 'The German troops will never cross the Belgian frontier. . . . Never. . . . Never. . . . Never.' "[10]

In her biography of her husband, Lucy Masterman denies that Masterman made any such prediction. It seems that Hueffer was seeking some retroactive support for the wild stories about German bankruptcy that he narrated in his propaganda books. Mrs. Masterman also denies the story that Hueffer and Violet Hunt circulated that the entire party had been shadowed during the trip by the German secret service in the mistaken belief that the Mastermans were the Winston Churchills. As she points out, there was no resemblance between the two couples.[11]

Hueffer published his first reactions to the war in *The Outlook*, a journal of current affairs. In the 8 August 1914 issue he writes, "I should feel no triumph in a German victory over France. I think I should cut my throat if the German fleet destroyed the British fleet; I should mildly like France to get back the Rhineland. . . . I hate to hear people talk of the overbearingness of Austria and the like. Why Austria—and the German Empire too—are at Death's door—are fighting for national existence against a gigantic Slav confederacy." He goes on to berate all the combatant nations for their lack of chivalry in their expressions of nationalism and to blame the democratic governments for misleading their populations. "For the present war as I see it," he concludes, "is simply a product of the indefinite, mysterious, and subterranean forces of groups of shady financiers working their wills upon the ignorant, the credulous, the easily swayed electorate."[12]

In an article of 15 August Hueffer predicted that the war would go on for eight years and argued that the proper expression of the situation should be left in the hands of Rudyard Kipling. But by 29 August he was deploring the intemperate language used by his fellow writers about the war, "I do wish that, so far as this country is concerned, this war could be fought in terms of 'the gallant enemy.' For I confess that when, as I have to do, many times a day, I read or hear that the chief sovereign of the confederacy opposed to us is a mad dog, I am rendered more miserable than I can express." This was too much for the editor of *The Outlook*, who firmly dissociated himself from such views in a footnote. "Gallant is as gallant does," he comments. "The English may be pardoned for not appreciating German 'gallantry' as displayed in Belgium and the North Sea."[13]

When Masterman asked him to write a propaganda book for Wellington House, Hueffer marched to the beat of a very different drummer. His messy personal affairs had left him very short of money, so he was grateful for the commission. In the resulting book, *When Blood Is Their Argument*, there are no more pleas for gallantry and moderation. The full-fledged propagandist took over. He wrote the book, as he did many others, rapidly and carelessly, employing as an assistant Richard Aldington, the impecunious imagist poet. Aldington later repaid the debt by mercilessly caricaturing Ford as Herr Shobbe in *Death of a Hero*.

Hueffer begins with an all-out attack on German scholarship and language, which he calls "the enemy of the European humanities"[14] and goes on to condemn German literature, art, and music. Since 1870, he claims, there has been no German art of any quality. He then argues that Germany was on the brink of bankruptcy before the war. He follows this by an attack on the whole German education system, which had spread the rot of Prussian culture throughout the world. As a counter to this system, Ford advances the ideal of the English public school, with its emphasis on amateurism, not only in sport but in all branches of life's effort. It is a curious spectacle to see this writer, who had spent much of his time before the war advocating professionalism in literature, demanding amateurism in the arts as well as everything else. In writing a book which condemned a whole culture, Hueffer was in effect advocating a doctrine of total war.

Hueffer's second propaganda book, *Between St. Dennis and St. George: A Sketch of Three Cultures* was written in part to counter Bernard Shaw's pamphlet *Common Sense about the War*. He calls the pamphlet an exercise in "sheer intellectual dishonesty." For good measure Hueffer attaches an appendix to his book in which he attacks all the noted pacifist intellectuals, including H.N. Brailsford, Fenner Brockway, Norman Angell, and Bertrand Russell, whom he lumps together under the label "pro-Prussian apologists."[15]

Between St. Dennis and St. George has a claim to be the most interesting propaganda book of the war because it employs the fictional technique that Hueffer and Joseph Conrad had perfected in their earlier collaboration, which they called *progression d'éffet*. The narrative moves in an impressionistic and apparently disconnected anecdotal manner as in *The Good Soldier*, but it is carefully centered on the theme of comparing the three cultures of France, England, and Germany, always at the expense of the third.

It begins with a scene in which Hueffer is campaigning in the peaceful countryside around Berwick-on-Tweed in a by-election against Sir Edward Grey. It proceeds through a disquisition on golf-clubs, suitcases, and an obscure assassination at a place called Sarajevo, to a celebration of a society almost entirely free from violence. All this time, the chapter ends, Germany had been arming against England. "I wish Germany did not exist," Hueffer concludes, "and I hope that it will not exist much longer. Burke said that you cannot indict a whole nation. But you can."[16]

Next he makes another attack on the German language, on the "incredibly filthy" corruption of German politics, and on the obscenities of German journalism. Then he launches into his praise of French culture. "For in the whole world," runs a typical statement, "it is only France that incontestably matters."[17] For Hueffer the essence of French achievement can be summed up in the word style. This was his justification for his ten-page attempt to translate the first sentence of Flaubert's *Un Coeur Simple*. Why all this effort? "I can only answer," writes Hueffer, "that the exact use of words seems to me the most important thing in the world. We are in the end governed so much more by words than by deeds."[18] This remark seems ironic when it is set against the verbal excesses of *Between St. Dennis and St. George.*

The book concludes with a celebration of those English counties closest to France, Kent and Sussex, and with a special invocation to Henry James. Hueffer's intent here is to celebrate the romance culture that England shares with France. It is part of a racist argument in which the inflated virtues of France and England are pitted against the exaggerated vices of Prussia.

Even given that Hueffer needed the money Masterman's assignments offered, it is hard to justify the line he took in them. In the preface to *When Blood Is Their Argument*, he states forthrightly that he wrote against Prussianism "with a hatred inspired by a cruel and cold indignation."[19] Thomas Moser believes that Hueffer's chauvinism at this time came out of his passionate need to claim his English identity and reject the German part of his heritage.[20] But he was too proud to change his German name while the war lasted, and he did not become Ford Madox Ford until 1919.

Whatever Hueffer's private reasons for his professed hatred of things German, there were others less quick to anger who joined the propagandists. Surely the most unlikely of all the recruits to the ranks of Wellington House was the Oxford classical scholar and poet, Gilbert Murray. As a close associate of Bertrand Russell before the war, he had long been an advocate of peace, and as late as July 1914, he had been one of the signers of Russell's protest against Britain's involvement in the coming war. But, by his own account, Grey's speech in the House of Commons on 3 August 1914 turned Murray round, and he became an enthusiastic supporter. He quickly wrote a pamphlet published in the Oxford Series in August 1914, called "Thoughts on the War." This, like many of his propaganda pieces, was later published in the collection *Faith, War, and Policy* (1918).

"Thoughts on the War" contains some remarks so unexpectedly bloodthirsty that the reader can only assume that Murray had been swept up by the massive current of war hysteria. "For my part," he writes, "I find that I do desperately desire to hear of German dreadnoughts sunk in the North Sea. . . . When I see that 20,000 Germans have been killed in such-and-such engagement, and next day that it was only 2,000, I am sorry."[21] And yet, Murray feels that he can go on from that statement without contradiction to write that there must be no hatred of Germany. Britain, he believes, must fight the war without thoughts of revenge or aggrandisement and go to the peace table determined to establish a new concert of Europe.

Some of the reasons for Gilbert Murray's turnaround from the peace to the war party are given in his long defence, *The Foreign Policy of Edward Grey*, a 127-page pamphlet published by the Oxford Press in 1915. It was specifically designed to answer the attacks on Grey by H.N. Brailsford and Bertrand Russell. In the opening pages of the pamphlet, Murray confesses that up to 1914 he had not seriously believed that Germany was unalterably aggressive, but that the government there, as in England, was in the hands of the wiser part of the nation. "I have derided all scares," he goes on, "and loathed . . . all scaremongers and breeders of hatred. I have believed (as I still believe) that many persons now in newspaper offices might be more profitably housed in lunatic asylums. And I also felt that although I could not tell exactly what the Government ought to do, they surely could produce good relations between Great Britain and Germany if only they had the determination and the will. And now I see that on a large part of this question—by no means the whole of it—I was wrong, and a large number of the people whom I honour most were wrong."[22]

Murray also explains how he came to feel that Germany was courting war and summarizes the peace-seeking foreign policy of Sir Edward Grey. As Bertrand Russell points out in a rejoinder, this whitewash of British foreign policy makes Germany completely responsible for beginning the war. Such an assumption of moral superiority could lead all too easily to a demand for total victory over the forces of evil and a refusal to consider the question of peace negotiations.

Murray soon became the most effective propagandist against the peace movement. In his best-known pamphlet, *How Can War Ever Be Right?*, he attacks all the pacifists' arguments. Even without Germany's violation of Belgian neutrality, he claims, it would have been necessary to go to war against her growing hegemony in Europe. After some detailed arguments against the pacifists' justifications of non-aggression, he makes grand claims for the moral benefits of the current war: it brings out qualities of heroism, self-sacrifice, and endurance in the people. "This is the inward triumph," he writes, "which lies at the heart of the great tragedy."[23]

Murray continued his argument for the moral benefits of war in an address called "The Evil and the Good of War" to the National Congress of Free Churches in October 1915. After deploring the growth of hatred caused by the war—particularly among the Germans—he says: "How these people have ever induced themselves to commit the crimes in Belgium which are attested by Lord Bryce's commission, or even to organize the flood of calculated mendacity that they pour out day by day . . . all this passes one's imagination."[24] The English, he asserts self-righteously, were incapable of such things.

The benefits accruing from the war were, he thought, clear. The relations between classes had improved; the relationships between the Allied nations had also improved. In addition, people had learned to think and feel in a more profound and primitive way. This last was reflected in the way people spoke and wrote—"the language of romance and melodrama has now become true." Honour, patriotism, dying for England, King and Country, these words and phrases were no longer broken fragments of the past but living expressions of the heroic age in which the nation was now living. England is "a community in which one man dies for his brother. . . . It is for us that these men are dying, for us the women, the old men, and the rejected men."[25]

By such arguments as these, Gilbert Murray spoke and wrote his way through the war. At the request of Wellington House, he lectured extensively in Britain and in Scandinavia, and he also wrote propaganda when he was asked. Masterman's successor, John Buchan, enlisted him to serve as the president of an informal Anglo-American society and often pressed him to write for and give interviews to the American press. In addition, Murray showed an amazing timidity in his other work. To maintain his classical interests he decided to produce *The Trojan Women*. But before doing so, he wrote to ask Buchan's permission to proceed. Buchan replied somewhat ironically: "I do not see any reason why 'The Trojan Women' should not be produced at Birmingham. The audience who will attend the Repertory Theatre is not likely to be driven into pacifist fury by Euripides."[26]

On the other side, most men whose consciences dictated that they had to protest against the war, like Bertrand Russell, found themselves caught in a cruel dilemma (plate 17). In his *Autobiography*, Russell speaks of himself as one "tortured by patriotism." The early successes of the German army were horrible to him. "I desired the defeat of Germany as ardently as any retired colonel. Love of England is very nearly the strongest emotion I possess, and in appearing to set it aside for the moment, I was making a very difficult renunciation." It became all the more difficult when he found that many of his friends who had desired neutrality for Britain became warriors overnight when their country declared war. Gilbert Murray, he notes with amazement, "went out of his way to write about the wickedness of the Germans, and the superhuman virtue of Sir Edward Grey." Russell knew that Belgium would inevitably be involved if war came, and he "had not supposed important publicists so frivolous as to be ignorant on this vital matter." What surprised him even more was that "anticipation of carnage was delightful to something like ninety per cent of the population."[27]

So with a passionate conviction unusual in this apostle of reason, Russell felt called upon by God to protest the war. "As a lover of truth," he writes, "the national propaganda of the belligerent nations sickened me. As a lover of civilization, the return to barbarism appalled me." Nightmares of death, chaos, and disillusion haunted his sleep.

Those few in sympathy with Russell, including Philip Morrell and some other M.P.'s, began meeting in Morrell's house in Bedford Square. These meetings led to the founding of the pacifist group, the Union of Democratic Control. Russell soon found that other outlets for his pacifist activities were denied him. Massingham, the editor of the *Nation*, turned round on the war as soon as it began and refused Russell's articles. But he did print a letter on 15 August 1914 in which Russell protests against Britain's share in the anticipated destruction of Germany. Russell deplores the blood lust of the British and the atavistic national greed and hatred fostered by governments, the press, and the upper class as a distraction from social discontent. He also blames the armament makers, the influence of the "foul literature of glory," and the slanted textbooks of history. In particular, he blames the government for not revealing the secret agreements made with the French, and Sir Edward Grey for his evasions in diplomacy. The editor attached a note to the article dissociating himself from these sentiments.[28]

Even at Trinity College, Cambridge, his colleagues had begun to treat him with coolness, especially after the sinking of the *Lusitania*. Since so few undergraduates were in residence, Russell had time for pamphlet writing, and he contributed a stream of articles to the *Atlantic Monthly*, many of which upset the Foreign Office. He also wrote a reply to Gilbert Murray's long defence of Grey, called *The Policy of the Entente, 1904-1914*. Using the same documents as Murray, Russell ridicules the notion that Grey had been the Angel of Peace in his time. He is especially hard on Grey's refusal to promise neutrality if Germany, on her part, guaranteed both the integrity of France and the neutrality of Belgium.

In the spring of 1915, Lady Ottoline Morrell brought about a meeting between Russell and D. H. Lawrence at one of her famous houseparties at Garsington in Oxfordshire. At first the two men got along famously and planned together a series of lectures on religion, politics, morality, marriage, the state, and war. But after Lawrence had made some insulting and intemperate comments on a draft that Russell sent him, it became clear that the opposed temperaments of the two ruled out any possibility of collaboration. In spite of their common loathing for the war, they soon became sworn enemies. Nevertheless, Russell went ahead with the lectures, which were given early in 1916 and published later in the year under the title *Principles of Social Reconstruction*. The reader can understand Lawrence's anger about the draft for the book is for the most part unsatisfyingly abstract.[29]

One chapter, however, "War as an Institution," incisively conveys Russell's thinking at the time. He blames German envy and English pride for causing the outbreak of the war. It would have been wisest for the two nations to have set about concluding peace as soon as the stalemate in the West set in. Failing such a settlement, the ultimate solution to militarism would be a parliament of nations with power to alter the distribution of territory. He claims the monotony of office and family life caused the ennui which led to release in war and invokes William James's idea of the "Moral Equivalent of War" for a partial solution. Beyond that, there should be a system which gave men more control over their own lives as the syndicalists advised as a means of institutionalizing conflicts within the political system. Another necessity was to eliminate the idea of the glamour of war from education, to play down nationalism, and to work towards an international peacekeeping force.

In the same year, 1916, Russell published a collection of the articles that had appeared in various journals in Britain and America, *Justice in War-time*. The most eloquent and important piece in the collection is "An Appeal to the Intellectuals in War-time." It is in effect a plea to intellectuals not to allow themselves to be used by the state for propaganda purposes. "In modern times" he begins, "philosophers, professors, and intellectuals gener-ally undertake willingly to provide their respective governments with those ingenious distortions and those subtle untruths by which it is made to appear that all good is on one side and all wickedness on the other."[30] He exempts Bernard Shaw and Romain Rolland from this charge and pleads with other men of learning to act like them and seek out the truth and the falsehood on their own and the enemy's side. "Allegiance to country," he claims, "has swept away allegiance to truth."[31] As an example, Russell adduces atrocity literature. Russian and German atrocities had no doubt occurred, but he thinks that instances had been far less numerous and less unnatural than was universally believed. At the root of the problem was man's fundamentally irrational belief that the victory of one's own side was of "enormous and indubitable importance, and even of such importance as to outweigh all the evils involved in prolonging the war." And yet, he continues, for all its vastness, the war is trivial. "No great principle is at stake," he writes, "no great human purpose is involved on either side. The supposed ideal ends for which it is being fought are merely part of the myth." The spectacle of the nations fighting was like that of a meaningless battle between two dogs in the street. What a shabby cause for intellectuals to lend themselves to!

The release of the aggressive instinct was, he says, linked closely to the sexual drive. One symptom was the exaltation of much of the male population. Russell foresaw that as the war continued there would be an increasing passion, so that finally "a weak and relaxed dissipation" would succeed its terrible concentration.[32] In the course of this debasement, all the power of science would be called upon to supply engines of destruction. Scientists also had to remember their higher duty to mankind before they too were swept into the passion for destruction. So Russell, with a devastating accu-racy in foretelling the course of the war and subsequent peace, called on his fellow intellectuals to withdraw their complicity in the growing nightmare. But he was a Canute commanding the tide to stop rising. The vast majority of his fellow writers were sunk to their necks in the passions and propaganda of their countries.

In another essay, "War and Non-Resistance," Russell takes his philosophy to its logical extreme. He advocates a national non-resistance to aggressors.

Let the enemy invade if they want to. Afterwards, there will be passive resistance to the conquerors until the attempt to impose a foreign domination fails. Such conduct would be the way-stage to world government. In this essay, Russell's reason had turned into a wide-eyed utopianism that had almost no relevance to contemporary realities. It is as if in his intellectual isolation and his passion for peace, his common sense had been submerged. He seemed to realize this himself, for he subsequently gave up writing long philosophical and political articles about the war and wrote only short pieces for pacifist organs.

No doubt Bertrand Russell's social position as an heir to an earldom and fellow of Trinity gave him a relative immunity that could be claimed by few of his fellow pacifists. The official propagandists alternately ignored and ridiculed him. In the end, Russell had to court prosecution and imprisonment to earn publicity for his cause. By that time, late in the war, he had no audience. These voices in the wilderness, as is traditionally the case, remained in the Great War, still, small, and largely unheard.

A more typical and widely shared response to the outbreak of war than Russell's came from the critic, biographer, and librarian of the House of Lords, Sir Edmund Gosse, who was not at the Wellington House conference. Nor was he asked, it seems, to write for the government. His propaganda essays appear to have been voluntary, an outbreak of pent-up emotion. They were published in *The Edinburgh Review* from the outbreak of war on and collected in 1916 under the title *Inter Arma*. The title was drawn from the latin tag "Silent leges inter arma"—ignore the law in time of war—an appropriate enough theme for Gosse's purpose.

In the preface to the book, he states that the British people were, on 4 August 1914, "awakened out of an opiate dream of prosperity and peace."[33] For him it was a time of tremendous excitement and eagerness about preparations for battle. Literature, he claims, must equal this excitement in order to be read at all. The first essay, "War and Literature," develops this train of thought in a manic way. "War is the great scavenger of thought," he proclaims. "It is the sovereign disinfectant, and its red stream of blood is the Condy's Fluid that cleans out the stagnant pools and clotted channels of the intellect. . . . We have awakened from an opium-dream of comfort, of ease, of that miserable poltroonery of 'the sheltered life.' Our wish for indulgence of every sort, our laxity of manners, our wretched sensitiveness to personal inconvenience, these are suddenly lifted before us in their true guise as the spectres of national decay; and we have risen from the lethargy of our dilettantism to lay them, before it is too late, by the flashing of the unsheathed sword."[34]

In this remarkable passage, there is the clearest expression of the relief, the gratification even, that the coming of war brought to this representative of a generation of men-of-letters who were not, as Gosse says unctuously later on, to "enjoy the signal privilege, the envied consecration, of actual fighting."[35] Underneath his metaphorical language is a sense of the prewar English mind as a kind of sewer or opium den, stinking with rottenness and decay. The euphemistic sword is also the scalpel which is to cut the decay from the fleshly body of England and restore it to psychic health.

Subsequently, Gosse goes into an hysterical appraisal of the probable effect of war on arts and letters. He foresees the end of "current literature" for the duration. "There can be no aftermath," he asserts. "We can aspire to no renewal. The book which does not deal directly and crudely with the complexities of warfare and the various branches of strategy will, from Christmas onwards, not be published at all."[36] Gosse envisages that all the writers of Britain will dress in the uniform of militarists and propagandists and say farewell to *belles lettres* until the end of the war. It was a bloodthirsty and apocalyptic vision of the mission of literature in wartime, and it went far beyond what Wellington House was prepared to propagate.

"War and Literature" was published in October 1914. In a pendant to it, written six months later, after the first flush of hysteria had abated, Gosse is forced to revise his estimate of the role of literature in wartime. He swings round to a defence of the continuation of scholarship and scientific enquiry. With complacency, he surveys the revival of current literature and recondite learning. After the first interruption, it is wonderful, he thinks, how little the intellectual energy of the nation had been disrupted by the war. The *Journal of Egyptian Archaeology* goes on enlightening its readers and "while gentlemen of the highest erudition continue to discuss *Newton's Hypothesis of Ether and Gravitation* I feel I should demean myself if I despaired of the Republic."[37]

The business of literature, then, proceeds as usual. Gosse looks forward to a continuation of the old order in which "all that is genuine in literature and science would hold its own." He goes on, "No brilliant effusion of talent, no exploration of new fields, can be expected or even desired. But we shall, I think, see a quiet persistence along the old paths, and we may be comforted by the disappearance of a good deal that was merely histrionic. The self-advertising mountebank will grow tired of standing on his head in the empty market-place." Just to make sure that nobody misses the meaning of his last remark, Gosse firmly crosses his t's. "We may very probably hear," he predicts, "very little more about 'vorticists,' " as the Ezra Pound-Wyndham Lewis group were known. On the other hand, the branches of learning that do not depend upon self-advertising would be less affected than Gosse had earlier believed when first the war had "thundered upon us out of a sky which seemed to be, relatively, not less blue than usual."[38]

In Gosse's revised opinion, then, part of the sewage to be cleaned out of

Britain's system by the war is avant-garde literature and other self-advertising trash. The old order would assert itself when the palmy days of peace arrived, and it would not be annoyed again by the *arrivistes* of the arts.

As William C. Wees has shown in *Vorticism and the English Avant-Garde*, the young artists that Gosse alluded to posed a real threat to the establishment writers since they were determined to destroy that outmoded world of the Edwardians, by violent means if necessary. *Blast* was their manifesto; vorticism and futurism — international movements — their methods. These movements threatened the relevance and prestige of the older artists. The coming of war fulfilled the futurists' expectations but almost destroyed their movement. Gosse must have received some satisfaction from the fact that *Blast* ceased publication in 1915; many of the writers and artists, being young, joined up or were conscripted. The older artists once again took over the leadership of public opinion. In their propaganda as well as in their art they held firm to traditional values. These were quite congruent with the antiquated military tenets of the cavalry officers who were in senior positions both in the War Office and at the front.

With the old order reaffirmed, Gosse could proceed to the usual business of the propagandist, the ritualistic essays on "The Unity of France," "The Desecration of French Monuments," "War Poetry in France," and, something to show that the neutrals really *were* on our side, "The Neutrality of Sweden." These essays contain little that is different from what has been examined already. The effect of the entire volume, however, is to leave the reader amazed that Gosse could believe that a cataclysm as huge as the World War could leave things so little changed, that it could act even as a means of returning literature and learning back to the good old days of Edward or Victoria when skies were eternally blue.

5

PROPAGANDA IN AMERICA

*Untried men who live at ease will do well to remember that
there is a certain sublimity even in Milton's defeated archangel,
but none whatever in the spirits who kept neutral, who remained
at peace, and dared side neither with hell nor with heaven.*
THEODORE ROOSEVELT, 1915

The most complex and important role of Wellington House was to persuade the people of the United States that the Allied cause was just and necessary, that they should support the Allied war effort and, ultimately, that they should join the war on the Allied side.

To do this required delicate handling. Most Americans were taken completely unaware by the war, and few had any interest in European affairs. The words of George Washington's farewell address had in the late nineteenth century become an abiding principle of American foreign policy: "Europe," he said, "has a set of primary interests, which to us have none, or a very remote relation.—Hence she must be engaged in frequent controversies, the causes of which are essentially foreign to our concerns." Public opinion on the war soon developed into three distinct positions: the overwhelming mass of opinion was neutral or indifferent, the second position was pro-Ally, and the third, pro-German. President Wilson himself was sympathetic to the Allied cause, but he was the leader of a party which became bitterly divided over the issue. The secretary of state, William Jennings Bryan, was determinedly neutral. Wilson also wanted to appear neutral as long as possible in order to keep his hands free to act as a peacemaker. The population of the midwest and most people in the far west were isolationist, as was much of the labour movement, which had strong ties with the pacifist Socialist Party.

It was the task of British propaganda to turn isolationist and neutral sentiment around in favour of the Allies, to combat the German propaganda effort, and at the same time strenuously to avoid appearing to influence

American policy. Nothing could more strengthen the neutral or pro-German elements than obvious attempts by the British government to work upon American opinion. It was of the essence then that British propaganda should be covert and apparently unofficial. Sir Gilbert Parker and his assistants took great care to make it appear that pro-Allied propaganda emanated largely from the spontaneous overflow of generous emotions by Americans themselves on behalf of the Allied cause, which soon became identified with the cause of civilization itself. The wisdom of this policy was glaringly illustrated by an incident that took place shortly after the outbreak of war when Masterman tried direct publicity by writers.

He knew that both James Barrie, the famous creator of Peter Pan, and A. E. W. Mason, the popular adventure writer, had considerable followings in the United States. He suggested to them that they make a trip to America as goodwill ambassadors. With high hopes and ambitions, they set sail on the *Lusitania* on 12 September 1914 (plate 18). According to Barrie's biographer, they did not quite know what was expected of them: "Somehow they were to state the British case, and Barrie saw more coming from it than this. He felt he was representing the Government, and that he and Mason were secret agents, that once more he was a power behind the scenes, and he didn't entirely disregard the possibility of bringing America in on the Allies' side."[1]

Plate 18 Sir James M. Barrie.   Plate 19 Theodore Roosevelt, 1915.

In his somewhat sensational book, *Why We Fought*, C. Hartley Grattan credits their mission with great success, claiming that their literary reputations advanced the British cause "on an unknown number of professors."[2] In fact, the expedition was a fiasco. The press caught word of their mission and blazoned it in Britain and America. No one in Wellington House had bothered to clear it with Sir Cecil Spring-Rice, the British ambassador in Washington. Naturally, he was furious. He asserted that the mission would only embarrass the authorities and "would be bound to provoke counter-demonstrations, and had indeed already been the subject of attacks in the pro-German press."[3] He repudiated the mission entirely. Poor Barrie and Mason made an humiliating *volte-face*. Barrie was forced into outright lying in order not to reveal the ways in which the British government was using writers to further the cause. In an interview for the *New York Times*, Barrie denied that there had been any official backing for their visit. He and Mason, he asserted, were in the United States "purely for social reasons," since they were too old to be in the fighting services.[4]

The incident was the first of many occasions on which the Foreign Office and Wellington House found themselves at loggerheads since each was always appearing to invade the other's departmental territory. Subsequently, until much later in the war, Masterman was careful to send as his ambassadors writers who had some military connections and who could talk with some authority and from first-hand experience about the war. Later, John Masefield and Ian Hay used the lecture circuit to advance the Allied cause in America under the guise of informative talks about particular campaigns.

From this point on, British civilian writers were employed indirectly to write newspaper articles, pamphlets, and books to be distributed in America. Wellington House did, however, try another covert method early in the game to rally American sympathy for the cause. Early in 1915 there appeared *Sixty American Opinions on the War*, a compilation of extracts from books and articles, private letters and letters to newspapers written by Americans prominent in the arts, universities, politics, business, and journalism expressing sympathy for the Allies. The opinion ranges all the way from that of a professor of Latin at Chicago, William Graham Hale, who wrote that the United States should enter the war at once on the side of the Allies, to Albert Bushnell Hart's view that the United States should remain strictly neutral but hold Germany responsible for beginning the war and for the destruction of Belgium.

The book shows how quickly American academics had swung against Germany. Many of them had received a pamphlet written by Professors Eucken and Haeckel of the University of Jena defending Germany's role in the war. This pamphlet revealed to several of the contributors a complete collapse of that scientific and objective attitude for which German scholarship had been valued. Robert Underwood Johnson apparently summed up the opinion of many when he wrote: "The German propaganda, although aided by Bernard Shaw, is making no headway. People read, laugh, and are of the same opinion still."[5]

A repeated theme of the collection was the appeal of the Anglo-Saxon heritage shared by Britain and the United States—the subject of impassioned, if somewhat maudlin, verse and of more judicious praise of British principles of law and liberty. Another theme was German barbarism, described by John Burroughs, the naturalist, as highway robbery, and by John Jay Chapman as a form of insanity. William Dean Howells contributed a letter in support of the Allies and Henry James had some rich praise of "grand old England." Many of the men who were of continuing assistance to the cause of interventionism were represented in the collection: James Montgomery Beck, Richard Harding Davis, Morton Prince, Sinclair Kennedy, and Theodore Roosevelt. *Sixty American Opinions on the War* was a triumphant vindication of the Allied cause. Presumably, few or none of the contributors knew that the whole collection had been made, published, and distributed by a propaganda agency of the British government.

One of the most effective supporters of the British propaganda efforts in the United States was the war-horse of Oyster Bay, Theodore Roosevelt, who was himself one of the most indefatigable writers in the United States on the side of the Allies (plate 19). His powerful emotions about the war endowed him with the ability to see all sides of the question from a single point of view. He had no sympathy at all for Woodrow Wilson and his complex political difficulties with a deeply divided nation. Roosevelt used much of his immense energy in trying to arouse the United States to action in the face of German aggression, and he threw himself into an unending round of speeches and article- and letter-writing.

He often used his friend, Ambassador Sir Cecil Spring-Rice, as a means to advise the British government on how to handle American public opinion. One suggestion, promptly taken up, was that the American people be given a chance to see the facts and arguments concerning alleged atrocities in Belgium.[6] This was one of the strongest pressures in producing the notorious Bryce Report, which Roosevelt, an old friend and admirer of Lord Bryce, seems to have accepted without demur.

His first contribution to propaganda about the war was a series of newspaper articles that were collected under the title *America and the World War* in January 1915. Roosevelt uses the apocalyptic language common to the time and expresses his "infinite sadness because of the black abyss of war into which all these nations have been plunged."[7] The war has revealed beneath the "smiling surface of civilization the volcanic fires" gleaming red in the gloom.[8] To him the disaster is like that of the *Titanic*, the great ship which hit an iceberg and sank in 1912. In the face of the war, it is the duty of the United States, Roosevelt says, to arm itself and stand up for international law and the rights of small nations. Though he is proud of the German blood in his veins, he strongly condemns Germany for her aggression in Belgium and adds that this aggression should be a lesson for the United States, whose policy should be to stay neutral and strongly armed.

The event that changed Theodore Roosevelt from an advocate of armed neutrality to an interventionist was the sinking of the *Lusitania*. His fury knew no bounds. "This represents not merely piracy," he writes, "but piracy on a vaster scale of murder than any old-time pirate ever practiced. . . . It seems inconceivable that we can refrain from taking action in this matter, for we owe it not only to humanity, but to our own national self-respect."[9] He believes that Wilson and Bryan are morally responsible for the loss of all the American lives in the sinking and hopes that such knowledge would drive them into a declaration of war. When no such declaration was forthcoming, he poured out his contempt for Wilson and Bryan in many speeches and letters. He believed that the American role in the European war should be the outstanding issue of the presidential election of 1916 and campaigned to get the nomination on that basis. Too many Republicans feared, however, that the issue would alienate voters, particularly German-Americans. Roosevelt lost the nomination to Charles Evans Hughes. He had to satisfy his fighting spirit by other means and set about raising a division of mounted riflemen to be commanded by himself and officered in part by his four sons. When the United States did finally enter the war, to Roosevelt's immense chagrin, Wilson refused the offer of a completely equipped division. There was later a grim satisfaction for him in the fact that all four of his sons did get into the war. One of them, Quentin, was shot down and killed behind the German lines in July 1918.

It is very probable that Roosevelt was also instrumental in the publication by Wellington House of two books by his old friend, Mrs. Humphry Ward, then a popular British novelist. Her two propaganda books, *England's Effort* and *Towards the Goal* are in the form of letters to him, although in the first he is not named as the correspondent. Lord Rosebery wrote the introduction to the first book and warned of an influence also feared by Roosevelt, "hyphenated Americans who preserve Prussian sympathies."[10] Mrs. Ward's ritual disclaimer of help from the British government seems even on the face of things thin, for she was given tours of war industries, the Western Front, and Royal Naval vessels. She writes sentimentally of an England in which workers are happy putting in long shifts in the factories, of women doing men's work making munitions, and of cheerful troops going up the line to give battle. Looking out from a hill over the front line, she feels: "There in those trenches is *The Aggressor*—the enemy who has wantonly broken the peace of Europe, who has fouled civilization with deeds of lust and blood, between whom and the Allies there can be no peace, till the Allies' right arm dictates it."[11] Mrs. Ward's biographer claims that a year after its publication, "it was asserted by many Americans with every accent of conviction, that but for *England's Effort* and the public opinion that it stirred, President Wilson might have delayed still longer than he did in bringing America in."[12]

Mrs. Ward's second book has a preface by Roosevelt in which he makes a savage attack on pacifism and salutes an England awakened by the war. By the time *Towards the Goal* was published, in early 1917, the public had some inkling of the enormous casualties suffered by the British army. It contains an elegy to the dead: "Their young bodies—their precious lives—paid the price," she writes, "And in the Mother-heart of England they lie—gathered and secure—for ever."[13] Much of the rest of the book is taken up with details of German atrocities in occupied villages and towns of France. She self-righteously claims that British, French, and Italian troops would be incapable of such behaviour. "We feel that we are terribly right," she complacently concludes, "in speaking of the Germans as barbarians: that, for all their science and their organisation, they have really nothing in common with the Graeco-Latin and Christian civilization on which this old Europe is based." Theodore Roosevelt had nothing but praise for this sentimentality and moral superiority.

Americans living abroad joined their voices to the pro-Allied writers in the United States. They were among the most passionate advocates of American intervention, and they formed a valuable, if unofficial, cadre of propagandists for the Allies. Henry James and Edith Wharton were the most effective among them, the former being especially influential because of his reputation among his peers, both in Europe and America. His essays in time of war were collected by Percy Lubbock and published under the title *Within the Rim* in 1918. They were largely pieces written for one or another charitable cause, appealing for support or volunteers. The reader is struck again and again in reading these essays with the apocalyptic vision with which James viewed the Great War. In one essay he tries to compare it to the American Civil War, but the analogies break down: "one swung off into space, into history, into darkness, with every lamp extinguished and every abyss gaping."[14] James believed that Germany intended to impose her rule on the world, not excluding the United States. But here Germany had made a great mistake: "the treasure of our whole unquenchable association" between England and America would defeat her.[15]

In "Refugees in Chelsea," the apocalyptic note is loudest. In a vivid narration, James portrays the Belgians surprised by the ruffianly Germans

Plate 20   Henry James at Seventy: Portrait by John Singer Sargent.

and forced to flee their homes in darkness and despair. Never had there been, to him, such a revelation as this "Belgian ideal of the constituted life, dismembered, disembowelled, and shattered, which had so supremely to represent the crack of doom and the end of everything."[16] It is a skilfully worded, fairly factual appeal, illustrated with telling anecdotes and free from atrocity stories, except the mention of the German fondness for firing on the insignia of the Red Cross, "a view characteristic of their belligerent system at large."[17] Partly as a result of James's efforts, the Norton-Harjes ambulance unit attracted the services of many idealistic young Americans, mostly from Harvard, Princeton, and Yale, including e.e. cummings and John Dos Passos.

The final essay in *Within the Rim* is called "France." It first appeared in *The Book of France* (1915), published in aid of French War Charities. The essay is Henry James's last tribute to French civilization, in praise of the organic wholeness of France, "whose name," James writes, "means more than anything in the world to us but our own." The country sums up for him "the life of the mind and the life of the sense alike." It is the duty of the civilized world to pay its debt to France by joining in the war against Germany, which is organized, rather than organic, "merely mechanical and bristling compared with the condition of being naturally and functionally endowed and appointed." James ends the essay with an image of France "bleeding at every pore," but still "erect . . . incalculable, immortal."[18]

Along with the image of the erect but bleeding spirit of France was presented that of a peaceful, pastoral England, transformed now so that the country seems to be in the throes "of some great religious service, with prostrations and exaltations, the light of a thousand candles and the sound of soaring choirs."[19] Germany, on the other hand, is imaged as a despoiling ogre, clad in the spiked helmet of the Uhlan, ravaging and destroying everything in his path. It is not true, as Violet Hunt claims,[20] that Henry James sacrificed even his style for the sake of the cause, but he did sacrifice something which he held to be as sacred: his objectivity.

He made another great sacrifice for the Allies: abandoning a principle of a creative lifetime at the urging of Sir Gilbert Parker, he allowed himself to be interviewed by the *New York Times* for a piece that was published on 21 March 1915. However, as Leon Edel notes, the interview must have been substantially written or rewritten by James himself for the marks of his style are overwhelming. He used the interview to appeal again for funds and for volunteers to the American Ambulance Corps; it was also a hymn of praise to the spirit of England and a warning to the United States that the country could not shirk its duty much longer.

James recalled that there had been times on the Western Front when there had been as many as five thousand casualties in twenty minutes. At the thought of such horrendous figures, the interviewer noted, James broke off, paused, and then resumed on a prophetic note. "One finds in the midst of all this, it is as hard to apply one's words as to endure one's thoughts. The war has used up words; they have weakened, they have deteriorated like motor car tires; they have, like millions of other things, been more overstrained and knocked about and voided of the happy semblance during the last six months than in all the long ages before, and we are now confronted with a depreciation of all our terms, or, otherwise speaking, with a loss of expression through an increase of limpness, that may well make us wonder what ghosts will be left to walk."[21]

So James anticipated the devaluation of language under the pressure of both the horrors and the propaganda of war. Significantly, it chanced that Ernest Hemingway saw these words in the *New York Times* interview and copied some of them down on one of the manuscript pages of *A Farewell To Arms*. They were not, however, included in the published novel. Michael S. Reynolds, in his book on the manuscripts of the novel, speculates that Hemingway may have intended to use the passage as an epigraph, but in the end, feeling that the epigraphs to *The Sun Also Rises* had misled readers, decided to use none for the later novel.[22] It is possible, though unlikely, that Hemingway saw the interview when it was first published and was thus influenced by James to join the ambulance corps when he was old enough,

two years later. It is more probable, however, that he discovered the interview during the 1920s and that he then apprehended its significance on the
question of language. In any event, as Reynolds notes, *A Farewell to Arms* is
in part an answer to James's question about what words would remain.
"Abstract words such as glory, honor, courage, or hallow," Hemingway
writes, "were obscene beside the concrete names of villages, the numbers of
roads, the names of rivers, the numbers of regiments and the dates."[23]

The friend and disciple of Henry James, Edith Wharton, threw herself into
the war effort with tremendous energy, working long hours on charitable and
hospital work, organizing her fellow writers to aid the cause, and making
tours of the front lines and rear hospitals. General Joffre liked to conduct his
operations in a secrecy that even his own government could not pierce. But
early in 1915, the French Red Cross asked Edith Wharton to make a tour of
some military hospitals near the front in order to publicize the need for
medical supplies. What she saw gave her the idea that she should spread the
news about the French war effort to her countrymen by a tour of the front
lines. Intervention on her behalf by powerful French officials finally persuaded Joffre's chief of staff to allow her the tour; he also realized that any
military secrets that Wharton might unwittingly betray would have lost their
value by the time of publication in magazine form several months later.[24]

The articles appeared in *Scribner's Magazine* during 1915 and were collected for publication in a volume called *Fighting France* immediately
afterwards. Small wonder that Barbara Tuchman used the book for one of
her sources in writing *The Guns of August* since it is marked by close
observation as well as passionate commitment. The men, the terrain, the
havoc, and the boredom are all accurately described as well as the patriotism
and the high sentiment. What is missing, of course, is the horror and the fear
and the filth. The French are praised as an anti-militaristic but warlike
nation, "with the ardor, the imagination, the perseverance that have made
them for centuries the great creative force of civilization."[25] As frontispiece
to the book is a photo of the formidable figure of Mrs. Wharton, impeccably
dressed, armed with a long umbrella, standing in front of a log and brush-
work rampart. Behind her a couple of French officers peer through peep-
holes at the enemy. The picture is called "A French Palisade." The title does
almost as much justice to the figure in the foreground as it does to the
rampart behind (plate 21).

In the midst of her other work Edith Wharton decided to try to raise funds
for the hostels and charity organizations trying to look after the needs of
refugees from Belgium and Flanders by publishing a literary anthology. She
called it *The Book of the Homeless* and had it published in Europe and the
United States for the benefit of the American Hostels for Refugees and for
the Children of Flanders Rescue Committee.

Plate 21   Edith Wharton: A French Palisade.

The Book of the Homeless came equipped with every possible blessing and accolade. It had a commendatory letter from General Joffre, an introduction by Theodore Roosevelt, and a dazzling list of contributors. These included Sarah Bernhardt, Laurence Binyon, Paul Bourget, Rupert Brooke, Paul Claudel, Jean Cocteau, Joseph Conrad, Vincent D'Indy, Eleanora Duse, John Galsworthy, Edmund Gosse, Thomas Hardy, W. D. Howells, Henry James, Maurice Maeterlinck, Alice Meynell, Paul Elmer More, Edmond Rostand, George Santayana, Igor Stravinsky, Mrs. Humphry Ward, Barrett Wendell, Edith Wharton, and W. B. Yeats. Contributors of art work included Max Beerbohm, Jacques-Emile Blanche, Cézanne, Charles Dana Gibson, Claude Monet, Renoir, Rodin, and John Singer Sargent. Mrs. Wharton's energy was so great that she solicited all these manuscripts, scores, and art work, edited them, translated the French and Italian pieces, wrote a preface, and had the manuscript ready for the press before the end of 1915.

Unfortunately, the emotions of the day militated against high artistic standards. To name just a few, Claudel came up with an empty and sonorous poem called "The Precious Blood," Howells with a totally sentimental piece of verse called "The Little Children," Edmund Gosse with a mixture of anecdote and bluster called "The Arrogance and Servility of Germany," and Galsworthy with a cloying piece of fake pastoral called "Harvest." Joseph

Conrad contributed a sombre piece called "Poland Revisited," an account of his escape from Poland on the outbreak of war and an attack on German militarism.[26] Rostand offered a poem that would have been more fitting had it been uttered by Cyrano de Bergerac. Its first stanza runs:

> Gashed hands of children who cry out for bread—
> While as the flames from sacred places rise
> The Blond Beast, hideous, with blood-shot eyes
> And obscene gestures mutilates the dead.[27]

The majority of the literary contributions run in this vein, trotting out tired clichés of hate and revenge against the Hun.

That this is not true of all the contributions is owing partly to the fact that some writers obviously sent in what they had unused in their files—material which in some cases had no reference to the war or to Belgium—and to a tiny minority who refused to be drawn into the vortex of propaganda. The most notable example of these is William Butler Yeats, and it is much to Wharton's credit that she printed his offering at all.

A Reason for Keeping Silent

> I think it better that at times like these
> We poets keep our mouths shut, for in truth
> We have no gift to set a statesman right:
> He's had enough of meddling who can please
> A young girl in the indolence of her youth
> Or an old man upon a winter's night.[28]

In the slightly revised version in *The Collected Poems*, Yeats, remembering the redoubtable solicitor, ironically re-entitled it "On Being Asked for a War Poem." This terse and pithy piece stands in vivid contrast to the inflated verbiage which surrounds it and makes it all the more striking by its standing alone.

One of the most effective means by which the expatriates influenced public opinion in the United States was by mail. Edith Wharton kept up a stream of letters to influential friends, and Edith Wharton Societies were established in several eastern American cities. Henry James also employed his great skills as a letter-writer to rouse his friends to action. As Percy Lubbock says, "To all who listened to him on those days it must have seemed that he gave us what we lacked—a voice; there was a trumpet note in it that we heard nowhere else and that alone rose to the height of truth."[29] James's war letters to America, an ample selection of which are published in Lubbock's edition of *The Letters of Henry James*, were widely circulated.

One of his correspondents was Owen Wister, who was deeply influenced by James's passion and rhetoric. James talked of a world that he and Wister had shared now annihilated by the war, creating an unbridgeable chasm. In a letter of 25 September 1914, he urged Wister to spread the news in America about the plight of the Belgian refugees and to compare "the hacking and hewing, the insolence of violation, the burning and ravaging and plundering and blackmailing of Germany on the one side, and on the other . . . the making of this island into a huge pitying lap or breast for the millions . . . of the stricken, the trampled, the despoiled and maimed and crazed! Casually call attention, but for all it's worth, to this interesting opposition, and let it percolate—also for all it's worth!"[30]

Spurred on by these letters, Owen Wister, who was the author of the first classic western, *The Virginian*, sat down to write *The Pentecost of Calamity*. The Belgians, French, and British had risen to combat what Wister calls "the new Trinity of German worship—the Super-man, the Super-race, and the Super-state." But what had the United States done? In the face of naked aggression, the United States maintained silence and complete neutrality or followed in Wister's words "Maxims of low prudence, masquerading as Christianity."[31] America had neither spoken out in the cause of liberty, nor begun to arm. Wister asserts that if the United States wishes to have any voice in the council of nations, any hope in maintaining a peaceful world, she has to stand up and be counted. He ends: "Perhaps nothing save calamity will teach us what Europe is thankful to have learned again—that some things are worse than war, and that you can pay too high a price for peace; but that you cannot pay too high for the finding and keeping of your own soul."

The text of *The Pentecost of Calamity* as published in book form had some significant differences from the earlier one published in the *Saturday Evening Post* in which Wister took a much more restrained tone about American neutrality. Theodore Roosevelt was an old friend of Wister's, and after reading the magazine articles, he wrote at once to tell him that Wilson and Bryan were totally at fault for not protesting Germany's violation of the Hague Conventions in her invasion of Belgium and that it had been inexcusable for the administration not to have taken decisive action after the sinking of the *Lusitania*. On receipt of the letter, Wister "made several additions" to the proofs of his book which made it a much tougher critique of American policy. When it came out, Wister sent the first copy to Roosevelt, who replied: "As an American none too proud of his country's attitude for the last thirteen months, I am grateful to you, for the sake of my own self-respect, because you have written so burningly and so nobly."[32]

The Pentecost of Calamity was widely distributed and made a considerable impression. A large part of this distribution and consequent success was through the initiative of Wellington House. Macmillan, Wister's English publisher, wrote on 4 January 1916: "I send you herewith the Dutch and French editions of 'The Pentecost of Calamity.' Although these editions have Nelson's imprint I understand that they were really prepared at the instance of the British Government."[33] Sir Gilbert Parker expressed his thanks to Wister "for the splendid work you have been doing for the Allies in the publication of 'The Pentecost of Calamity.' It is a very remarkable piece of writing, and it cannot fail to do (as I understand it has done) a vast amount of good in the United States."[34] Sir Gilbert made sure that it was also widely distributed in Britain.

Wister was one of the writers who promoted an attempt to form a nucleus for a national mobilization of the literary resources of the United States to aid Theodore Roosevelt in his fight for "Americanism"—or what soon became interventionism. The writers in support of this movement included George Ade, Rex Beach, Winston Churchill (the novelist), Hamlin Garland, Hermann Hagedorn, Don Marquis, and Booth Tarkington.

The voices of all these literary Americans, both in and outside the country, greatly influenced the move of public opinion in the United States out of indifference, isolation, and neutrality and finally into war. As J. D. Squires has written: "Fired by such notions [that German soldiers cut the hands off Belgian children] about the behavior of the enemy and by others equally absurd, the American people launched themselves into war with an emotional hysteria that can only be understood by realizing the power of propaganda in generating common action by a nation under belligerent conditions. Those who did not accept the war ideology were usually few in number and always quite impotent."[35]

Between 1914 and April 1917, the efforts of the interventionists gradually undermined the attempts by Woodrow Wilson to act as mediator between the belligerent powers. Blundering German diplomacy and clumsy propaganda also did much to undermine her case, and the increasing tolls made by U-boats on neutral shipping alienated many Americans. Wilson made his final attempt to end the war by diplomacy in his "peace without victory" address of 22 January 1917. Ten days later, however, the German government announced unrestricted submarine warfare. From then on it could only be a matter of time before the United States entered the war. Addressing the newly elected Congress on 2 April 1917, Wilson asked the people of the United States to "formally accept the status of belligerent which has . . . been thrust upon it by the Imperial German Government." Four days later, by a vote of 373 to 50, Congress declared war.

The American people, from August 1914 to the end of the war, heard little of the German side of the case. As Stanley Cooperman has said, "The success of scientifically organized Allied propaganda in the United States, which helped to create much of the subsequent opposition to political and aesthetic rhetoric, was certainly not matched by German efforts."[36] In 1920, H. L. Mencken sardonically noted: "When he recalls the amazing feats of the English war propagandists between 1914 and 1917—and their even more amazing confessions of method since— [the American] is apt to ask himself quite gravely if he belongs to a free nation or to a crown colony."[37]

6

PROPAGANDA FROM AMERICA

In all things, from first to last, without halt or change, [the Committee on Public Information] was a plain publicity proposition, a vast enterprise in salesmanship, the world's greatest adventure in advertising.

GEORGE CREEL, 1920

Although Woodrow Wilson felt the same need to create a propaganda agency on entering the war as had the British government, he and his appointees apparently made no attempt at the outset to establish a liaison with either Wellington House or its office in New York. The secrecy with which the British operation had been conducted had made it invisible even in Washington. A week after America's entry into the war, on 13 April 1917, Wilson created the Committee on Public Information and appointed George Creel its chairman, with the secretaries of State, War, and the Navy as the other committee members (plate 22).

Unlike Masterman, Creel later told his own story about the manifold activities of his committee in *How We Advertised America*, a brash, self-serving, but thorough and entertaining account of the country's first information agency. In *Words That Won the War*, James Mock and Cedric Larson sum up Creel's efforts well: "The Committee was America's 'propaganda ministry' charged with encouraging and then consolidating the revolution of opinion which changed the United States from an anti-militaristic democracy to an organized war-machine. This work touched the private life of virtually every man, woman, and child; it reflected the thoughts of the American people under the leadership of Woodrow Wilson; and it popularized what was for us a new idea of the individual's relation to the state."[1]

Comparing the way in which Masterman ran Wellington House to Creel's way with the Committee on Public Information reveals a good deal about national styles and priorities. Although both had been politicians, Creel had

Plate 22   George Creel shortly before the War.

spent most of his time as a publicist, promoter, and publisher, whereas Masterman had been devoted to literary and social enterprises. Masterman was diplomatic and self-effacing in style and worked brilliantly behind the scenes of public life. Creel was pugnacious and outspoken, often indiscreet. Masterman saw propaganda as a business for literary men and worked, particularly at the beginning, with the printed word, whether in book or pamphlet. Creel saw the war as a product which he had at all costs to "sell" to the public, and he was determined to use any means to get the job done.

Creel's organization had one immense advantage over the British propaganda efforts. Propaganda in Britain was fought for by a dozen different departments, and final integration into the Ministry of Information came too late to be really effective. The organization of the Committee on Public Information was, on the other hand, as Harold Lasswell has pointed out, "equivalent to appointing a separate cabinet minister for propaganda." Creel was, Lasswell adds, responsible "for every aspect of propaganda both at home and abroad."[2] He was thus relieved of the political infighting that dogged the various chiefs of British propaganda from Masterman to Bennett.

But at the same time Creel was under constant attack from Congress for his work was carried out with none of that cloak-and-dagger secrecy that masked the work of Wellington House. At first, as in the British operation, Creel worked with discretionary funds from the administration, but he let slip a foolish remark which brought the hounds of Congress barking at his heels. In a question period after a speech in New York about the attitude of Congress to his work, Creel replied, "I do not like slumming so I won't explore into the hearts of Congress for you."[3] This naturally brought about a full-scale attack on him, a demand for his dismissal, and for the dissolution of the CPI. Creel demanded a hearing before the House Appropriations Committee, which took place in June 1918. He was able to defend himself quite successfully and win an appropriation of $1,250,000 for the committee — about half of what he had been asking for.

At its peak, the Creel Committee employed 150,000 men and women in

Plate 23   The Creel Committee posters went in for sex and idealism as much as for atrocities.

the various branches. Among its many activities, the committee published the *Official Bulletin*, which disseminated government news. Dean Guy Stanton Ford from the University of Minnesota headed a division which prepared and circulated 105 pamphlets by scholars on the causes and effects of the war. There was a Film Division, a War Expositions Division, a Labor Publications Division, and a Pictorial Publicity Division under Charles Dana Gibson. The posters published by this division tended to be sexy and folksy in contrast to the grimmer admonitory posters published by British propaganda (plates 23 and 24). The Syndicate Features Division employed novelists and short story writers to write articles in support of the war for publication in the United States and abroad.

Plate 24   Another Creel Committee poster motif. A folksy version of the American working man.

In contrast to those who wrote for British propaganda, these writers were mostly of the second rank, even though Creel claimed that his office "gathered together the leading novelists, essayists, and publicists of the land, and these men and women, without payment, worked faithfully in the production of brilliant, comprehensive articles that went to the press as syndicated features." Among them were Samuel Hopkins Adams, Booth Tarkington, Mary Roberts Rinehart, Herbert Quick, Gertrude Atherton, Robert Herrick, Wilbur Daniel Steele, Ida Tarbell, Rex Beach, Virginia Boyle, and William Allen White. Most of their articles were short and relatively insignificant. One of the most successful was Booth Tarkington's "American Facts and German Propaganda," which was, according to Creel, "so vivid and attractive" that the British government made arrangements to reprint and distribute eight hundred and fifty thousand copies in England alone. It was also widely reprinted in other countries.[4]

However, it appears that little further effort was made to co-ordinate the British and American propaganda agencies. As late as November 1917 in a parliamentary enquiry into the Department of Information, Professor W. MacNeile Dixon, then in charge of the American section of Wellington House, was asked if the Americans had an operation corresponding to his department in Washington. Dixon replied: "Yes, but it has never got into proper working order. We have never been able to get in touch with it. It would be of great advantage to us if we could." By that time, the Creel Committee had been flourishing for eight months. Dixon's statement was blatantly false.

Pressed further on the question, Dixon was asked why it was not possible for Wellington House to be brought into contact with the propaganda department in the United States. Dixon then confessed that the department was forbidden by the Foreign Office to initiate any policy in America. "We have several times addressed a memorandum to the Foreign Office," he went on, "requesting that they should put us more closely into touch with the organisation in the United States. That is one of the points we can make considerable progress in, if only higher officials come to some arrangements about it." His questioner said that there was obviously some remissness somewhere. Dixon replied that the head of the Department of Information, Colonel Buchan, was attached to the Foreign Office and that any such move should come from him. Dixon then diverted the line of questioning into how Wellington House operated in the United States.[5]

It is clear from this exchange that no effort was being made by Buchan and his superiors to co-ordinate efforts with the United States. The Foreign Office perceived that the interests of the two countries in the coming peace would be different and that co-ordination in propaganda might lead to embarrassment later. Accordingly, Foreign Office officers evidently decided that bureaucratic non-co-operation was the way to prevent the spread of Wilsonian idealism and other ideas that might inhibit British policy at the peace conference. In January 1918, Creel sent a representative of his office, Mr. Rickey, to meet Colonel Buchan and discuss liaison. Buchan wrote to Creel on 1 February 1918: "It was a great pleasure to me to meet Mr. Rickey yesterday and to establish for the first time personal contact with your Department. You may be assured that we will do everything to meet your wishes and to give you the assistance here which you have so generously extended to us on the other side of the Atlantic."[6] Buchan apparently did nothing. The first conference on Inter-allied Propaganda did not take place until 14 August 1918. It was called at the initiative of Lord Northcliffe, acting as the head of a new propaganda agency at Crewe House. Northcliffe's efforts to promote a committee representing France, Great Britain, Italy, and the United States to co-ordinate propaganda were again apparently sabotaged by the Foreign Office. As late as October 1918, George Moore, who had been accredited by Creel to act as the agent of the CPI in London, reported that his work had been sabotaged, that American news had been minimized or killed outright, and that he had been told that the British Press Bureau should be the agency of issuance of American material. Strongly suspecting the hand of the Foreign Office, Creel instructed Moore to go directly to the minister for Foreign Affairs, Arthur Balfour, for help.[7] All to no avail.

So, to the end, the Creel Committee was obliged to pursue its own line. Its work, however, had been indelibly formed by what British propaganda had already accomplished in the United States. The CPI did not have to get men of the calibre of Bennett or Hueffer to write their material because the ideas and images they had created had become part of the stock-in-trade of the run-of-the-mill-propagandist. One example is the pamphlet written by a professor of English at Stanford, John S.P. Tatlock, called *Why America Fights Germany*. Its material was drawn straight from the report of the Bryce Committee and Arnold Bennett's pamphlet, *Liberty*. It tells the story of an imaginary invasion of America and the occupation of a small town in New Jersey, followed by pillage, rape, arson, and murder. "And every horrible detail," Tatlock concludes, "is just what the German troops have done in Belgium and France."[8] The pamphlet concludes with a stirring call for enlistment. According to Mock and Larson, it had a circulation of nearly three-quarters of a million copies.

Unlike Wellington House, the Creel Committee could not make collusive agreements with private publishers. Guy Stanton Ford explained the situation to Doubleday and Page & Co., Kipling's American publishers, who proposed a co-operative venture. Ford thought it an excellent idea but regretted "that we are working under some limitations which evidently do not apply to the activities of Sir Gilbert Parker and Professor MacNeile Dixon on behalf of the British government." These were limitations, Ford added, both of resources and of discretion.[9] Evidently, these were still the days of innocence and above-board dealing in the American propaganda services, a legacy, no doubt, of Wilsonian idealism. Nevertheless, George Creel himself appears to have been tempted to exceed this discretion in September 1918, when Upton Sinclair wrote to offer him a novel-in-progress.

Upton Sinclair, a life-long socialist and pacifist, had broken with the American Socialist Party on 11 April 1917, five days after America's declaration of war (plate 25). At its annual convention the party had adopted a platform denouncing the war and opposing enlistment. The platform said: "We brand the declaration of war by our government as a crime against the people of the United States, and against the nations of the world."[10] A minority report, supported by Upton Sinclair, opposed this resolution and urged the winning of the war as soon as possible to promote a democratic peace. When in a referendum the anti-war statement was approved by the membership twelve to one, Sinclair resigned from the party and began his own magazine *Upton Sinclair's*, a monthly in support of Wilson's policies. His pro-war novel, *Jimmie Higgins*, was meant to broaden the reach of this support by being published in book form as well as in his magazine. "What has occurred to me," Sinclair wrote to Creel, "is that the story ought to be used by the Government. It is exactly what the Government needs in order to win and hold the radical part of labor. . . . The book could be printed in a very large edition on light paper and with paper binding for about ten cents per copy. If the Government were to give it out to the ship workers, the miners, the lumbermen, and all those engaged on Government work, I believe it would do more to spike the guns of the Pro-German intriguers in the radical movement than any equal amount of pamphlets. The point is that people will read a story whereas they won't read the usual propaganda dope." He proposed that the government have the work translated into seventeen languages and distributed abroad. He would be glad to donate the book to the cause. He added that the British government had paid D. W. Griffiths a small fortune to have him make a propaganda film, and the American government would be getting Upton Sinclair for the cost of paper and ink, "so now get busy."

Creel wired back "Much interested. Send completed manuscript and scenario." Sinclair sent Creel half of the book on 26 September 1918, explaining that this half showed Jimmie as a violent pacifist, but only to make his conversion to a passionate volunteer for the army all the more dramatic. He believed that the book would influence labour to support Wilson in the belief that their conditions after the war would be improved by the President.

On 2 October Creel replied: "I have gone over your manuscript very

Plate 25   Upton Sinclair.

carefully, and have taken the whole matter up at length with the various Division heads. I am sorry beyond measure, but it is impossible for me to use the material in the manner that you suggest. We have never yet published other than the short official pamphlet, setting forth facts in the case. The whole proposition, aside from its many other difficulties, would be too expensive for me to handle. I am very sorry."[11]

Creel thus lost the opportunity to publish a book that had everything that Allied propaganda had been pushing thoughout the war—German guilt for starting it, an attack on militarism, atrocity stories, including the one about the soldier being crucified against a barn door, and praise for the war aims of the Allies. What stopped Creel was no doubt the strong socialist bias of the book and the realization that his department would be getting into hot water politically if it endorsed it.[12]

It must be presumed, then, that all the other propaganda efforts in fictional form, such as Booth Tarkington's novel *Ramsey Milholland* and his story "Captain Schlotterwerz," received no help from Creel. *Ramsey Milholland*, chronicling the story of a young man's conversion from indifference to passionate interventionism, culminating in his joining the army, is an obvious recruiting book. "Captain Schlotterwerz," a story of a German-American's conversion to a pro-Allied sentiment, was, according to Tarkington's biographer, turned down by *Collier's* because it was too propagandistic. The story was later published by the *Saturday Evening Post*, a journal that was eager throughout the war to publish pro-Allied material.

On the other hand, Creel promoted Tarkington's journalism, which was especially effective in the midwest where isolationist and pro-German sentiment flourished. Tarkington wrote many magazine articles advocating compulsory training for an army of a million men and calling for huge military appropriations. Tarkington had got into the propaganda business well before the United States entered the war. He wrote an article for the British press as early as June 1916 that was reprinted by the *New York Times Current History* under the title "Why Americans are Pro-Ally." In it he insists that "all normal and educated Americans have been from the beginning, and now are, 'pro-Ally.' " He dismisses all the others as "oddities" or "German-Americans" and so joins in the attack on the so-called hyphenated Americans. Tarkington goes on to claim that working against the American spirit is "something fermented of sloppy materials and waste, stirred and brewed into a gas by the ebullience of these times."[13] This fermentation, according to Tarkington, was going on within the Democratic party, presided over by the witch of the Democratic cauldron, William Jennings Bryan. Tarkington believed, however, that Bryan's attempt to raise a mob of pacifists would not succeed. Now, he maintained, the nation was bent on preparedness, whether for war or peace.

Two months before America entered the war, Tarkington went down into the market place to rally the people to the Allied cause. He joined an Indianapolis committee sponsoring a mass meeting to protest the deportation of Belgians to Germany for forced labour and wrote to the newspaper urging: "Whoever goes to that meeting is a voice—one more voice lifted in protestation against slavery . . . being actually and increasingly brought into existence in the year 1917 by the order of the German government."[14] Two thousand people turned out for the demonstration. Tarkington was also the chairman of the Indianapolis branch of the American Rights Committee. He was responsible for a resolution sponsored by the branch in March 1917 to urge Congress to enact compulsory military service. He expressed his feelings on the war more succinctly in a letter to George Ade: "I have a feeling of shame . . . that I'm not carrying a gun. . . . EVERYTHING'S been said and said. . . . I want my limber joints and good wind and dependable heart of twenty years ago. . . . I don't want to argue. I want to call 'em bastards and move towards the brick pile."[15]

Another novelist to enter the fray on behalf of the Allies early in the game was the Californian, Gertrude Atherton. She was one of those writers urging preparedness in 1915, and her letters found ready acceptance by the *New York Times*. In the summer of 1916 she went to France in order to write newspaper articles on the war work of American women. There she was co-opted into working for one of the war charities, partly through being told about the efforts of her rival, Edith Wharton. Subsequently, Atherton wrote a series of articles for the *New York Times* praising the work of her own *oeuvre*, "Le Bienêtre du Blessé" and appealing for funds. In one such article, she either invents or gives circulation to a particularly unpleasant atrocity story. She claims that there were something like eighty thousand French soldiers afflicted with tuberculosis who had been returned from German prisoner-of-war camps to France. "All the exchanged prisoners," she continues, "return not only in rags, but telling the dreadful story that they have been deliberately infected, by being made to sleep with consumptives and drink from the same vessels; also they have reason to believe they have been given the germ hypodermically. Many also come back with morphinomania, having been drugged in the German hospitals."[16] It must be added that when Atherton published the *Times* articles in book form in 1916 under the title *Life in the War Zone*, this tidbit was left out. Up to America's entry into the war, she constantly berated westerners for their "serene neutrality" and advocated armed preparedness.

After America came in, she notes in her autobiography, she was asked to write more propaganda articles "in order to help stimulate enlistment." She does not reveal who asked, but it was almost certainly George Creel. The articles are vengeful and bloodthirsty. In August 1918, for example, she advocates no mercy for Germany should the government sue for peace. "Better exterpate [*sic*] the whole breed," she writes, "root and branch. And this, unless the German people come to their senses, is what we propose to do."[17] "Virulent was a weak word for those articles," she admits in her autobiography. "As I look back I think I must have given much energy to the cultivation of hate, for it was a new and interesting passion. Heretofore I had always prided myself upon never condescending to hate anyone."[18] The hate certainly lent venom to her propaganda. She claims that the French government warned her that it would be wise to avoid the German frontier when she went to Switzerland since there was a price on her head. If this were true, many British and American writers would have had bounties on their scalps.

The hatred that Gertrude Atherton candidly admitted after the fact was the inevitable by-product of the contents of the propaganda disseminated by Wellington House and the Committee on Public Information. George Creel seemed unaware of this consequence as he went on selling the American public on the war as if it were some sovereign and indispensable product. He confidently expected to carry on his committee's work after the armistice in order to promote Wilson's efforts at the conference table and his post-war policies. But Congress, like Parliament in Britain, was out to get the propaganda agency, not only because of its manipulation of public opinion, but also because it could be used to promote the interests of the president in office. Creel wrote to Wilson on 20 May 1920: "As you know, the Republican majority in Congress destroyed the Committee on Public Information on June 30, 1919. . . . There is no question that the disruption and prevention of orderly liquidation was the deliberate intention of Congress."[19] Its records were dumped in vacant offices, and its former executives had to come to Washington to wind up their work at their own expense. As in Britain, many essential records were lost.

7

OVER THERE: DRAWING THE PAPER CURTAIN

This war is trivial, for all its vastness. No great principle is at stake, no great human purpose is involved on either side. The supposed ideal ends for which it is being fought are merely part of the myth.

BERTRAND RUSSELL, 1916

Throughout the war writers both in and out of uniform helped to sustain the illusion of present glory and coming victory that the High Command wished to present for the government and people of Britain as well as for the neutrals. In effect, the writers drew a paper curtain across the Western Front and the other campaigns behind which the armies fought grimly on. Even before the close of 1914, the Western Front had settled down into the deadly war of the trenches that was sustained until almost the end. Although Winston Churchill and a few other leaders kept pressing for greater efforts in other theatres of war, Flanders remained the highest priority. Against all the odds, the High Command kept on believing that breakthrough and victory could be achieved if they could only get their hands on enough men, guns, and ammunition.

The generals also believed that it was necessary to keep meddling reporters away from the front lines. This served the double purpose of ensuring that military plans and movements would not be revealed in the press and, equally important, of concealing the real conditions under which officers and men in the front lines lived, were wounded, and died. The degradation of the trenches remained the best-kept secret of the war, not properly revealed until the publication of the prohibited photographs and the memoirs, poetry, and fiction of serving soldiers.

By the spring of 1915, the routine communiqués from Army headquarters that the press were allowed to publish had become so boring, and the public so restive for first-hand news, that even the brass hats saw fit to relax their rules and allow a few carefully selected civilian correspondents into the front zones. They were closely escorted by military attachés, and their despatches were thoroughly censored. Soon afterwards, established writers were invited to go to the front and report their findings in the hope that their prestige and literary skill would put the best face on the war. A procession of these authors toured the front and rear areas, including Arnold Bennett, Rudyard Kipling, Conan Doyle, Hilaire Belloc, and John Galsworthy.

The propaganda agencies also used authors in uniform to write articles and fiction about the war, including John Masefield, John Buchan, Ian Hay, and the Canadian novelist, Beckles Willson. Only one author tried to buck the rigid censorship rules in writing his reports for the home front. This was Max Aitken, created Lord Beaverbrook in 1917. He combined the power of his civilian authority as a representative of the Canadian government and his privileges as a military officer to see and describe things that censorship proscribed. Even he ran into a great deal of trouble publishing his work. In order to be quickly published, authors had to be careful not to name individuals or regiments, to be vague about place, to be uncritical, not to reveal any information that would in any way disclose information to the enemy, and to be full of praise for Allied efforts and aims.

Of all the authors chosen by Wellington House for the tour of the front, Arnold Bennett was most adaptable to the needs of propaganda. He was the first choice and set off in June 1915. His tour (under the supervision of the French and British military authorities) resulted in the famous book, *Over There: War Scenes on the Western Front*, brought out under the Methuen imprint in the same year. Bennett's unpublished reaction to what he saw was later revealed by Frank Swinnerton: "I think he visited the front as a duty, and was horrified at what he saw and felt that he must not express that horror."[1] The three-week tour left Bennett so physically and emotionally drained that he was ill for weeks afterwards. In his book on Bennett's war years, *A Writer at War*, Kinley E. Roby attributes the illness to his drinking polluted water in France, but Bennett was sporadically unwell for months afterwards, at which times he was heavily depressed and felt "mysteriously and intestinally ill."[2] Probably his prostration was largely psychological in origin. The disparity between what he expected to see and what he saw, between the high-flown rhetoric of his own propaganda and the ugly realities of the front line, seems to have been too much for his mind to accept. Though Roby maintains that Bennett was not deeply affected by his experiences at the front, he admits that "it is difficult to understand" why he "made so little use of his experience at the fronts in his subsequent fiction."[3] The difficulty may be resolved by accepting Swinnerton's view that Bennett felt it all too deeply—and concluding that for Bennett to write about it was both too painful and too inimical to his work as a propagandist.

It is not true, as Roby claims, that Bennett "saw almost nothing in the trenches to excite his imagination with horror." There is a picture in his journal of one horror: of wheat "absolutely growing out of a German [corpse]."⁴ And in *Over There* there is another glimpse of a wrecked trench from the side of which projected the well-shod legs of German corpses. A terrible stench hung over the mess. Bennett called it a symbol, but he did not stay to explain. "With alacrity we left them to get forward to the alert, straining life of war."⁵ He quickly shut out the inevitable consequence of this straining life— rotting death. This suppression has considerably affected his later fiction.

Over There appeared first as articles in British and American newspapers. In the length of its chapters and in its discontinuity, the book form of *Over There* reflects its origins. Each piece contains the built-in clichés and stereotypes of such reportage. There is the usual reference to the "brutalized air" of German prisoners and the customary tribute to the urbanity and austerity of French officers.⁶ A fine flight of fancy embellishes an account he heard from an officer about a recently liberated stretch of the French countryside, which was found to be littered with liquor bottles and musical instruments: "groundwork," Bennett gloats, "of an interrupted musical and bacchic fete whose details must be imagined, like many other revolting and scabrous details which no compositor would consent to set up in type."

The city of Ypres lay just behind the salient, and as a logistical centre for troops and supplies, it was an inevitable target for German artillery. Bennett makes it simply the object of German barbarism and invents a little scene in which German soldiers rejoice in the planned destruction of the cathedral and the Cloth Hall. Roby claims that he seems to have been more moved by the destruction of buildings than by the killing of men. Certainly the destruction he saw released aggressive emotions in him that resulted in an hysterical condemnation of Germany and led him to advocate a policy of reprisals. "If, at the end of the war," he writes, "Cologne were left as Arras was when I visited it, a definite process of education would have been accomplished in the Teutonic mind."⁷ Perhaps the memory of the First World War helped to make reprisals an Allied policy after the blitz on London and Coventry. *Over There* is humane only when Bennett forgets his propaganda mission and describes with care and realism scenes at or behind the front. He had, too, a fleeting glimpse of real danger when the blast of a nearby shell made him believe, momentarily, that he had been hit.

He was given *de luxe* treatment by the generals and was wined and dined at the staff chateaux. With deep awe he approaches an interview with the commander-in-chief, who goes unnamed, like God in the Old Testament. He describes him reverently, even down to his "finger-nails full of character." As the commander-in-chief passes out of the house, Bennett thinks, "I have seen him!"[8] His name was Sir John French. Others had seen him, and studied him, more objectively than Bennett, and at the time this was written, July 1915, this slow-witted, indecisive, but stubborn general was on his way out, to be replaced by Sir John Haig. There is no hint in *Over There* of the troubles of and dissatisfaction with the British High Command, although these things were common knowledge in high places in England at the time. Nor is there any hint of the lamentable failures in liaison with the French, of which Bennett must have been particularly conscious. It is impossible to agree with Kinley E. Roby that Bennett never "defended a policy of suppressing the truth in order that the government might escape embarrassment."[9] It would have been far wiser for Bennett to have kept quiet about Sir John. His sycophantic praise of incompetence, though supportive of the *status quo*, could only have hampered the effective prosecution of the war.

The War Office rather than Wellington House organized Rudyard Kipling's tour of the Western Front in August 1915. Out of it came some of the most violent propaganda written by any British writer in the Great War. He published his impressions as newspaper articles and collected them in the same year under the title *France at War*. The book is prefaced by Kipling's curious poem of 1913, "France," in which he argues that Britain and France were bound to make excellent allies because for centuries they had been such fixed enemies:

> We were schooled for dear life's sake, to know each other's blade.
> What can blood and iron make more than we have made?

Apparently the pen could make more than both, for at a stroke all the enmity was transformed into undying loyalty and friendship. *France at War* is both lyrical about France and brutal about those Kipling called "the Boche."

Kipling generally uses a stereotyped French soldier or an old woman as his mouthpiece, but the sentiments about German Satanism are unmistakably his own. " 'We — you and I,' " says one soldier, " 'England and the rest — had begun to doubt the existence of Evil. The Boche is saving us.' "[10] This remark is surely one of the frankest expressions of the psychological need that many then felt (and many still apparently feel!) for an enemy. "The Boche," or whomever, clears the ground of moral uncertainties and confusions. Having made such a definition, Kipling can proceed to the damnation of that enemy without scruple. He outdoes all his competitors in his reaction to the ruins of Rheims. He asserts: "Rheims is but one of the altars which the heathen has put up to commemorate their own death throughout all the world." The cathedral had been used by the French as a dressing station for the wounded, but the enemy had continued his shelling and set it on fire. On the floor and on one of the pillars was a scorch-mark — all that was left of a German major.

Kipling devoutly hopes that the mark will be left for the edification of future generations. As that staunch friend of the Allies, Richard Harding Davis, points out, "Mr. Kipling's hope shows an imperfect conception of the purposes of a cathedral. It is a house dedicated to God, and on earth to peace and good-will among men. It is not erected to teach generations of little children to gloat over the fact that an enemy, even a German officer, was by accident burned alive."[11]

Kipling, however, makes the cathedral an object lesson for the war. His mouthpiece at Rheims, a French woman, "tells" him " 'This is not war. It is against wild beasts that we fight. There is no arrangement possible with wild beasts.' " Rheims reinforced his conviction that there could be no settlement with the Germans. Only total victory could be contemplated. "This is the one vital point which we in England must realise," he proclaims.[12]

Kipling's tour of the front released that lust for revenge which was often the mainspring of his worst writing as well as some of his best. Having duly noted the tales of German atrocities during the advance through France and Flanders, he goes on to discuss the German soldier on the defensive. "The Boche does not at all like meeting men whose womenfolk he has dishonoured or mutilated, or used as protection against bullets" he writes, in his formulaic fashion. "It is not that these men are angry or violent. They do not waste time in that way. They kill him." The rhetorical trick of denying the very emotions that trigger Kipling's own hate is common in his propaganda writings. It was no doubt an effective way of both masking and engendering those same emotions in his readers. The visit to the front gave Kipling a welcome opportunity to indulge in a fantasy of violence in which the French soldier became the sentimental and outraged hero and the German the bestial object of his revenge. The beauty was outraged French womanhood. Kipling did not overlook the chance to have a crack at English pacifists: "But there is very little human rubbish," he savagely observes, "knocking about France to hinder work or darken counsel."[13]

Watching a group of German prisoners allowed him to exercise his fancy about their nature. This was the breed, he thought, which had raped, sprayed petrol on and ignited property, and voided their excrements on the persons and belongings of their captors. "They stood there outside of all humanity," Kipling writes in tones of scorn, "Yet they were made in the likeness of humanity."[14] Against these animals stand the great civilization of France and the line of defence which stretches from the Channel to the Alps. "It is the rampart put up by Man against the Beast," Kipling exults, "precisely as in the Stone Age. If it goes, all that keeps us from the Beast goes with it."[15]

The high rhetoric of Kipling's praise for French valour and self-sacrifice degenerates at one point into an anti-climax that would be comic if it were not so earnest. "France," he asserts, "has discovered the measure of her soul. . . . One sees this not alone in the—it is more than contempt of death—in the godlike preoccupation of her people under arms which makes them put death out of the account, but in the equal passion and fervour with which her people throughout give themselves to the smallest as well as to the greatest tasks that may in any way serve their sword. I might tell you something that I saw of the cleaning out of certain latrines."[16]

France was not the only venue for Kipling's wartime activities. He had long been a favourite of the Royal Navy, and in 1915, the Admiralty asked him to visit the auxiliary vessels and smaller craft, which were apt to be neglected in favour of the more glamorous battleships, cruisers, and destroyers (plate 26). *The Fringes of the Fleet* is the propaganda book which came out of his visit. It presents to the reader a picture of a kind of *Stalky and Co.* navy, with boys sailing around in their little ships playing elaborate jokes on the Germans. The boyishness and the fun only emphasize the superiority of the Royal Navy over the German fleet. "It is no lie," he claims, "that at the present moment we hold all the seas in the hollow of our hands. . . . Nor is it any lie that, had we used the Navy's bare fist instead of its gloved hand from the beginning, we would in all likelihood have shortened the war. . . . It is no lie that we continue on our inexplicable path animated, we will continue to believe till other proof is given, by a cloudy idea of alleviating or mitigating something for somebody—not ourselves."[17] This elaborate circumlocution is meant as irony against the government policy of respecting neutral rights to trade with belligerent nations, to which Kipling was bitterly opposed. From the start, he was all for total war on the sea. This policy would undoubtedly have ruined British relations with the United States and undermined Britain's high moral position in the war.

Later on, in May 1917, Rudyard Kipling visited the Italian front and subsequently wrote *The War in the Mountains* as an account of that experience. The first part of the narrative was suppressed at the request of the British government because it contained one of Kipling's customary intemperate outbursts against young men who had not joined up. This section was printed from the manuscript in *The Reader's Guide to Rudyard Kipling*. The attack on "the young civils [men] in such elegant costumes . . . with the beautiful ladies at lunch and tea" might have upset some influential Italians. The artistic purpose of this section, however, is clear. It was meant to show that "Rome is Rome"—the corrupt city of all the ages—and that up there in the mountains all is work and courage and light. Even at this point in the war, Kipling could still drum up enthusiasm for the glory of the enterprise.

Kipling went through the area just north of the plain of Udine where many Italian soldiers lay buried. "They lie, as it were," he intones, "in a giant smithy where the links of the new Italy are being welded under smoke and flame and heat."[18] He continues on lyrically about the Italians' road-building efforts, their skill, humour, and devotion to service in the face of immense difficulties caused by the spring thaw. "No one is hurried or over-pressed," he writes, "and the 'excitable Latin' of the *Boche* legend does not appear."[19]

Kipling went further north into the mountains, beyond Gorizia, where he saw preparations for the coming offensive. "The heathen mountains in front, had yet to be baptized and entered on the roll of honour, and one could not say at that moment which one of them would be most honourable, or what cluster of herdsmen's huts would carry the name of a month's battle through

Plate 26   Rudyard Kipling carried at a canter around the quarterdeck after giving a reading on board *H.M.S. Majestic.*

the ages."[20] The painful irony of this statement in the light of the defeat suffered by the Italian forces in this area six months later is inescapable to the modern reader. Even more ironic is the contrast between the rhetorical and abstract nature of Kipling's prose and the concrete, laconic force of Hemingway's account of the retreat from Caporetto in *A Farewell to Arms*. No "cluster of herdsmen's huts" was to carry the name of any glorious battle in future ages. But the names of villages were to Hemingway one of the few real things in a universe of empty words like "sacrifice" and "in vain." It is irresistible to record one final irony. "On the simple principle that transportation is civilisation," Kipling says, "the entire Italian campaign is built, and every stretch and curve of every road proves it."[21] What the roads were to prove, of course, is that they were just as vital to an army in retreat, and for invaders, as the broken columns reeled back on Udine in the face of the German attack of October 1917.

Sir Arthur Conan Doyle was also a persevering tourist of the front lines, and he became an ardent publicist for the Allies. His writings, however, seldom had the vengeful quality of Kipling's propaganda. Although Conan Doyle had often been a severe critic of British military policy, he became an ardent defender of it during the war and, like Kipling, seemed to believe what the generals told him and to trust their judgment. His largest enterprise in the war was the writing of a six-volume military history. It was better informed than most other such efforts, but he had of course to conform to the requirements of censorship, and it was permeated by an unflagging optimism. In his histories, Allied losses in ground, men, and material were constantly underplayed and German losses just as constantly exaggerated.

Throughout the war, Conan Doyle was an indefatigable proponent of cavalry or, rather, what he called mounted infantry. He was one of the promoters of the fantasy which was to haunt British strategists throughout the war—the idea of a cavalry breakthrough—dramatized by a well-known poster (plate 27). It was a fantasy which strongly appealed to the British High Command, who were mostly cavalry officers. It was later to earn the well-deserved scorn of H. G. Wells. "Ten thousand well-mounted, well-trained riflemen," exulted Conan Doyle in an essay called "The 'Contemptible Little Army,'" "young officers to lead them, all broad Germany before them—there lies one more surprise for the doctrinaires of Berlin."[22]

Conan Doyle's work as a historian and reporter created a demand for his appearances at the front. In the early summer of 1916 Lord Newton, then in charge of propaganda at the Foreign Office, a competitor of Wellington House, asked him to visit the Italian front and write about it. Conan Doyle refused because, he said, he had nothing with which to compare the Italian front, not having seen any other. So Newton got Conan Doyle sent out to the British sector of the Western Front. He dressed in his imposing uniform as

Plate 27 Recruiting poster. The idea of a cavalry break-through haunted Conan Doyle, and many British generals, throughout the war.

deputy-lieutenant of Surrey, which made him look like a general, and he received red-carpet treatment all the way. He then went on to visit the Italian front and later the French sector of the Western Front (plate 28).

These three visits not only provided material for his military history, but also gave rise to *A Visit to Three Fronts*, published in 1916. This book was intended as a morale booster for the Allies. It is full of praise for the fighting

Plate 28   Conan Doyle on the Italian Front, 1916.

spirit of the armies and pious hopes for future victories. The material was revised somewhat for inclusion in his autobiography, *Memories and Adventures*.

Conan Doyle was better equipped to write about this experience than
most literary tourists of the front. But while he gets down to the practical
problems of trench-holding, logistics, and administration, all three Allies
continue to appear as stereotypes. On the British front there are the fresh-
faced public-schoolboy officers and the bronzed troops, quietly heroic; all

are cheerful, resolute, and steady. General Haig is given high praise. It is significant that in his revision for the autobiography, Conan Doyle admitted that Haig's officers' mess "was the dullest in France."[23] He probably quite unwittingly put his finger on the general's central weakness. Lacking a sense of humour, Haig also lacked a sense of proportion. This led to his grim and deadly idea of attrition—a sterile military policy which treated armies as millstones to grind down the enemies' resistance. But while the war lasted, Haig was above criticism.

Conan Doyle also did his bit for the myth of the romance of the trenches. He went into what he lyrically called "the most wonderful spot in the world—the front firing trench, the outer breakwater which holds back the German tide."[24] So the trench became the moral as well as the physical bulwark against the Hun. For visitors to the front, who were in and out of the line in usually ideal conditions, this was easy enough to say. It was very different for the troops with their wearing round of trench duties in all sorts of weather.

Conan Doyle was briefly under fire during an artillery duel, and he conveys the excitement of the occasion. Again, his experience was very different from the tension and depression inevitably attendant on exposure to shellfire over a long period. In stark contrast to his pictures of heroic British fighting men is his impression of some conscientious objectors who were doing their bit in working parties behind the line. Even these "half-mad cranks," as he scornfully labels them, "whose absurd consciences prevent them from barring the way to the devil" seem to be "turning into men under the prevailing influence." With condescension and prejudice, Conan Doyle adds: "I saw a batch of them, neurotic and largely bespectacled, but working with a will by the roadside. They will volunteer for the trenches yet."[25] He had no doubt of the salutary moral influence exerted by the fighting line.

Conan Doyle turned up on the Italian front at a quiet time— some months before the retreat from Caporetto—so he had a pleasant visit to the trenches north of Udine and in the mountains (plate 28). He was able to report back to England on the fine state of Italian morale and wrote the usual description of the courage and high spirits of the troops. He adds, "on the whole, however, it may be said that in the Austro-Italian war there is nothing which corresponded with the extreme bitterness of our western conflict. The presence or absence of the Hun makes all the difference."[26] Conan Doyle flattered himself that his own bulky presence on the Italian front had been a fillip to the soldiers' morale. They had read of the Allies, but they never saw any. His self-importance rather carried him away later on, when, in his autobiography, he theorized that if the Italians had seen more of Allied visitors, the disaster at Caporetto might not have happened.

Conan Doyle had one bad moment on his trip to the French front when a fiery little French general demanded at lunch one day: "Sherlock Holmes, est-ce qu'il est un soldat dans l'armée Anglaise?" After an awful hush around the mess table, Conan Doyle stumbled out with, "Mais, mon general, il est trop vieux pour service."[27] This exchange may well have given Conan Doyle the idea of pulling Holmes out of retirement to do his bit for the war effort.

He notes with some relish a certain savagery among the French soldiers, which he put down to the fact that the Germans occupied a substantial part of France. He looks forward to the day when French bayonets would sweep forward to kill the invaders. After three days of inspection, the party returned to Paris, Conan Doyle leaving the French troops with this resounding message. "Soldiers of France, farewell! In your own phrase, I salute you! Many have seen you who had more knowledge by which to judge your manifold virtues, many also who had more skill to draw you as you are, but never one, I am sure who admired you more than I. Great was the French soldier under Louis the Sun-King, great too under Napoleon, but never was he greater than today."[28] The romance of war lived on in this rhetoric.

Paul Fussell has brilliantly analysed how literary language consistently obstructed truthtelling about the war and how easily writers lapsed into cliché and the passive voice when it became necessary to describe casualties or defeat. By 1916, also, the propagandists had established a vocabulary of high-flown abstractions which could be used to conceal the truth, romanticize the action, and fictionalize the outcome. A solid genre of what Bertrand Russell aptly called "the foul literature of glory" established the conventions in which the writers chronicled the succession of stalemates, defeats, or meagre successes that plagued the Allies throughout 1915, 1916, and 1917. It became the job of the writers in uniform to counter the gloom that the public in Allied and neutral countries felt as some of the facts about these reverses filtered through the screen of censorship. Concomitantly they helped stifle any sense of realism about the war — realism which might have substantially changed the strategy of the generals and the diplomacy of the politicians.

Among those who were used to provide false views of disasters was the well-known poet and novelist, John Masefield. He was thirty-six in 1914, but he was anxious to work for the cause. He was at the Wellington House conference in September, but he wished to take a more active part than many of his fellow writers. So he signed up for the Red Cross and served for a time in France. He then went to the Dardanelles expedition with an ambulance unit where he had a ringside seat at the elaborate and costly disaster (plate 29).[29]

In January 1916, Wellington House called upon him to make a lecture tour in the United States. One of his tasks was to try to judge the extent of the German influence on the midwest. On his return, he reported that he had been heckled from time to time about the Dardanelles expedition and asked

Plate 29   John Masefield.

Plate 30   Lt. Col. John Buchan, 1916.

if he might write about the subject in order to counter the bad image of the event in the United States and elsewhere. The resulting book was *Gallipoli*. His technique in the book is to avoid the main issue consistently. Not a word is said about the blunders in grand strategy and little about the tactical plans of either the military or naval command. Masefield also plays down the opportunities missed and the terrible delays which cost the expedition the essential factor of surprise, the main reason for the heavy casualties when the assault finally took place. Masefield's task was to show the glory and minimize the failures. He considered the campaign "not as a tragedy, nor as a mistake, but as a great human effort, which came, more than once, very near to triumph, achieved the impossible many times, and failed, in the end . . . from something which had nothing to do with arms nor with the men who bore them."[30]

Here he shifted the blame with a vengeance, largely into the laps of the gods, who supplied bad weather at crucial times. But this report was far from the whole truth. General Sir Ian Hamilton, in charge of the operation, wasted a whole month reorganizing the transports in Alexandria, giving the Turks ample time to strengthen what had up till then been inadequate defences. By the time he got back to the Dardanelles with his force, the Turks were ready for him.[31] Masefield was quite right in saying that they presented a formidable barrier to the attacking troops. He concentrated much of his lyric power on his description of the panoply of Allied arms. When the fleet and the transports finally gathered at Lemnos to stage the assault, he writes: "No such gathering of fine ships has ever been seen upon this earth, and the beauty and the exultation of the youth upon them made them seem like sacred things as they moved away."[32]

This is all very well, but all the beauty in the world did not make up for the lack of training in landing on a hostile coast or for inadequate assault weapons. Gallipoli was a saga of improvisation at best, colossal blundering at worst. The troops were set an impossible task at most points of landing, and the irony was that many of the survivors had to attack against equally formidable defences on the Somme a year later. Masefield ignored the blundering and concentrated on his ace card—the spirit of the troops. "All that they felt," he writes, "was a gladness of exultation that their young courage was to be used. They went like Kings in a pageant to their imminent death." This smacks of the overwrought lyricism of the war poems of Rupert Brooke, who died of blood poisoning en route to the Dardanelles.

John Masefield drew on the pastoral tradition for another book he wrote for the government, *The Old Front Line*. This was supposed to be an account of the Battle of the Somme, but the army authorities denied him access to brigade and battalion diaries—material too revealing in 1916 and '17. Instead of the battle account he had intended, he writes a retrospective summary in which that whole dismal episode is distanced by nostalgia and elegy. "There is nothing now to show," he writes of Gommencourt, "that this was one of the tragical places of this war."[33] The Germans had abandoned the whole area to take up stronger positions on the Hindenburg line, so *The Old Front Line* reads like a naturalist's field guide to a neglected area of countryside. "In a few years time," Masefield writes, "when this war is a romance in memory, the soldier looking for his battlefield will find his marks gone. Centre Way, Peel Trench, Munster Alley, and these other paths of glory will be deep under the corn, and gleaners will sing at Dead Mule Corner."[34] The topography of the battlefield is described in detail, with many pastoral similes and scattered references to heroic actions. The book ends where it should properly have begun: with the first wave climbing over the parapets on 1 July 1916, "having done with all pleasant things, advancing across No Man's Land to begin the Battle of the Somme."

Wellington House found another fine soldier-publicist for the glories of Allied campaigns in John Buchan, the publisher, historian, novelist, and former young imperialist with Lord Milner in South Africa. He soon became one of the most successful and prolific authors of war literature and was incorporated into the official effort (plate 30). His entire *History of the War* is a work of propaganda, consistently giving the most positive slant to the news from all fronts of the war. For example, in Volume V, published late in 1915, Buchan writes cheerfully, "Trench warfare cannot last indefinitely. The enemy cannot fall back forever on new trench lines. . . . The reason is that human powers are limited . . . and the steady pressure of those winter weeks, barren as it might seem in brilliant results, was more vital to our ultimate success than any spectacular victory."[35] Equally cheerful is his estimate of casualties for 1914, which appears in the same volume. "There can be little doubt," he writes, in one of his favourite formulae, "that the Germans, especially in the West, lost out of all proportion to their opponents." It would be truer to say that his figures were out of all proportion to common sense. The Germans, he estimates, suffered in that year 1,300,000 killed and wounded. In that same time, he reckons, the British suffered only 100,000. On the basis of these figures, Buchan quite rightly concludes, "We can therefore regard the long-drawn Battle of West Flanders as an Allied gain."[36]

In the autumn of 1915, Buchan was commissioned as lieutenant in the Intelligence Corps and was often in France as official *rapporteur* for the War Office. By March 1916 he was a major, shuttling back and forth across the channel, drafting communiqués and compiling summaries of the fighting for the use of the press and Wellington House. He also found time to give optimistic speeches to various groups. In one such of 16 March 1916, called "The Future of the War," he gives his customary sunny explanation of events, military, political, and financial, states that the German war machine was running down, and predicts that there would be a crisis in the next three months, followed by a decisive defeat of the Germans both on land and sea. Out of the victory would surely emerge a more democratic society in England. If this were to happen, he winds up, "this war may rank as one of the happiest events in our history."[37] The next few months instead saw defeat on the Somme, the standoff at Jutland, and the loss of much of the spirit and many of the men who might have made a better England afterwards.

John Buchan was a prime victim of that "irony of circumstance" which Paul Fussell discusses at length in *The Great War and Modern Memory*. In June 1916 Kitchener's New Army began to mass itself along the Somme front in preparation for the assault, which was meant to take the German first and second-line trenches and, quite possibly, roll up the enemy lines in a decisive defeat that was expected to bring about the end of the war.

In spite of the reverses that Buchan had already witnessed in France, particularly at Loos, he shared the infectious high spirits of this volunteer army, which was the élite and pride of Britain and the Empire. On 1 July and subsequent days, the army was embroiled in terrible debacle, but with an extraordinary tenacity and doggedness Buchan managed to hold on to his belief in victory in the face of all the bloody and outrageous facts of loss that he saw and heard about.

In late June he went out to G.H.Q. in France to cover the imminent "Big Push," as it was universally called before the event. "It's a mad romantic place," he wrote his wife on 27 June. "I have just had luncheon at a little inn in the courtyard in an old French walled town on the top of a hill. And I breakfasted in Portland Place. I came over with Belloc. He had taken the sacraments . . . in case he was blown up, but we have survived and it was all for nothing."[38]

There was no time for such lighthearted comment when the Battle of the Somme began three days later. The book that Buchan wrote about the battle is an expansion of his account of the battle in Volume XVI of *The Nelson History of the War*. The volumes were called *The Battle of the Somme: First Phase* and *The Battle of the Somme: Second Phase*, published in 1916 and early 1917. He managed to win the battle single-handed, for certainly no other Englishman came anywhere near doing so. The account contains all the ringing clichés and exaggerations of the genre, and by representing that almost unmitigated hell in such glowing colours, Buchan falsifies the whole military situation on the Western Front. By his omissions and exaggerated claims he makes not only the common soldier but also the commanding generals look superb.

In an introductory section Buchan describes the good spirits and harmony of the army units before the battle in language rich with the imperial vision. This army is "the flower of the manhood of the British Empire, differing in origin and antecedents, but alike in discipline and courage and resolution."[39] Then Buchan gets down to the attack, which begins with a massive bombardment. This is followed by the first massed infantry assault at 7:30 A.M. on 1 July over what Buchan says is a twenty-five mile front. It was actually eighteen. Even the British Official History points out that it was a bad mistake to attack on such a long front instead of concentrating heavy assaults on selected points of the enemy line. General Sir Henry Rawlinson was the architect of this plan to advance on a broad front after a prolonged artillery barrage which was supposed to destroy the enemy's trenches. Haig believed that the plan was wrong, but, being a cavalryman, he did not overrule his subordinate, who had a long experience with infantry tactics, largely in earlier wars. Buchan writes of this first assault: "The British moved forward in line after line, dressed as if on parade; not a man wavered or broke ranks; but minute by minute the ordered lines melted away under the deluge of high explosive, shrapnel, rifle, and machine-gun fire."[40]

The same phrase about how the orderly lines "melted away" is used in the Official History in describing an attack on Beaumont Hamel. Paul Fussell acutely compares such terms to a "merciful soft focus, as in the cinema" that cloaks the brutal reality of the countless deaths.[41] So confident had the British commanders been of the effectiveness of the bombardment that there had been no reconnaissance of the ground. The troops were ordered over the top into a complete unknown. Carrying packs weighing at least sixty-six pounds, they walked out in full daylight into uncut wire, over ground badly broken up by shellfire. German machine-gunners, emerging from deep dugouts to set their weapons in place, were presented with the incredible target of several waves of British and Empire troops moving in close order towards them. The consequence was not a battle but abattoir slaughter.

Buchan dignifies the massacre with such phrases as "the splendid troops . . . shed their blood like water for the liberty of the world."[42] His troops are always "bronzed," are "quick to kindle to a fight," "formidable," and so on. Barbara Tuchman has aptly called this sort of language the typical "verbal nobility" of British military history. The reality behind these fine words was the desperate struggle of the troops to survive the suicidal tactics of their generals. "The strength of our plan," Buchan explains, "lay in its deliberateness, and the mathematical sequence of its stages."[43] This was precisely its main weakness. It substituted mathematics for common sense and provided neither flexibility nor room for the initiative of front-line commanders either to exploit success or accept failure. As Basil Liddell Hart observed, "1916 marked the nadir of infantry attacks, the revival of formations that were akin to the eighteenth century in their formalism and lack of manoeuvring power."[44]

By evening most of the survivors were back in the trenches from which they had started that morning with such high hopes. Of about 110,000 men who made the assault, 57,540 were casualties, 20,000 of them killed. No wonder that a recent military writer has asserted: "July 1, 1916 was the blackest day in the history of the British Army."[45] The German army on that day, on the other hand, according to a recent writer, suffered only 8,000 casualties.[46] That represents a loss rate of seven to one in Germany's favour, whereas the British at the beginning of the battle outnumbered the Germans by the same ratio! Buchan made his usual large claims for German losses. At the attack on Montauban alone, he asserts, the "6th Bavarian regiment lost 3,000 out of a total strength of 3,500."[47] Buchan himself was safe in the rear along with the generals. He wrote his wife that evening: "A perfect summer day and larks are singing above the bombardment; as I walk back an old fellow is selling oranges to the transport drivers: a queer thing war, and a damned silly thing."[48]

The defeat should have given Haig pause. Liddell Hart notes that even as late as 5 June Haig had warned Rawlinson that if his attack met with considerable opposition, he might decide to suspend it and proceed with another he had planned at Messines. Liddell Hart surmises that the bulldog element prevailed in Haig's makeup, and he decided to go on with the slaughter. Buchan continues his narrative in praise of these terrible tactics.

The next major assault was on 14 July on a four-mile front about which Buchan writes triumphantly: "The attack failed nowhere. In some parts it was slower than others, where the enemy's defence had been less comprehensively destroyed, but by the afternoon all our tasks had been accomplished. . . . The audacious enterprise had been crowned with unparalleled success." Cavalry was called in for the first time since 1914. "That cavalry should be used at all," exults Buchan, "seemed to forecast the end of the long trench fighting and the beginning of a campaign in the open."[49]

Buchan makes it sound like a major advance. But what was the reality? There were some initial successes, writes Liddell Hart, and when the cavalry was brought up, "roseate expectations pictured open warfare on the skyline, but once more it proved to be a mirage in the military desert." The attack faltered. German reserves came into action, and late on the next day several of the positions were evacuated under pressure of counterattacks. Two more months of nibbling attacks were to take place before the positions were regained. The surprise storm of the Somme "Bastille, on July 14th," Liddell Hart concludes, "brought the British to the verge of a strategic decision; thereafter their efforts degenerated into a battle of attrition."[50]

Ignoring these bleak facts in concluding his first volume, Buchan claims that Germany had exhausted her capital of defences during the battle: "Thenceforth, the campaign entered upon a new stage, and the first stage, which in strict terms we call the Battle of the Somme, had ended in an Allied victory. . . . Today Germany is the Allies' inferior."[51] He also asserts that German casualty figures were as high as those of the Allies. Of the many photographs that adorn the book, none shows a wounded or dead British soldier. The verbal equivalent of this cover-up is the unnamed padre whom Buchan quotes, "The Germans may write on their badges that God is with them, but our lads—they know."[52] If this remark was ever made, some of the lads must have wondered what kind of God this was.

Liddell Hart observes that after the attacks of 14 July faltered, "Nearly two months of bitter fighting followed, during which the British made little progress at much cost, and the infantry of both sides served as compressed cannon-fodder for artillery consumption."[53] Buchan chronicles these two months in his sequel, *The Battle of the Somme: Second Phase*. In spite of the appalling losses his troops had suffered, Haig was still optimistic about achieving a breakthrough. To help achieve this aim, Haig called on the tanks, which many critics have asserted was his major strategic error. He was able to use only thirty-two of these machines, nine of which got through with the front line of infantry in the surprise attack on Flers. Buchan makes much of this local success, but the reality was that Haig had squandered a secret weapon, which might well have had a devastating effect if it had been used in a surprise attack in force.

In another attack on the right of the line, the Guards division lost heavily. Among those killed was Raymond Asquith, the son of the prime minister, a scholar and poet, to whom Buchan, an old friend, paid tribute in words which were to become part of the formula of Great War commemoration: "Debonair and brilliant and brave, he is now part of that immortal England which knows not age or weariness or defeat."[54] His death contributed to the political collapse of his father in December 1916. More nibbling attacks finally gained the high ground which was the Germans last complete line of defence, yet their stubborn resistance offered little hope for a real breakthrough.

Buchan saw it differently. "A fortnight of fair bright days would suffice for a crowning achievement. The hope was destined to fail. The guns were scarcely silent after the great attack on the 26th when the weather broke, and October was one long succession of tempestuous gales and drenching rains."[55] Haig would have done well to have stayed where he was on high ground, commanding the enemy's positions, but he kept up the attack down the hill. When the attack finally petered out, he had condemned his troops to a winter in the appalling stench, filth, and discomfort of flooded trenches, linked by a tenuous network of duckboards from which a slip could often bring death by drowning. Like Masefield, Buchan used bad weather and bad luck to excuse failures of generalship, but he concludes that in spite of all, Haig had achieved what he wanted: "We did what we set out to do; step by step we drove our way through the German defences. . . . Our major purpose was attained. . . . It was not the recapture of territory that we sought, but the weakening of the numbers, *matériel*, and *moral* of the enemy."[56]

And what were the facts? Martin Middlebrook gives them succinctly: "On 14 November the battle ended. No one could ever agree on the final casualty figures, but it is certain that in the 140 days that the battle had lasted, Britain's share was over 400,000. For this loss, Haig's troops had advanced exactly six miles and were still four miles short of Bapaume, which the cavalry had hoped to take in the opening attack."[57] Many critics agree with A. J. P. Taylor's view that, strategically, "the battle of the Somme was an unredeemed defeat."[58]

If anything can redeem the memory of the battle, it is the incredible courage and determination of the men who fought it, on both sides. But the British and Empire junior officers and men were under no illusions about the waste and mismanagement to which they had been subjected by their generals. Just before his death in battle, an Australian officer who had fought courageously from the beginning, wrote in a letter of the "murder" of many of his friends "through the incompetence, callousness, and personal vanity of those high in authority." Liddell Hart quotes another Australian who wrote: "For Christ's sake, write a book on the life of an infantryman, and by doing so you will quickly prevent these shocking tragedies."[59] Instead, they got Buchan's whitewash, *The Battle of the Somme* in two volumes.

A little later Buchan wrote a similar defence of the Battle of Jutland. It is instructive to contrast his account of the battle (which he compared with the Battle of Trafalgar!) with Arthur Marder's account of it in the third volume of *From Dreadnought to Scapa Flow*. According to Marder, there was no Nelson touch in the Battle of Jutland. "Initiative, fearlessness, responsibility, were sadly lacking among the flag officers and captains," he writes, "One sees it everywhere."[60] Buchan made the British admirals look as good on paper as he made the generals and thus helped perpetuate their command.

He knew well enough the facts of both battles. He was privy to all the despatches and had friends in both services. One of them, Stair Gillon, was a captain in an infantry brigade on the Somme and later became Buchan's assistant at the Department of Information. Gillon bitterly condemned the bad staff work which led to the deaths of many of his men.[61] The strain of duplicity evidently told on Buchan as it did on Bennett. He suffered severe gastric pains after the Somme and almost died from an attack in October 1916. In February 1917, he was operated on for an ulcer and could not return to his duties for some time.

But even after the war, he was unable to admit responsibility for his evasions. A potted version of his history of the war was severely criticized for its inadequacies by Lloyd George and others. As late as 1940, he was still praising Haig. Admitting that the general had made mistakes, he still asserted that Haig showed himself to be "remarkably receptive and prescient."[62] Even in Buchan's own files at Queen's University there is a document casting doubt on this. It is a copy of a secret brief prepared by Haig for the War Office in 1927, advocating the continuing value of cavalry units and defending their role in the Great War!

Another writer on the Allied side was able to present a truer account of various battles. Sir Max Aitken was given the rank of lieutenant-colonel and appointed himself Canadian Eye Witness when he went out to G.H.Q. in France in March 1915 to observe and report on the activities of the First Division of the Canadian Expeditionary Force.[63] In the reports which Aitken sent back to be printed in Canadian and British newspapers, he regularly gave the names of units and of officers and men engaged in battle in defiance of censorship rules. Very soon, the Canadian units were getting the best publicity of any of the units fighting in France, to the growing anger of the other Allied governments. Late in 1915, Aitken gathered together his despatches and, with a little help on his style from Rudyard Kipling, published the first volume of *Canada in Flanders, the Official Story of the Canadian Expeditionary Force*.

Although Aitken admitted mistakes and acknowledged casualties, he did gloss over failures in Allied strategy. For example, most of the first volume of *Canada in Flanders* is devoted to the 2nd Battle of Ypres, in which the Canadians heroically filled the gap left by French colonial troops after the Germans first released poison gas. As Liddell Hart points out, the Ypres salient should never have been allowed to stabilize in the first place, since that great loop in the line formed "one huge artillery target" in which casualties were enormous and largely unnecessary.[64] Beaverbrook makes no mention of the fact that the Allies should have fallen back, as the fighting commanders had recommended, on a straight line in front of Ypres.

This situation did allow Aitken to make the most of heroic stands by Canadian troops and to raise a rallying cry for more recruits. He was at least as eager an imperialist as Kipling or Buchan. Writing *Canada in Flanders* gave him a glorious opportunity to celebrate the unity of the Empire as Canada's gallant sons proved their manhood alongside their British brethren. For him it was Canada's great chance to emerge from colonial status to become a nation in its own right. The agenda hidden in *Canada in Flanders* is the claim of the Canadian government to have a stronger voice in the conduct of the war, a voice bought with the blood of its soldiers. Ironically, through his rhetorical treatment of battle and death, burial becomes baptism. "The wave that fell on us around Ypres," he proclaims, "has baptised the Dominion into nationhood—the mere written word 'Canada,' glows now with a new meaning before all the civilised world."[65]

Aitken had hoped to publish the second volume of *Canada in Flanders* in July 1916, but the book was held up by the censors, even though much of it had already been printed in the newspapers. He complained to Sir Robert Borden, the Canadian prime minister, to no effect, so he then launched a campaign against the censor's actions in the form of a confidential memo addressed to influential friends in Canada and Britain. His analysis of the changes demanded by the censor shows clearly how the system managed to suppress even a moderately realistic account of what was going on at the front. The changes would have taken all the drama and bite out of Aitken's reports. For example, "The presence of wounded men in a crowded trench passes the limits of horror" was changed by the censor to "The presence of wounded men in the trench makes it far worse." Aitken's mild criticism of the staff on issues of shell shortages, of tactics, and of the conduct of individual units had all been deleted. For example, the censor took out a reference to the Northumberland Regiment failing to improve their trenches for the Canadian relief.[66]

Ultimately, Aitken's intense lobbying was effective, and the book was published as written in January 1917. The censor had won a partial victory by the delay, since the account had lost its immediacy in the wake of the larger drama of the Somme. By that time Aitken was busy organizing Canada's propaganda efforts in London. The country's continuing colonial status is emphasized by the fact that Ottawa did not set up its own information service until near the end of the war. Aitken handed over *Canada in Flanders* to Captain Charles G. D. Roberts, the poet and novelist. Roberts had a more romantic view of battle than Aitken. He combines some medieval mythology with his interests as a naturalist to gloss over such bitterly fought battles as Courcelette and the disastrous assaults on Regina and Desire trenches. Roberts ends the third volume of *Canada in Flanders* with a brio that could have been shared by few of the surviving Canadian soldiers stuck in the winter mud of the Somme valley. "To the Canadian Battalions," he writes, "the impregnable and the invincible had come to mean a challenge which they welcomed joyously. They knew the utmost of which men were capable was now confidently expected of them. How gloriously they were to justify that high expectation, on the dreadful Ridge of Vimy, amid the bloody slag-heaps of Lens, and along the fire-swept crest of Passchendaele, remains to be told in the succeeding volumes of their story."[67] Apparently even such realism as Roberts conveys was too much for the censors, who held up the third volume for a long time, as the references to battles of 1917 show. Such delays rendered book publication useless. No further volumes of *Canada in Flanders* appeared.

Another Canadian novelist, Beckles Willson, had been appointed to Aitken's staff in London to help organize the Canadian War Records. The men quarrelled, and Aitken took advantage of the illness of the war correspondent of *The Daily Express* to get rid of Willson by sending him out to France in his place.[68] Obviously Willson was less concerned with realism than Aitken, and his articles for the *Express* were praised by Sir Gilbert Parker and Conan Doyle. Masterman had them collected and published under the title *In the Ypres Salient, the Story of a Fortnight's Fighting, June 2-16, 1916*. It was probably published the same year, thus scooping Aitken's second volume of *Canada in Flanders*. Willson took for his model the vague and sonorous battle accounts of John Buchan, even prefacing the book with a quotation from the *Nelson History*, full of the clichés about "sacrifice," "consecrated ground," "hallowed," and so on. Unexpectedly, however, in a prefatory note, Willson lets slip the information that "Ypres and the Salient are chiefly retained for sentimental reasons." He justifies this position on the curious ground that "this whole War was avowedly waged, in the first instance, for sentimental reasons."[69] Willson's account contains no criticism of Allied strategy or tactics. He dramatizes the fighting spirit and valour of the Canadian troops in a brief epic which gains a certain artistic unity from a pattern of fighting in which Germans bombard the Canadian trenches and then capture them; the Canadians bombard the same positions and recapture them. There is no hint of the waste and futility of such bloody work.

Between them the civilian writers and those in uniform created a myth about the Western Front which held sway at home and among the neutrals until the end of the war. Censorship ensured that little bad news would pass, but the writers exceeded mere complicity in the illusions created by censorship. They embellished the tales of barbarism and blood-lust on the part of the Germans, suppressed reports of staff incompetence, and sustained the myth of the high quality of British leadership.

Soldiers returning to Britain on leave were astounded at the beliefs about the war held by the civilians. Many, like Robert Graves, found conversation with their parents all but impossible. A war neurosis prevailed, fed by the work of the propagandists. This neurosis insisted on the continuing need for the sacrifices at the front until total victory had been achieved. Most people showed little awareness of what conditions were really like in the trenches. The curtain of evasions and misconceptions was so thick that few serving soldiers could pierce it with the accounts of their own experiences.

No doubt the writers felt that for the sake of civilian morale it was necessary to keep the curtain firmly closed. But did they never pause to consider the long-term effects of concealing the blunders made by army staff and High Command? Did the deaths of cherished friends and relatives not make them wonder if all the sacrifices they wrote about were futile? The answer is surely that these men of sensibility must have felt despair at the discrepancy between what they knew and what they wrote. Apparently, a patriotism almost mystical in its power and an overmastering belief in the necessity of total victory kept them at their work of propaganda.

8

FICTION AS PROPAGANDA: WAR STORIES

One thing is worse than a long war, and that is a long peace.
IAN HAY. 1917

Just as the absence of hard news from the front made it expedient for the propaganda services to send authors on reporting missions, so that same lack caused writers to create fantasies about what was going on. In most cases these fantasies were spontaneous; in others, it is clear that the fictions received official backing. The public appetite for stories about the war was very strong; people had a craving to know about the fighting and to see their faith in the moral and physical strength of the Allies reflected in an accessible form. Many members of this public were gullible and uncritical, as is shown by the quick acceptance of wild rumours that circulated in Britain in the early months of the war. The most famous of these rumours was that thousands of Russian troops, some with snow on their boots, had been seen passing through Britain on their way to the Western Front in sealed trains. Spy scares, rumours of invasions and of imminent, mass Zeppelin raids flourished. Writers seized on these opportunities to satisfy the craving for sensation. However, one of the most successful propaganda myths of the war was created quite inadvertently and unofficially.

Late in August 1914, reports about a battle around the small mining town of Mons began reaching London. A British force had successfully held off a vastly superior German army before retreating in good order. On 29 September a short story by Arthur Machen, titled "The Bowmen," appeared in *The Evening News*. The story is a clumsy, circumstantial narrative apparently told by a soldier who fought at the Battle of Mons. With his unit surrounded by Germans and on the point of being overwhelmed, he suddenly remembers the dinner plates of a London vegetarian restaurant that he had frequented. The plates were decorated by the figure of St. George and the motto *Adsit Anglis Sanctus Georgius*: "May St. George be a present help to the English." Involuntarily the soldier repeats this motto and feels "something between a shudder and an electric shock pass through his body." Then he hears a tumult of voices crying " 'St. George! St. George!' " and " 'Harow! Harow! Monseigneur St. George, succour us' " and similar cries. The soldier sees in front of him "a long line of shapes, with a shining about them." A cloud of arrows flies through the air, and suddenly ten thousand Germans lie dead on the field without visible wounds. The German attack fails, and "the man who knew what nuts tasted like when they called themselves steak knew also that St. George had brought his Agincourt Bowmen to help the English."[1]

The story is the most obvious fantasy, and any claim to seriousness seems to be deliberately undercut by Machen's comic insistence upon the vegetarian restaurant and by the linguistic mixups of the Bowmen's cries. Machen himself was utterly astonished when his potboiler was at once taken up by the masses as gospel truth and his mythical bowmen transformed into angels—a word which does not occur in his story. *The Evening News* was showered with requests for reprint permission, particularly by parish magazines, and Machen was asked by several psychical research journals to reveal his sources. Variants of the story appeared in other papers and magazines, and many distinguished clergymen preached about the angels. In the popular mind, the myth grew in a short time to be the universal experience of the British Expeditionary Force at the Battle of Mons.

After some months of vainly trying to stem the tide by correspondence, Machen reprinted his story in a little book containing three other stories of equally improbable visions called *The Bowmen and Other Legends of the War*. In an introduction, he explained that, as a Christian, he did not deny miracles, but he did deny the miracle of the Bowmen because he had created it himself, and he knew of no shred of evidence to support the current stories about the Angels of Mons. The story's genesis came out of his imagining the "inferno of fire" in which the British troops must have been fighting. These thoughts became mixed with a memory of a ghostly Kipling story (probably "The Lost Legion"), further compounded with the medieval strain in his work which he got from reading G. K. Chesterton. Having quickly finished the story, he was greatly disappointed with the result, thinking it to be "an indifferent piece of work."[2] He was therefore astounded at the success of the tale, which he now felt had gone quite out of his control. It had dawned on him that, "if I had failed in the art of letters, I had succeeded, unwittingly, in the art of deceit."[3] He blamed the churches for exploiting the stories. They had preached not the eternal mysteries, "but a two penny morality, in changing the Wine of the Angels and the Bread of Heaven into gingerbeer and mixed biscuits."[4]

Machen's disclaimer had no effect, and a flood of pamphlets and books pursued the legend, including one by Harold Begbie, who quickly rushed into print *On the Side of the Angels: A Reply to Arthur Machen*. Begbie attacked Machen's callousness in ignoring the depths of suffering caused by the losses at Mons and "the intense eagerness for consolation" in England.[5] No doubt, Begbie asserted, Machen was receiving telepathic messages from some wounded or dying soldier as he thought about the battle. The proof of this is the evidence of a man who survived the battle. There is such a man, Begbie proudly announced, a Lance Corporal———. The unnamed witness was the device almost invariably used by Lord Bryce's Committee on Alleged German Outrages. The reality of Lance Corporal———is attested to by no less than the Lady Superintendent of the Red Cross, Miss Courtenay Wilson, who had it from a nurse, who had it from the lance corporal in hospital. Begbie alleges that he knows of two other soldiers who could confirm sighting the Angels. He also knows a nurse, Phyllis Campbell, who had met two men in a hospital who claimed that they had seen St. George in the sky, turning the Germans back. They knew it was the saint because they had seen his face "on every quid they'd ever had."[6]

Miss Campbell herself shortly produced a book boosting Begbie, called *Back of the Front*. Various officials vouch for the authenticity of the book in prefaces and letters, and Begbie himself appears on the dust jacket, portentously: "I am on the side of the angels and on the side of Miss Campbell." *Back of the Front* is yet another atrocity book with accounts of Miss Campbell in France meeting a trainload of Belgian refugees, most of them Bryce-Report victims— women with their breasts cut off, headless babies, and so on. There follows a highly embroidered version of the Angels of Mons, who are now accompanied by Joan of Arc, St. Michael, and golden clouds. Exalted soldiers know that they have seen St. George, because they "were familiar with his figure on the English sovereign, and had recognised it."[7] Genteel literary English thus irons out Begbie's salty and more apparently authentic version. *Back of the Front* concludes with the usual litany of hate against the bestial, machine-like Germans and with a hymn of praise to a France, "filled with Holy Vengeance." Campbell does not deign to mention units of the British army, let alone any names, to document her work, and so this Angels of Mons clincher peters out into dreary nonsense.

This anti-climax did not prevent at least five more books being published on the topic supporting the angels during the war. Afterwards the angels appeared in the iconography of countless British and Commonwealth war memorials. Historians too have also taken the side of the angels. Even as late as 1966, A. J. P. Taylor remarked, "The Battle of Mons was the first British battle; and the only one where supernatural intervention was observed, more or less reliably, on the British side. Indeed, the 'Angels of Mons' were the only recognition of the war vouchsafed by the Higher Powers."[8]

On the contrary, there is no single shred of hard evidence to support the angels. The whole story seems to be the product of a mass hysteria generated by gullible or unscrupulous men and women. It fed what Begbie rightly called "the intense eagerness for consolation" of a shocked and bewildered people, who were looking for divine intervention in what was obviously going to be a long and murderous struggle.

It was appropriate that Machen should invoke the spirit of Kipling's "The Lost Legion" when he came to write "The Bowmen," for Kipling's militaristic writings established conventions and provided models for many of the fictions of the Great War. However, Kipling's own early war stories on this conflict were written not from the military, but from the civilian point of view, as befitted his own experience. The first of these was published as early as February 1915, and it is a direct response to the Bryce Report atrocity stories. "Swept and Garnished" concerns an elderly, rich German woman, Frau Eberman, who comes down with the flu in her immaculately tidy Berlin apartment. In her fever she believes that a group of ragged, bleeding children come to the apartment, asserting that they are from a devastated Belgian village. They claim that thousands like them have been killed by the Germans. She persuades them to leave. Later her maid enters to find her mistress on her knees cleaning the floor with a lace cover from a radiator "because," she explains, "it was all spotted with the blood of five children—she was perfectly certain that there could be no more than five in the whole world—who had gone away for the moment . . . and Anna was to find them and give them cakes to stop the bleeding, while her mistress swept and garnished that Our dear Lord when He came might find everything as it should be."[9]

Angus Wilson sees the story as a parody of the Victorian sentimental tale of the kind old lady and finds it "a masterly parable of cosiness brutally dispersed." But the psychology of the story is badly flawed. Frau Eberman seems to be genuinely unaware that "thousands" of children had been killed in Belgium. She could only have had a vision of the suffering children if she had had such guilty knowledge. After all, Lady Macbeth tried to scrub out the bloodstains only after she had been racked by pangs of guilt from actual murders. As J. M. S. Tompkins has said, "the suffering of children was a dangerous incentive to Kipling," and it seems that this little waiting company "were rather an inflamed vision of his own rather than a likely hallucination of the old lady."[10]

Kipling's fantasies of revenge did, however, produce one masterpiece: "Mary Postgate," also published in 1915. In this story Mary, a spinster lady's companion, has brought up her mistress's nephew, Wynn, from the age of eleven and looked after him until he entered the Royal Flying Corps. Soon afterwards, at the age of twenty, he is killed on a training flight. Mary goes to the local village to buy paraffin with which to burn the young man's books, toys, and other effects in the fire, "that would burn her heart to ashes." A German bomb falls nearby and kills a nine-year old girl. Mary observes "the ripped and shredded body" before it is covered by a sheet. She then returns home in order to light the bonfire and discovers a badly injured German aviator lying by a nearby tree. Obviously in agony, he asks in broken French for a doctor. Mary replies " 'Nein . . . Ich haben der todt Kinder gesehn.' "[11] ["No . . . I have seen the dead child."] She runs to fetch Wynn's service revolver and points it at the German. The aviator, however, is past resistance, and she returns to building her bonfire. But he groans again, and she cries, " 'Stop that, you bloody pagan,' " echoing a phrase of Wynn's. Wynn, she thinks, "was a gentleman who for no consideration on earth would have torn little Edna into those vividly coloured strips and strings. But this thing hunched under the oak tree had done that thing." As the fire burns, the German slowly dies in agony.

"Now a woman's business," Mary reflects, "was to make a happy home for—for a husband and children. Failing these—it was not a thing one should allow one's mind to dwell upon—but— ." Failing these she sees what her work must be—work which no man would ever have done—that is to take revenge on one who was Wynn's enemy and who had destroyed a child (plate 31).

The sexual connotations are made quite clear by Kipling in his description of Mary's emotions. As she waits, "an increasing rapture laid hold on her. She ceased to think. She gave herself up to feel. Her long pleasure was broken by a sound that she had waited for in agony several times in her life. She leaned forward and listened, smiling." That sound is the death rattle, and when it ceases, Mary appears to have an orgasm: "Mary Postgate drew her breath short between her teeth and shivered from head to foot." " '*That's* all right,' says she contentedly, and went up to the house." She breaks her routine by having a hot bath before tea. Her mistress observes her lying relaxed on the sofa and pronounces her "quite handsome."[12]

The tale is breathtaking in its horror and convincing in its psychology. The frustrated old maid, shaken to her dry depths by the death of her beloved charge, Wynn, and then by that of the little girl, finds her revenge in the only way she can, by officiating as a vestal virgin of sacrifice. Kipling was acute in seizing on the idea that this was work no man could do and creating the particular circumstances which could bring such a horror to pass. The story is, as its defenders have stated, an account of the pathological behaviour of a totally repressed woman, but it is far more than that. Kipling seems to justify the act, to portray Mary with sympathy as well as understanding. By drawing

RED CROSS OR IRON CROSS?

**WOUNDED AND A PRISONER
OUR SOLDIER CRIES FOR WATER.**

THE GERMAN "SISTER"
POURS IT ON THE GROUND BEFORE HIS EYES.

THERE IS NO WOMAN IN BRITAIN
WHO WOULD DO IT.

THERE IS NO WOMAN IN BRITAIN
WHO WILL FORGET IT.

Plate 31   This poster makes an ironic comment on Kipling's story, "Mary Postgate."

on a deep level of myth, he makes of the tale a parable for the times. Mary undergoes a spiritual conversion for a war which, as Kipling says at the outset of the story, "unlike all wars that she could remember, did not stay decently outside England and in the newspapers, but intruded on the lives of the people whom she knew." When she discovers the injured flyer, she thinks he is a British airman, for the uniforms are similar, but then she sees his scalp, which is "as pale as a baby's, and so closely cropped that she could see the disgusting pinky skin beneath." The flyer at once becomes something alien and repulsive, to be referred to henceforth only as "it."

The usual stiff upper lip and punctilio of the British will not do for this war. Mary becomes an exemplary "bloody pagan," brandishing her weapon in front of the sacrificial fire while her enemy slowly dies. She also assumes the role of the vengeful mother for whom "civilized" forms of warfare do not apply. As Angus Wilson has pointed out, the reader has to accept the "possibility that a fine and subtle work of art can also be propaganda written in a spirit that we find repulsive."[13] The point was driven home by Kipling himself when he put his poem of hatred "The Beginnings" right after "Mary Postgate" in his collection *A Diversity of Creatures*:

> It was not part of their blood,
> It came to them very late
> With long arrears to make good,
> When the English began to hate . . .
>
> It was not preached to the crowd,
> It was not taught by the State.
> No man spoke it aloud,
> When the English began to hate. . . .[14]

   This is apparently Kipling's response to the German "Hymn of Hatred." In these very lines he gives the lie to his own statement: "It was not taught by the State." With the aid of propagandists such as Kipling, hatred was taught by the state. "Mary Postgate" is the most vivid testament of hatred to come out of England in the Great War. Released from that context, however, it can be read as a great, and appalling, work of art.

   Kipling's subsequent war stories were written from a military point of view, presumably as he came more and more to identify with the soldiers and sailors on active service. "Sea Constables: A Tale of '15," however, is analogous to "Mary Postgate" in being a revenge story. It also reflects the admiration that Kipling had shown for the Royal Naval Volunteer Reserve officers in *The Fringes of the Fleet*. "Sea Constables" is set in a hotel dining room where a group of these officers in civilian clothes are luxuriating in their first decent dinner in weeks. Kipling sets up the tensions and ironies in the story early by having an American millionaire and music-hall actress at a nearby table make audible remarks about these men being war-shirkers. The actress sings patriotic songs which, according to one of the officers, "make the aunties weep."[15]

   The officers' talk is all shop, of the kind that anyone without experience of the sea would find baffling. They tell a rambling story, which they take up in turn, about following a "newt" — a neutral freighter — which they all believe is carrying a cargo of oil destined for re-fueling U-Boats. The captain is obviously an American, like the actress and the millionaire. All his efforts to escape their attentions are frustrated by their relentless harassment, which includes firing guns all round him. Finally the "newt" is driven into an Irish port where the exhausted captain collapses with bronchial pneumonia. When the last of the pursuing R.N.V.R. officers goes on board to check his papers, he is asked by the sick captain to ferry him to a doctor, for there is not one in this small port.

The officer refuses and, told that he is thereby condemning the captain to death, replies, courteously, "Try to be reasonable, sir. If you had got rid of your oil where it was wanted, you'd have condemned lots of people to death just as surely as if you'd drowned 'em."[16]

The officer does not, like Mary Postgate, stay to watch the captain die, but he has the satisfaction of seeing the newt's flag at half-mast the next morning. His fellow-officers obviously believe that he has acted with propriety. They end their dinner with the toast: " 'Damnation to all neutrals.' " Kipling showed in *The Fringes of the Fleet* how much he disapproved of his country's correct treatment of neutral shipping. "Sea Constables" is his private revenge on those who made a profit from trading with England's enemies. C.E. Carrington believes that the subject of the story is "the moral degradation that infects even decent, law-abiding citizens in war-time."[17] Kipling appears himself to have been so infected, and, through his R.N.V.R. officer, he took the law into his own hands.

Other writers introduced propaganda into their fiction far more subtly than Kipling. John Buchan took full advantage of the spy scares rampant in wartime Britain and found a huge audience for his succession of Dick Hannay adventures, *The Thirty-Nine Steps*, *Greenmantle*, and *Mr. Standfast*. Writing the thrillers was an escape from his arduous official duties. *The Thirty-Nine Steps* came out in the summer of 1916, and soon afterwards, Buchan found himself among Britain's most famous novelists.[18]

The Thirty-Nine Steps is written to a formula that stood Buchan in good stead for all his remaining thrillers. The complicated chase sequence is central to the novel; the rest is a mixture of derring-do and high intrigue. The premise on which the series is based is expressed early in *The Thirty-Nine Steps*: "Away behind all the Governments and the armies there was a big subterranean movement going on, engineered by very dangerous people."[19] At the centre of the hidden web is the master spy who has to be outwitted by the colonial adventurer, Dick Hannay. Buchan expressed the mode well himself through the remark of one of the characters in *The Thirty-Nine Steps*: " 'By God!' he whispered, drawing his breath in sharply, 'it is all pure Rider Haggard and Conan Doyle.' "[20]

Another ingredient gave the book and its successors a strong moral dimension. This is the narrative scheme based on Bunyan's *Pilgrim's Progress*. Christian Dick travels from the City of Destruction—the spy network—to the Celestial City—Allied victory—defeating the German Appolyon on the way.[21] *The Thirty-Nine Steps*, *Greenmantle*, and *Mr. Standfast* served several functions for Buchan. In the first place, they were extensions of his propaganda work, painting the Germans in the bright colours of ruthless aggressors, militarists, and exploiters, full of plots and wickedness. In the second place, they released him from his largely desk-bound work as propagandist into regions where his swashbuckling surrogate Hannay could score freely off the Germans, participate in a cavalry charge, and ultimately command a division in the field, as well as become a master counterspy.

The novels also gave Buchan a chance—not taken too often— to state his own view of the conduct of the war instead of the official one. The *personae* of his characters allowed him to evade responsibility for his critical remarks. For example, Buchan had witnessed the disaster of the Battle of Loos, and in *Greenmantle*, his American character, Blenkiron, says: " 'We in America respect the fighting of the British soldier, but we don't quite catch on to the de-vices of the British Generals. We opine that there is more bellicosity than science among your highbrows. That is so?' "[22] Hannay does not contradict him.

Greenmantle also shows that Buchan had none of the fantasies of vengeance that can be found in the propaganda of Bennett and Kipling. Fleeing from his pursuers in a German forest, Dick Hannay is given shelter by an old woman who looks after him when he falls ill. "That night," Hannay reflects, "I realised the crazy folly of war. When I saw the splintered shell of Ypres and heard hideous tales of German doings, I used to want to see the whole land of the Boche given up to fire and sword. I thought we could never end the war properly without giving the Huns some of their own medicine. But the woodcutter's cottage cured me of such nightmares. I was for punishing the guilty and letting the innocent go free. . . . To be able to laugh and be merciful are the only things that make man better than beasts."[23] The Hannay thrillers took Buchan and his readers away from the deadly stalemate of the Western Front to a war where there is continual movement and excitement. They were often found in the kit of men at the front.

Conan Doyle also took advantage of the spy scares to bring Sherlock Holmes out of retirement once more. Conan Doyle was egged on, no doubt, by the fiery French officer, who had asked him if the great detective had joined up. In "His Last Bow" (1917), Holmes is at first extremely reluctant to give up his hardearned leisure. Only the personal intervention of the prime minister persuades him to buckle on his deerstalker.

The story takes place at the beginning of August 1914. Von Bork, the chief German spy in England, is packing up to leave with his rich cache of British war plans, maps of dock facilities, sites of ammunition factories, and so on. The chief secretary of the German legation has come down from London to congratulate him on his work and to tell him that war is just around the corner. Von Bork now has only to await the appearance of his chief source of information, Altamont, who has the key to all the Royal Naval signal codes. Von Bork then intends to return to Germany. As soon as the secretary leaves, Altamont appears. He hands over—a *Handbook to Bee-Keeping*—overpowers Von Bork, and ties him up.

Altamont is, of course, none other than Sherlock Holmes. He later explains to Watson, in the usual fashion, how he has pulled it off. " 'It has cost me two years, Watson, but they have not been devoid of excitement. When I say that I started my pilgrimage at Chicago, graduated in an Irish secret society at Buffalo, gave serious trouble to the constabulary at Skibbareen and so eventually caught the eye of a subordinate agent of Von Bork, who recommended me as a likely man, you will realize that the matter was complex.' "[24]

This is more than can be said of the story which, because of its propagandistic intent, is without the brilliance and skill of the classic Sherlock Holmes tales. Not only has Holmes caught Von Bork; he has netted all his agents too. All the information that Von Bork has already transmitted to Germany is fake. At the beginning of the story, after the master spy has been congratulated by the German first secretary on the success of his mission, he replies: "[The British] are not very hard to deceive. . . . A more docile, simple folk could not be imagined." He has reckoned without Sherlock Holmes. The great detective supplies the epilogue in his usual omniscient fashion as he looks out from Von Bork's windows over the sea.

'There's an East wind coming, Watson.'
'I think not, Holmes. It is very warm.'
'Good old Watson! You are the fixed point in a changing age. There's an east wind coming all the same; some such wind as never blew in England yet. It will be cold and bitter, Watson, and a good many of us may wither before its blast. But it's God's own wind, nonetheless, and a cleaner, better, stronger land will lie in the sunshine when the storm has cleared.'

Sherlock Holmes, too, subscribed to the doctrine of the moral benefits of war.

Just as Conan Doyle returned to his best-known character, Sir James Barrie tried to use his most congenial genre, the drama, to inspire the people at home. On his return from the fiasco of the American goodwill tour, Barrie immediately embarked on a play that would convey his thoughts on the war and also promote among the British public an appropriately warlike spirit. The result, *Der Tag*, produced just before Christmas, 1914, proved to be almost as much of a fiasco as his tour. This theatrical fustian portrays the Emperor of Germany, encouraged by his Chancellor and ignoring the pleas for peace made by the Spirit of Culture, declaring war on France and Russia.

He is quite sure that dull and sluggish Britain will not enter the war. He dreams of the day when, France and Russia having been crushed, the German army will cross the channel to destroy Britain. And then the final stroke: " 'Carve America in great mouthfuls for my colonists.' "[25]

The play is full of the banalities of current propaganda; Germany is a ruthless militarist power; the Allies are spotless in their virtue. The sentimental imagery is reinforced by an overwrought emphasis on the moral benefits of war. Superimposed on all this is a rather sickly mysticism based on the current legend of the Angels of Mons. Barrie's biographer writes justly that he was "full of feeling that he couldn't quite express. And to tell the truth, it was all rather dull."[26]

Barrie's other writings of the period are collected in *Echoes of the War* (1919). All four sketches are full of patriotic clichés and the sentimentality that the conflict invariably induced in his writing. The second sketch, "The New Word," depicts an ineffably reticent English-middle-class family coping with the situation of seeing a young son off to the front. Mother says to her son, Roger: " 'I wouldn't have had one of you stay at home, though I had a dozen sons. That is, if it is the noble war they all say it is. I'm not clever, Rogie, I have to take it on trust. Surely they wouldn't deceive mothers.' "[27] Interestingly, this statement embodies those feelings of doubt about British propaganda that Barrie seems to be trying to assuage. What if it were not the noble war that it is cracked up to be? Roger's father has no such doubts. Moreover, he is striving to bring out "the new word" of the title. Finally he casts his "grenade": " 'I'm fond of you, my boy.' " Roger squirms and properly rejects an implied offer of an embrace, but he manages a "dear Father" before leaving. Such emotional expansiveness is, in Barrie's view, one of the benefits of the war.

Two of the other sketches in *Echoes of the War* appear to have been written later on, after two of Barrie's favourite godsons had been killed in action and he had lost other friends and relatives. They are not about aggression and revenge, but about death and reconciliation. "Barbara's Wedding" concerns the marriage of a nurse to an army captain, who had been her uncle's gardener. Her original intended, from her own social class, has been killed in battle. His best friend, a young German army officer, was killed in the same battle. The incident underlies, in a Hardyesque way, the irony and pointlessness of the war, as well as the way it is helping to break down class barriers. In "A Well-Remembered Voice," Barrie experiments in spiritualism, a common manifestation of the period. While a bereaved mother and a medium wait in vain for a message from her dead soldier son, the spirit comes to visit and comfort his father instead. The heaven from which the dead son speaks is, appropriately enough, a replica of an English public school in which Germans and English are united in the same house.

Barrie had intimations of forgiveness and reconciliation long before most of his contemporaries.

Barrie's sketch is one of many fictions which reveal the powerful influence of the public school in the British perception and waging of the Great War. Ian Hay, a thirty-eight-year-old popular novelist and former schoolmaster, volunteered for the army at the outbreak of war. He saw service on the Western Front with the Argyll and Sutherland Highlanders, rose to the rank of captain, was awarded the Military Cross, and mentioned in despatches. His fictionalized account of the raising, training, and early battle experience of a unit of Kitchener's New Army, K(1), which he called the Bruce and Wallace Highlanders, was published serially in *Blackwood's Magazine* in 1915 and collected as *The First Hundred Thousand* in 1916.

As Paul Fussell notes, the archetypal school yarn, Kipling's *Stalky and Co.*, is the model for Hay's book.[28] In fact, as recently as 1914, Hay had written an enthusiastic review of the novel. The tone of *The First Hundred Thousand* is farcical: practical jokes are always in order; emotion must never be expressed; high sentiments are out. The more senior officers are the equivalent of housemasters and usually nicknamed (Wagger for Wagstaffe is typical); the junior officers are the prefects, and the men are partly grown-up versions of the younger boys—down to the unwashed knees beneath their kilts. Instead of the house or the school, it is the regiment that demands unquestioning loyalty; instead of rugby or cricket, war becomes "the great game," in which effort and sacrifice for the team are given without question.

The First Hundred Thousand captures the high spirits and devotion to duty of that early citizen-army and did much to establish the myth of the volunteer soldier for the home front: he is a man off-handedly brave, carelessly efficient, and incurably philistine. Fighting the war is seen as quite a lot of fun, really, with the occasional casualty adding the spice of danger to the action. All in all, the war is "a good thing," as a conversation in the mess indicates. Wagstaffe says:

'War is hell and all that, but it has a good deal to recommend it. It wipes out all the small nuisances of peace-time.'
'Such as—?'
'Well, Suffragettes, and Futurism, and—and—'
'Bernard Shaw,' suggested another voice. 'Hall Caine—'
'Yes, and the Tango, and party politics, and golf maniacs. Life and Death, and the things that really are big, get viewed in their proper perspective, for once in a way.'
'And look how the War has bucked up the nation,' said Bobby Little, all on fire at once.'[29]

On the other hand, the war is a serious business, as the men discover when they reach the front. Outside their billets there is a tree. "Not many months ago," the narrator observes, "a party of Uhlans arrived here, bringing with them a wounded British prisoner. They crucified him to that self-same tree, and stood around him till he died. He was a long time dying."[30] Hay here transposes the familar story of the Crucified Canadian to a British context to generate the appropriate spirit of revenge.

The crucified soldier serves another purpose too, for beneath the genial, sometimes farcical, narrative lies the same model which informs Buchan's spy thrillers— *The Pilgrim's Progress*. There are several direct allusions to the book and the spirit of sacrifice typified by the crucifixion. There is "the dogged band of Greathearts" who hurl back the foe at the Battle of the Marne; malingerers and backsliders are discharged from the regiment, while Christian Bobby Little, the hero, strives ever upwards to be the perfect second lieutenant. These references are reinforced by the church parades devoutly attended by the troops. The fight against the Hun, as he is usually referred to by Hay, is a battle against the forces of Apollyon, and victory is the Heaven to be achieved after much toil.

The simplistic scheme afforded by Hay's version of the allegory allows him to proceed to blame and praise without scruples. He is scathing about union leaders who dicker about wages before taking their coats off to work and about lazy munitions workers who deny the troops adequate artillery support by their failure to produce enough shells. On the other hand, Hay's heroes are brave and simon pure. Bobby Little is filled with dreams of glory that he never dares utter, and young Lochgair, "heir to a thousand acres," stands up on the parapet of his trench to encourage his troops. Since he is 6 feet 3 inches tall, naturally enough he is shot. His dying words are straight out of vaudeville: " 'Carry on, Major!' he murmurs faintly. 'I'm all right.' "[31]

The book ends with an account of the Battle of Loos, which A. J. P. Taylor has called "simply useless slaughter, with the British losing two and a half times as many men as the Germans."[32] Hay regards it as a glorious scrap, although he does admit large losses. The main feature is a set piece about a trench held for a time against great odds by part of the Scottish Division. "When the final advance comes, as come it must, and our victorious line sweeps forward, it will pass over two narrow, ill-constructed, shell-torn trenches. In and around these trenches will be found the earthly remains of men—Jocks and Jimmies, and Sandies and Andies—clad in the uniform of almost every Scottish regiment. That assemblage of mute and glorious witnesses marks the point reached, during the first few hours of the first day's fighting by the Scottish Division of 'K(1).' "[33]

The First Hundred Thousand was written in the first months of enthusiasm for the New Army, when it seems that Hay could genuinely believe that victory was around the corner—and he could truly think of uniforms still undecayed in the triumphal advance. The keenness and patriotism of men like Hay made his schoolboy enthusiasm possible and even his uncritical acceptance of the poor generalship at Loos understandable. The mixed scheme drawn from schoolboy fiction and *Pilgrim's Progress* had an immense appeal, and the book sold in the hundreds of thousands to a public eager for accounts of the war. It was, after all, what the public wanted to believe was going on in Flanders, and the censorship made it difficult for them to discover any other version. Hay's problem, as he went on with his trilogy, was that he was locked into this romantic formula, and his subsequent books became increasingly divorced from the realities of the Western Front.

Masterman at once saw the value of such a writer for official propaganda. He was seconded from the fighting front to Wellington House in 1916 and employed there on various writing assignments for propaganda and liaison purposes. He also continued his propaganda fiction in *Carrying on—After the First Hundred Thousand* and *The Last Million*, an account of American troops coming to join in the war. Hay was also employed to make stirring speeches about the fighting front in Britain and the United States. In the course of his lecture tours, he spoke to audiences of over a quarter million people.

In *Carrying on—After the First Hundred Thousand* Hay makes a valiant attempt to pick up the pieces after the Battle of Loos. Few of the old battalion are left, it seems, and those who have survived are "finer-drawn" and "less chubby"—or less like schoolboys, presumably. "War is a great maturing agent," as the narrator says.[34] Enough of the old gang are still around to carry on the narrative thread, but somehow these characters do not carry as much conviction as before, and they disappear for long stretches while Hay describes comic aspects of trench warfare and life in billets. The crucified soldier motif is replaced by the legend of the life-sized figure of Christ on the cross standing in a devastated village with its face untouched, although the body is riddled with bullets. "Throughout the length and breadth of France you will see the same thing," the narrator claims. "Agnostics ought to come out here for a 'cure.' "[35]

While *The First Hundred Thousand* had been a hymn to volunteerism, *Carrying On* is high in its praise of conscription, and the moral benefits to be gained from fighting. "If the present scrap can only be prolonged another year," Wagger sagely observes, "the country will receive a tonic which will enable it to carry on for another century." "One thing is worse than a long war," he adds, "and that is a long peace."[36]

The book concludes with a partial account of the Battle of the Somme. The regiment performs valiantly, of course, and, miraculously enough, both Wagstaffe and Bobby Little survive as the "last of the old crowd." Bobby comes away with a Military Cross and a leg wound which gives him a permanent limp, while Wagstaffe has a D.S.O. and an empty sleeve. These wounds were both aesthetically acceptable and sufficient to give both offi- cers permanent base duty until the end of the war. Hay gives his readers the stock picture of captured German troops with their shifty eyes and curiously shaped heads. "They move like over-driven beasts," Hay comments. "We realize now why it is that the German Army has to attack in mass."[37] Bobby Little and Wagstaffe have a long conversation about the effects of "the Somme victory" and how they hate being out of the war, but they continue to stress the benefits the war was bringing to Britain, which would continue afterwards when the country would be invaded by "several million of the wisest men that she has ever produced—the new British Army." *Carrying On* ends with the comic convention of a marriage. Bobby Little, appropri- ately bashful, marries a nurse, with Wagstaffe acting as his best man.

Hay's war fiction is just as much fantasy as Machen's Bowmen legend or the spy stories of Buchan and Conan Doyle. Kipling's revenge-stories, although they have more of the trappings of realism, are equally part of a fantasy based on stereotypes of the Germans with bestial or criminal natures. In other words, these fictions of war illustrate the non-fiction propaganda myths which the Wellington House writers were publishing in pamphlet and book form. Buchan's and Conan Doyle's stories were escape fiction of a relatively harmless kind. The hatred preached by Kipling was more corrosive. The most misleading accounts of the war were written by Ian Hay, appar- ently from first-hand experience and a fine war-record. He snatched victory from the reality of defeat at Loos and the Somme and created moral benefits out of the waste, squalor, and bloodshed of the trenches. It is as if Hay and other popular fictionists who followed his lead with similar jocular tales of battle created a brightly painted façade of glory behind which the armies fought on in the terror and degradation of the real war in Flanders.

9

HOME FIRES BURNING LOW:
FICTION AS AN ESCAPE FROM PROPAGANDA

Perhaps the frame of society was about to collapse.
ARNOLD BENNETT, 1918

For many writers, wearing the mask of the propagandist took considerable psychic toll. They knew that they were selling out to the state, even if they did not articulate that knowledge. The state could exact its tribute through commissioned propaganda articles and books; patriotism could command unquestioning loyalty and disregard of facts. The mask of fiction, however, also offered a shield for reflection, for question, for irony and debate, for the exploration of private problems instead of public issues, even for despair. Not even the draconian powers of the Defence of the Realm Act could compel entire assent to the war, nor exercise complete censorship over the imagination. The seeds of disillusion—abundantly harvested in the postwar period—were sown quite early in the minds of writers whose propaganda efforts were directed towards exciting and uplifting the peoples of the Allied and neutral nations in support of the war.

In 1915, Ford Madox Hueffer published his two inflammatory propaganda books, *When Blood Is Their Argument* and *Between St. Dennis and St. George*. He also published the masterpiece which he wanted to call *The Saddest Story*, but which the publishers changed to *The Good Soldier*, for obvious reasons. In the same year he and Violet Hunt wrote a curious book, which is now almost unknown and unobtainable, *Zeppelin Nights*. This is nothing less than a public airing of the couple's long quarrel over Hueffer's joining the army, masquerading in the form of *The Arabian Nights*. It would be more accurate to call *Zeppelin Nights* a London *Decameron*, written to beguile the hours of waiting for the expected plague of Zeppelins.

Zeppelin Nights begins on an apocalyptic note. For many it is a strange time of tension. "There was no panic; only London lay, breathing heavily," Hueffer and Hunt write, "oppressed by a nightmare such as the most ferocious minds of the darkest of the Dark Ages did not dream of."[1] The nightmare is not so much physical as psychological. Many have terrible fears, compounded by anxiety about the German attack on France and the imminence of devastating night raids on London: "Cellars were no refuge; no cellar can hide you from the thought of millions of men in danger of death or of civilisations crumbling like the inner volcanoes in eruption. From those thoughts the only refuge is in 'diversion.' "[2]

The function of *Zeppelin Nights* is to provide a diversion to the group of friends who gather at what was obviously the home of Hunt and Hueffer, South Lodge on Campden Hill, to talk, drink whisky, and eat sandwiches on the flat roof in the summer nights of 1915 among the leaves of the lime trees. So they beguile time until 2 A.M., after which it is too late for the Zeppelins to reach London and return to Germany in safety. The stories are told by "Mr. Serapion Hunter" and "Mrs. Candour Viola, the young widow whom Serapion loved." They are, in effect, fables about how civilization got into its present state, largely through the neglect of the arts, artists, and visionaries. One example is St. Joan, who was martyred in part because she wished to unite England and France. The stories are punctuated by exchanges with Americans in the audience "behaving like neutrals" and reports of deaths at the front of friends of those present.

Serapion is distressed by these reports. " 'It isn't right; it's a wrong system,' " he insists. He is forty-one (Hueffer's age in 1915) and maintains that he is young enough to serve at the front. His friends insist that it is much more important for him to write than to fight. Candour breaks in: " 'Oh, I tell him that, I tell him that. . . . But it's on his nerves all the time. . . . He can't really bear to see the young boys go. He says it's all wrong. . . . They have had nothing of life; and he's had his whack! He says it's a medieval system, taking the young first—because men were worn out at twenty-four in 1330 and they last years now. All nonsense! All nonsense!' "

The friends encourage Viola in her protest against Serapion's joining up. The very idea of the artist, "with his love of luxury, his preoccupation with style, his vanities and his selfishnesses," dressed in khaki is ridiculous. Besides, the War Office would never accept "the sacrifice of his brilliant life."[3]

The stories continue between the arguments, and the arguments get fiercer as the nights stretch on and the Zeppelins do not appear. One of the listeners, a politician probably modelled on Masterman, loses his temper when an Irishwoman berates Serapion for his unabashed patriotism. " 'I'm sick of the lot of you,' " he rages, " 'Pro-Germans and Free-Loveists and Ulster

Bloomsbury and Sham Labourites. Look here; this country is a house where people are dying—dying slowly. You keep out of it. You hold your tongues.' " The tirade goes on at length, illustrating clearly the deterioration in the public temper during the year of setback and stalemate, 1915. It ends with the politician's words: " 'I wish to God I was in the poison gas and out of all these filthy jobs!' "[4]

As the book proceeds, its tone becomes increasingly ironic. One of the last stories is about a contractor, Mr. Duke, who gets terribly excited about the outbreak of the Boer War in 1899 and is swept up in the jingoism of the time. Exempt himself, of course, he cries out at a patriotic play in a London theatre: " 'Three cheers for Tommy Atkins, the Man that does the work!' And with the sound that came he sat down, at peace. He had voiced, he had led the people; he had made history."[5] It is hard not to read the story as an allegory about Hueffer himself contracting to write propaganda while the soldiers go off to fight and die.

The book's last story is an account of the coronation of King George V in a fine blaze of parade, pageantry, and colour. It is a demonstration of all the pomp and circumstance of England and a symbol of patriotism. Serapion is overcome by his own telling of the tale and breaks out at the end: " 'Damn it all, haven't I for forty years or so been in the ruling classes of this country; haven't I enjoyed their fat privileges, and shan't I, then, pay the price?' "

The politician asks why he is making so much fuss, and Candour cries out, " 'Oh, don't you understand? . . . Serapion enlisted this morning. He put his age down at thirty-three and they jumped at him.' And she went out of the room crying."[6]

Hueffer really did enlist in the Welch Regiment on 30 July 1915, and he was immediately commissioned through the efforts of his influential friends. His motives were mixed, but there can be no doubt that he felt a strong obligation to his country and to the young men fighting and dying in France. He really believed, too, in his own oft-repeated phrase: "Men have no rights: only duties." All the same, it must have been a relief to get away from the demands of Violet Hunt, an increasingly impossible mistress. Most of all, his enlistment was an escape from the financial and patriotic necessity to write propaganda for C. F. G. Masterman's office. He had voiced, he had led the people enough. The inherent hypocrisy of urging young men to go out and fight while he sat safe and secure in London, still a relatively young man, finally proved too much for his conscience. He was one of the few of that generation of British writers and propagandists who crossed the abyss and went to the fighting front.

His going out to France had an appropriate blessing. It was the last time that he saw Henry James, on 14 August 1915, in St. James's Park. James embraced him, and said: " '*Tu vas te battre pour le sol sacré de Mme de*

Staël!' " ["You are going to fight for the sacred soil of Mme de Staël!"]

"I suppose it was characteristic," Hueffer reflected years later, "that he should say "de Mme. de Staël"—and not of Stendhal, or even of George Sand! He added—and how sincerely and with what passion—putting his hand on his chest and just bowing, that he loved and had loved France as he had never loved a woman!"[7]

As time wore on, writers and public alike knew the war would not soon end, and some of the most eager propagandists began to reflect more deeply. Among them was H. G. Wells, who had spent the early months of the war turning out article after article, mostly of a propagandistic nature. One of the most strident pieces he ever wrote—and one that returned to plague him in later years—was *The War That Will End War*, which he used as the title for a collection of his articles that he brought out early in 1915. That title became an ironic catch phrase for subsequent generations. Even at the time it raised some ridicule. G. K. Chesterton sagely remarked: "To tell a soldier defending his country that it is The War That Will End War is exactly like telling a workman, naturally rather reluctant to do his day's work, that it is The Work That Will End Work."[8] But Wells the propagandist had in those early months of war entirely taken over from Wells the scientist and critic. "I was intensely indignant at the militarist drive in Germany," he admitted in his *Autobiography*, "and, as a convinced Republican, I saw in its onslaught the culminating expression of the monarchist idea. This, said I, in shrill jets of journalism, is the logical outcome of your parades and uniforms! Now to fight the fighters." Shrillness is indeed the tone of *The War That Will End War*. There were to be no more Kaisers, no more Krupps, no more diplomacy after this war. It all sounds like a schoolboy released from school for the holidays.

In *The War That Will End War*, Wells is obsessed with the importance of spreading his ideas. The King, the churches, and the press are not doing it, so *somebody* has to convince people that the business of the war is not killing men, who could be replaced, but killing ideas. In a doctrine later to be taken up and twisted by Goebbels and other Nazis, he writes: "The ultimate purpose of this war is propaganda, the destruction of certain beliefs, and the creation of others. It is to this propaganda that reasonable men must address themselves."[9] And yet, underlying all this show of bravura is Wells's recurrent sense of nightmare. The pamphlet ends: "There have been moments in the last three weeks when life has been a waking nightmare, one of those frozen nightmares when, with salvation within one's reach, one cannot move, and the voice dies in one's throat."[10]

H. G. Wells wrote many newspaper articles in support of the war effort in the course of the next year. He took a leading role in the pamphlet battle against pacifists and conscientious objectors. Lytton Strachey and Bertrand Russell were outraged by his unscrupulous attacks, and Clive Bell could not bear to meet Wells for years after the war. Wells also had a bitter row with Bernard Shaw over his pamphlet *Common Sense about the War*. On the other hand, as the campaign in Flanders settled into the stalemate of the trenches, his flood of articles and letters to the press began to bore him and he gradually lost his sense of certainty. He turned back to fiction as a means of conveying his ideas and emotions. *Mr. Britling Sees It Through*, published in 1916, was, he wrote in his *Autobiography*, an attempt to convey "not only the astonishment and the sense of tragic disillusionment in a civilized mind as the cruel facts of war rose steadily to dominate everything else in life, but also the passionate desire to find some immediate reassurance amidst that whirlwind of disaster."[11]

Mr. Britling Sees It Through is indeed a passionate book, perhaps the most deeply felt that Wells ever wrote. It found a large audience on both sides of the Atlantic. Lovat Dickson calls it "demonstrably the most auto-biographical of all his novels,"[12] and yet it brilliantly universalizes, in the creation of Mr. Britling, an intellectual, middle-class "little Briton," who sums up the thoughts and emotions felt by many of his kind in the opening months of the war. Matching's Easy, Britling's Georgian red-brick house, so like Wells's Easton Glebe, was also analogous to Shaw's Heartbreak House, an emblem of old England before the cataclysm of war.

The opening pages of the novel give a splendid picture of that leisured, secure England of June 1914, of long talks on shaven lawns, vigorous games, and prodigious meals. On the day of the assassination at Sarajevo, Britling says, " 'You see we live at the end of a series of secure generations in which none of the great things in life have changed materially. We've grown up with no sense of danger—that is to say, with no sense of responsibility. . . . All this—"Mr. Britling waved his arm comprehensively"—looks as though it was bound to go on steadily for ever. It seems incredible that the system could be smashed.' " The irresponsibility of his generation is later given metaphorical extension in Mr. Britling's remark that the English are "everlasting children in an everlasting nursery."[13]

Mr. Britling's various activities as an artist, as an irresponsible driver, and as an adulterer symbolize the preoccupations of the Edwardian world, which are made to seem careless and self-indulgent. The opening of the book recapitulates the historic quarrel that Wells had had earlier with Henry James over the purpose of the novel. The war sharpened Wells's sense that the novel was something for *use*, not for the sake of art alone. The use of *Mr. Britling Sees It Through* was to clear the ground of the Victorian and Edwardian laxities which, Wells thought, had done so much to make the war possible. The most obvious symbol of that world was Claverings, the country house where imperious and incompetent members of the ruling class gather and make fatuous statements to each other. But Claverings is only part of a whole heedless society. Mr. Britling compares the even tenor of village life with the quick growth of preparations elsewhere to fight the war as reported in the newspapers: "It was a display in the sphere of thought and print immeasurably remote from the real green turf on which one walked, from the voice of the church bells . . . that sounded their ample caresses in one's ears, from the clashing of the stags who were beginning to knock the velvet from their horns in the park, or the clatter of the butcher's cart and the respectful greetings of the butcher boy down the lane."[14] Even in the quiet activities of village life are the unperceived emblems of conflict and death, the rutting stags and the butcher's cart.

Sunk in his amours and concerns, Mr. Britling has been unaware of the coming storm. The war wakes him up, and he goes through a series of visions and re-visions about it. One of the earliest is the familiar one, best expressed by Edmund Gosse, that the war is somehow a cleansing draft, a reviver for a tired civilization. Such a mood leads Britling to the rapid writing of "And Now War Ends." But this facile view does not last long as the real nature of the war breaks in on Britling's consciousness. The immense German army sweeps down on France and Flanders, inflicts terrible defeats on the Allies, and supposedly commits unspeakable atrocities on the civilian population. The German people are shown to have a deep hatred for the English. Britling has thought that this is a war forced upon the world by the German ruling classes, but he is obliged to revise his views. His opinion of Germany as "a right pleasant people in a sunny land" cannot be reconciled with "the massacres at Dinant, the massacres at Louvain."[15]

Britling's involvement in the war becomes more immediate when his old aunt is killed in an air raid on a coastal town and he sees for the first time the real horror and stupidity of modern warfare. He becomes thirsty for vengeance. A different emotion takes over when, soon afterwards, his son enlists as a private, pretending that he is two years older than he is, and is soon one of the millions in the trenches. Wells's version of the war in Flanders is different from the one peddled by John Buchan. Britling becomes increasingly disillusioned with British leadership as his son writes him about what is going on at the front. After the failures in the Dardanelles and defeats and missed opportunities in Flanders, Britling concludes that the British staff work is poor and that all the amateurishness in the Army and the ruling class are coming home to roost. There is blundering, waste, incompetence, and a complete disdain for science and the imagination. The only minister who comes in for any praise from Mr. Britling is Winston Churchill.

As the stalemate drags on, Britling comes to be less and less sure of his moral grounds. He sees now that Germany is fighting with discipline, skill, patience, and steadfastness, with economy and science. On the other side, France is resolute, but Russia and England are careless, negligent, and uncertain. The war seems now essentially futile. A deep pessimism grips Britling's mind. He wonders whether the basis of life itself is evil.

The crisis of the novel occurs when Britling's son is killed in action. Britling goes through a terrible, incommunicative period of loss and mourning before groping his way towards some kind of faith that can sustain him. He begins to dream of new world order, redraws the map, and plans means of eliminating wars forever. Soon afterwards, his former secretary is also reported killed. The secretary's young wife is inconsolable. She is convinced that there can be no God, or, if there is, he is like "some idiot who pulls off the wings of flies."[16] Britling consoles her, assures her that there is some meaning in life, and, by his tinkering with a world atlas, persuades her that it is worth going on. He presents her with his God, not the outworn God of Christianity, but a brand new one, fit for the times, who can make sense of this strife-torn world. This is the God whom Wells promotes in *God the Invisible King*, his next book, "more like a senior N.C.O.," as Lovat Dickson has aptly put it, "able to commune with the Commanding Officer, but definitely representing the men."[17] Miraculously, at this point, the young ex-secretary appears, minus a hand. He has escaped from a prisoner-of-war camp.

Then the German who had been tutor to Britling's sons is also reported killed. Britling sits down to frame a letter to the man's parents, in which he tries to justify and reconcile reality to "these boys, these hopes, this war has killed."[18] He makes many false starts and revisions, and when he ends there is some doubt that he will ever send the letter. As he puts down the last, broken phrases and then thinks about the coming reign of God, dawn breaks and a distant worker "whets his scythe." It is a suitably ambiguous ending for the novel, completed when the war was at its height, with no solution to its problems and horrors in view.

Some things in *Mr. Britling* are far too pat, like the return of the ex-secretary on cue and the joining up of the American, Mr. Direck, in the Canadian army, which wins him the hand of the romantic heroine, Cicely. But these devices of plot are not of central importance to the working out of the main theme of the book—the evolution of a representative, intelligent mind in relation to the first two years of the war. Wells did not spare himself or his countrymen in the analysis of that mind. It is frequently childish or adolescent, veering rapidly from vacillation to resolution; it is often bombastic and self-deceiving. Yet that mind is always struggling towards a greater understanding of the self and the meaning of the war. Best of all, this is a mind shedding the habits and ideas of an outmoded world and grappling with the chaos and opportunities of the new.

Along the way, Wells is discarding some of his stereotypes in the attempt to see beyond the blind and sterile animosities of the war. Yet in the letter Britling writes to the parents of the dead German tutor of his sons, he expresses Well's continuing condemnation of Germany for almost solely starting the war and his sense that it must end in a complete Allied victory. At the same time, he still looks forward to a post-war world of reconciliation and kindness.

Wells could continue to maintain such illusions because, in spite of his insights, he still had little idea of the nature of the war in Flanders. Robert Graves, on leave after seeing fierce fighting at the front in 1916, met Wells and records their unsatisfactory conversation. "At the Reform Club," Graves writes, "H. G. Wells, who was 'Mr. Britling' in those days, and full of military optimism, talked without listening. He had just been taken for a 'Cook's Tour' to France, and staff conductors had shown him the usual sights that royalty, prominent men of letters, and influential neutrals were allowed to see. He described his experiences at length, and seemed unaware that I and Siegfried [Sassoon], who was with me, had also seen the sights."[19] Nevertheless, *Mr. Britling Sees It Through* gave people in the United States and other nations a better understanding of the civilian view of the war than official propaganda.

Like H. G. Wells, Arnold Bennett spent much of his energy early in the war writing propaganda articles, to which he added committee duties for a variety of charitable and patriotic organizations. But he continued to write fiction, often as an escape from the pressing demands of the propaganda machine. Two of his novels of the period, *The Lion's Share* (1916) and *The Roll Call* (1918) have little to do with the war, but in the most notable book of the period, *The Pretty Lady* (1918), his submerged feelings about the war and its conduct find a measure of expression.

The pretty lady of the title is a French courtesan, Christina, who comes to London at the beginning of the war as a refugee from the Germans and becomes the kept woman of the other major figure, G. J. Hoape, known throughout the novel as G. J.: the hope seems to have been dropped from his character for much of the novel. There are many similarities between G. J. and Bennett: in the nature of their war work, their sybaritic tastes, their emotional coldness, their love of music, fluent French, and their age; but G. J. is by no means a self-portrait. He is a snobbish, proud, and conventional figure. Christine gives G. J. far more than the services of a courtesan: she loves him passionately, keeps him always at the head of her list of clients, and treats him splendidly. Finally he sets her up in a luxurious flat so that she can be kept for his exclusive use and pleasure. His coldness and his upper-class upbringing, however, make him suspicious and distrustful. When he sees her on the street, apparently soliciting, he casts her off without a second thought.

In effect, the two characters are the pegs on which Bennett hangs his views on the war. It was a bold stroke to give one such view to a prostitute. Bennett's devotion to realism was so strong that, according to George

Beardmore, as part of his research for *The Pretty Lady*, he spent an evening with a prostitute. Characteristically, for weeks afterwards, he was "haunted by fear of clap."[20] In consequence, perhaps, Christine is a convincing figure in spite of Bennett's execrable device of translating her French conversation into word-for-word English. The reader gets tired of all the "thee's" and "thou's." Her views are more realistic, as well as more compassionate, than those of G. J. She sacrifices her easy berth with G. J. by her search through the streets for a young soldier, Edgar, whom she hears calling her in a vision. Earlier in the novel she had helped this soldier, then an officer, when he was blind drunk. He is a clear case of shell-shock, although Bennett does not specify his condition. John Wain rightly calls him "doomed, mystical, tragic, an inhabitant of the apocalyptic landscape of the war."[21] Edgar provides a reminder of the horrors that Bennett had passed over almost completely in *Over There*. He is stripped of his commission for overstaying his leave and meets Christine once more before going out again as a private to France, where, presumably, he is killed. Christine conceives of this liaison in religious terms and imagines herself as a protégé of the Virgin Mary bringing succour to the afflicted.

This soldier's suffering presence in the novel contrasts starkly with that of the man-about-town, G. J., who has a pretty good war, particularly since his already substantial private income is considerably increased by his investment in a war industry. Midway through the novel—it is spring 1916—G. J. reflects: "Morally, he was profiting by the war. Nay, more, in a deep sense he was enjoying it. The immensity of it, the terror of it, the idiocy of it, the splendour of it, its unique grandeur as an illustration of human nature, thrilled the spectator in him. . . . The worst was over when Paris was definitely saved. Suffering would sink and die like a fire."[22] This is fine and good for the spectators like G. J. whose age and wealth keep them above either fighting or the hard labour in factories. But the inhumanity of the attitude with respect to those actually sinking and dying at the front is clear. Ironically, it reflects on the spectatorial attitude that Bennett had displayed in *Over There*.

Civilian smugness is also stressed earlier in the novel when at a charity committee the members express their condolences to the chairman, whose son has just been reported killed in France. The chairman proudly replies that he would sacrifice ten sons if he had them and gazes round the table as if to challenge any other member to question his sincerity. "However," Bennett adds, "nobody had the air of doubting that if the chairman had had ten sons, or as many sons as Solomon, he would have sacrificed them all with most admirable and eager heroism."[23] By constant juxtaposition of society men and women at their work of charity with glimpses of what these efforts are in aid of, Bennett ironically and savagely undercuts the posturings of the rich.

G. J. organizes an exhibition of society portraits, charging a guinea a head to raise funds for his charity. "All of both sexes," Bennett comments, "were comfortably conscious of virtue in the undoubted fact that they were helping to support two renowned hospitals where at that very moment dissevered arms and legs were being thrown into buckets."[24]

Throughout the novel, members of London's upper class are seen to be living careless and extravagant lives. As James G. Kennedy has shown, Bennett based two of his most extreme representatives of this class, Lady Queenie Paulle and Concepcion Iquist Smith, rather closely on Lady Diana Manners and Elizabeth Asquith, the daughter of the prime minister. Lady Diana's picture appeared almost weekly in *The Tatler* and *The Sketch*, and she was held to be Britain's reigning beauty. She also went in for the latest fashion in dress and interior design and was the model for all kinds of rakish and bohemian behaviour.[25]

Lady Queenie is thoroughly selfish and amoral and thoroughly aware of her power as a beautiful and striking woman. When G. J. reproaches her for the extravagance of her dress at the art show, she replies, " 'Good God! If I began to dress like a housemaid the Germans would be in London in a month. Our job as women is quite delicate enough without you making it worse by any damned sentimental superficiality.' " An army major responds, " 'She's right. . . . Why, what's all this'—he waved an arm at the whole scene—'what's all this but sex?' "[26]

This is an acute prevision of the later view that the Great War was in part a sudden release of sexual tension and antagonism. Lady Queenie is the first of her set to go in for wild interpretive dancing, African masks, and primitive colours in the palatial rooms of her father's house. Bennett ultimately shows what he thinks of her by having her killed by a piece of shrapnel in an air raid. Typically, she had disregarded warnings and gone up to the roof of the house to watch the spectacle in order to feel like a soldier at the front.

G. J. and Christine themselves narrowly miss being blown to bits in an air raid. They are separated after the explosion, and G. J. soon afterwards finds a child's bleeding severed arm on the street. A month elapses before he is able to mention this discovery to anyone. The incident parallels and emphasizes Bennett's own horror and reluctance to discuss what he saw at the front— other than to mention the well-shod legs of Germans sticking out of the walls of the trench.

The weakness of *The Pretty Lady* is that it presents its subject—the war—with a fragmented and contradictory vision, partly because the point of view is divided among G. J., Christine, and the ironic narrator. More fundamentally, none of these points of view seems adequate to interpret the whole experience—perhaps because Bennett himself was both too involved

with and too confused by the war. G. J. in particular is a centre of contradictory attitudes: an absurd figure at one moment, a stoic hero the next.
Bennett does not seem sure of how to treat him: as *un homme moyen sensuel*
or one intensely repressed and laconic. His war work is an attempt to escape
from his own selfish and indolent nature and even his means of staving off
feeling and passion by immersing himself in detail and routine.

Bennett also uses G. . as a mouthpiece for officially suppressed feelings
about the war and the way in which it was being conducted. During the
Battle of the Somme in 1916, as the novel draws to its close, G. J. reflects:
"The war was growing, or the sense of its measureless scope was growing. It
had sprung, not out of this crime or that, but out of the secret invisible roots
of humanity, and it was widening to the limits of evolution itself. It tran-
scended judgment. . . . The great new Somme offensive was not succeeding in the North. Was victory possible? . . . In his daily labour he was
brought into contact with too many instances of official selfishness, folly,
ignorance, stupidity, and sloth, French as well as British, not to marvel at
times that the conflict had not come to an end long ago through simple lack
of imagination."[27]

This is Bennett the novelist speaking out against Bennett the propagandist
in a voice strangely similar to that of H. G. Wells in protest against inefficiency.
Bennett, like Wells, seems to have thought that the war had brought society
to the brink of disintegration, which opened up the possibility of a new
integration better than the old. Near the opening of *The Pretty Lady*,
Bennett describes the grand funeral of General Lord Roberts in St. Paul's—a
funeral symbolic of the end of the old army and perhaps the old Empire—
attended by all the parade, pomp, and circumstance of a traditional and
hierarchic society. Near the close of the novel there is a scene in which the
Marquess of Letchford is treated contemptuously by the coroner at the
inquest on his daughter, Lady Queenie. His London house has been
commandeered by the government.

The old aristocratic order is falling apart. Women are emerging from their
traditional roles and taking over men's jobs in industry, commerce, and
government. This change is demonstrated by the one society woman who
comes through well in the novel, Concepcion Iquist Smith, whose name
implies regeneration. After her husband is killed at the front, she organizes a
canteen for the women workers of an arms factory in Scotland, then becomes
the secretary of G. J.'s hospital committee. G. J. reflects: "Perhaps Queenie,
deliberately courting destruction, and being destroyed, was the symbol of
society. . . . Perhaps civilisation, by its nobility and its elements of reason,
and by the favour of destiny, would be saved from disaster after frightful
danger, and Concepcion was its symbol."[28]

This is the only hope for the future that G. J. expresses in the novel. The flawed hero has otherwise shown no sign of regeneration. His self-righteousness and snobbery are starkly dramatized shortly after these grand reflections when he casts off his mistress and speaks of his desire to marry Concepcion.

Bennett makes Christine his effective moral agent, even though doing so uses the hackneyed device of a whore with a heart of gold. Unlike G. J., she does not judge or condemn, with the exception of the Germans, whom she execrates. She is warm and sympathetic. There is at the end nothing ridiculous in her belief that she is about the Virgin's business in seeking through the streets for her drunken and neurotic soldier. Her re-enactment of the role of Mary Magdalen transcends the intellectualizing of G. J. and points the way to a more effective regeneration than do his grandiloquent phrases.

The most significant aspect of *The Pretty Lady* is that it foreshadows some of the major themes and characters of postwar fiction. Bennett paints vivid scenes of the hedonism which was the consequence of the fear and tension of the war. One such scene takes place in a night club called the Guinea Fowl. The tables of the club are placed around the dance floor where "the figures of dancers whose bodies seemed to be glued to each other, pale to black or pale to khaki, |were| passing slowly and rhythmically across. The rag-time music, over a sort of ground bass of syncopated tom-tom, surged through the curtains like a tide of the sea of Aphrodite, and bathed everyone at the supper tables in a mysterious aphrodisiacal fluid."[29]

In this scene and others, Bennett begins to chart the vast changes in sexual and social mores that later became the territory of Huxley, Waugh, and other satirists of the 1920s. These changes are also conveyed by the fragmented, nervous, and impressionistic tones of Bennett's prose. Similarly, the drunken, shell-shocked Edgar prefigures McKechnie in Ford's *Parade's End*, and Lady Queenie Paulle is the prototype of the aristocratic bitches of postwar fiction like Ford's Sylvia and Hemingway's Lady Brett Ashley. Bennett clearly foresaw that changes in sexual roles and the hysteria and dislocation of the war would lead to severe psychological traumas. His frankness was too much for the mores of the time. The novel was strongly attacked for its alleged pornography, especially by the Roman Catholic church. W. H. Smith and Sons banned it from their newsstands.

John Galsworthy also experienced ambivalent feelings, and he expressed them in a novel he wrote in the latter part of the war. *The Saint's Progress* (1918) is about an orthodox Christian minister, Edward Pierson, who has two grown daughters, Noel and Gratian. Gratian's loyalties are clearly defined. She is married to an army doctor and is herself a nurse. Noel falls in love with a young second lieutenant and wants to marry him hurriedly before he leaves for the front. Pierson refuses his consent. Noel sleeps with him anyway and becomes pregnant. The young officer is soon afterwards killed in France.

Other main characters are Jim Fort, an old soldier, and a refugee Belgian artist, Lavendie.

The novel indulges in many discussions in which Galsworthy appears to be working out and dramatizing his contradictory feelings. Most of his own sentiments seem to have been placed in the mouths of the old soldier and the artist. Fort says, for example: " 'Philosophy seems to mean nothing nowadays. The one thing is to hate tyranny and cruelty, and protect everything that's weak and lonely. It's all that's left to make life worth living, when all the packs of all the world are out for blood.' "

Noel listens to this eagerly, for she knows that Fort is in part talking about herself. She has not been able to tell her father about her pregnancy since she knows that he will be both hurt and shocked. Fort goes on to say: " 'Why! Even we who started out to fight this Prussian pack, have caught the pack feeling—have got it hunting all over the country, on every sort of scent. It's a most infectious thing.' "[30]

Pierson disagrees. He echoes the refrain of the propagandists, arguing that the war has made everyone far more brotherly and tolerant than before. But Lavendie takes Fort's side. " 'I see all human nature now, running with gaping mouths and red tongues lolling out, their breath and their cries spouting thick before them.' " The minister is totally ineffectual in the debate and seems to represent Galsworthy's view of the declining power and influence of the church in general. The painter says of him: " 'To me, *monsieur*, he is exactly like a beautiful church which knows it is being deserted.' "[31]

Noel later goes to the home of the painter where he meets a Belgian soldier, who has become a little crazy from his experiences in the trenches. From him, Noel learns for the first time of the full horrors of the war. Lavendie comments: " 'Ah! this war! It seems to me we are all in the stomach of a great coiling serpent. . . . In a way, it is better out there in the trenches; they are beyond hate, they have attained a height that we have not. It is wonderful how they still can be for going on till they have beaten the Boche.' " Lavendie goes on to discuss the hope some soldiers have that they will come back and change the future of the world. He adds bleakly: " 'But it will not be so. . . . They will be ruled as they were before. The tongue and the pen will rule them; those who have not seen the war will rule them.' "[32]

After what she has learned, Noel is ready to revolt against her father's gentle tyranny and narrowly interpreted Christian morality. She has her baby openly, owning that she had never married her lover. After agonizing over the issue, Pierson lets her and the baby stay in his house and so outrages the opinion of his congregation by doing so that he is forced to resign from his church. He joins the army as a padre and is sent to Egypt. Pierson's last act in the novel is to try to console a dying soldier with the thought of God, but only a "flicker of ironic question" creeps over the boy's mouth. He says nothing more, but Pierson sees in the dying soldier's smile "the whole of stoic doubt, of stoic acquiescence."[33]

Saint's Progress is by no means among the best of Galsworthy's novels since it too often preaches about instead of dramatizing the issues. It is interesting, however, as a barometer of his feelings during the war, of his growing certainty that little of value would emerge from it, except, perhaps, the breakdown of old harsh moralities and rigidities. The title is ironic, as the saintly Pierson regresses towards ineffectuality. The pragmatic and healthy realism of Fort and Lavendie, who can see the essential bestiality of man and yet remain undismayed, becomes the only possible progress.

All these novels undercut, in one way or another, the ideas that these authors had expressed in their propaganda books and pamphlets. There is little here about the moral benefits of war, little celebration of military glory and sacrifice, little credence given to stories of Hun barbarism and atrocities. What emerges from these fictions is a more or less stoic acceptance of things as they are and a determination to keep going in the face of defeat and discouragement. Curiously enough, the question of ending the war through negotiation is never seriously discussed. This option seems to have been closed off by the pressure of propaganda even from the intimacy of fiction.

10

NEW BROOMS OF PROPAGANDA

*I daresay every one of those Government officials would have
died for England without any fuss at all. But he would not have
it suggested that some twopenny leaflet should pass through
another little cell in the huge hive of Whitehall, without making a most frightful fuss.*

G. K. CHESTERTON, 1936

As effective and hardworking as Charles Masterman was at his job of
running British propaganda, it was inevitable that he should come increasingly under fire as the war continued. According to Ivor Nicholson, Masterman
had warned his colleagues at Wellington House at the outset that "they
would have to labour in secret and be subject to criticism of all kinds, just
and unjust, to none of which they could reply." Nicholson added, grimly,
"this prophecy was amply fulfilled."[1]

It was essential that the propaganda operation should be run under a thick
cloak of secrecy, so that the effort should appear purely spontaneous and
private. Ironically, the more successful Wellington House was in keeping
under cover, the less that was known about all those books and pamphlets
apparently published by private firms, the more it was criticized. Only a few
members of cabinet knew about Masterman's techniques of operation. In
the House of Commons, few M.P.'s knew the extent of Britain's propaganda
work. Most thought that the government was doing little or nothing, and
there were repeated calls for greater effort. Consequently, Wellington House
was subjected to an almost continual round of cabinet and parliamentary
enquiries which had to be held in camera.

As if all this were not enough for the Wellington House officials, the
Foreign Office, the Admiralty, the War Office, even the Home Office,
thought that they should be allowed to run their own propaganda machines.
Their officers constantly attacked Wellington House and petitioned cabinet
for a free hand. G. K. Chesterton's book *Barbarians in Berlin* was translated

into Spanish. He commented in his *Autobiography*: "The fools who baited Masterman would have published it with a Union Jack cover and a picture of the British Lion, so that hardly one Spaniard would have read it, and no Spaniard would believe it. It was in matters of this sort that the rather subtle individuality of Masterman was so superior to his political surroundings."[2]

Since propaganda was run on discretionary secret service money supplied directly from the Prime Minister's Office, there was bitter competition for the funds, and frequent charges of wastefulness were levelled against Wellington House. The press resented the censorship of news exercised by Masterman's office and constantly complained, with justice, that the freedom of the press was being eroded. Masterman, whose rather closemouthed personal style had always earned him a bad press, was used to the pressure and was able to survive as long as Asquith, who trusted him, remained in office. But Masterman ran afoul of Lloyd George early in 1915. He indiscreetly tried to be nominated for a Welsh constituency without consulting the man who controlled them all—Lloyd George. According to Frances Stevenson, Lloyd George said, on 24 January 1915, "I have knifed Masterman today."[3] Presumably, he meant that he had at least in part destroyed his credibility with the cabinet. Although there was a degree of reconciliation later in the year, Masterman never regained Lloyd George's confidence, and he was subsequently vulnerable in his office at Wellington House.

When H. H. Asquith fell from office in December 1916, it was only a matter of time before Masterman was demoted. There had been mounting dissatisfaction with Asquith's leadership since the fruitless slaughter of the Somme. Lord Northcliffe gave voice to it in his newspapers, but, A. J. P. Taylor affirms, it was Sir Max Aitken who successfully engineered the destruction of the Asquith government. The story is told brilliantly in Aitken's inside narrative of the intrigue, *Politicians and the War*.

When Lloyd George became prime minister, he ordered yet another enquiry into Wellington House and then sought to reorganize it. One of his new cabinet ministers was Lord Milner, an old friend and patron of John Buchan, who was still working on the staff of Sir John Haig. Milner pressed Lloyd George to appoint Buchan to head the proposed new Department of Information in place of Masterman. The prime minister was reluctant to do so, perhaps because he disliked the way that Buchan was covering up for the failures of the military leaders of the country, particularly Haig, about whom Lloyd George had no illusions. As early as October 1916, Lloyd George knew that the Somme offensive had been "a ghastly failure."[4] Later he tried, without success, to get the generals to change their unimaginative and wasteful tactics.

Finally, Lord Milner overcame Lloyd George's opposition, and on 9 February 1917, Buchan was appointed director of the new Department of

Information over Masterman's head. The latter became head of the production section at Wellington House, responsible for books, pamphlets, photographs, and the paintings and drawings by official war artists.[5] Another section was created for wireless, press, and cinema, and a third for political intelligence.[6] "I hear you are now Director General of Propaganda," wrote Buchan's old friend, F. S. Oliver, "and work day and night in the interests of Great and Greater Britain with the assistance of Little Britain; also that Masterman has been interned at your instigation, and that Gilbert Parker has been sent on to Samoa."[7] Certainly the old guard was changing, and a new and more openly aggressive style became the vogue for British propaganda. Geoffrey Butler took over the New York bureau from Parker, and with the greater allocation of money now being made, he was soon able to open other offices in the United States.

After Masterman's demotion, literary men played a smaller part in the propaganda effort of Great Britain. But he continued to promote their interests in any way he could. Writers were, in a sense, Masterman's constituents. D. H. Lawrence was harassed by the police, largely owing to suspicion of his German-born wife, Frieda von Richthofen. Masterman stepped in and stopped the harassment. As an alien neutral, Ezra Pound had been restricted by the police from free movement in England. Again Masterman was successful in interceding on his behalf. In September 1916, Pound sent a copy of his collection of poems *Lustra* to the Rt. Hon. C. F. G. Masterman, with the inscription, "In gratitude for swift delivery from the long arm of the law." Later on, after the United States had entered the war, Pound was told that he was too old to join the U.S. army. In a letter to Masterman of 26 June 1917, he expressed his willingness to do whatever he could for the war effort. "In view of the National service activity," Pound wrote, "perhaps the time has come when I might be given something to do, i.e. something suitable, without being what Ford calls 'bloody furriners stealing OUR jobs.' I believe my French, Italian, and Spanish are not too dilapidated, and I have some memory of mathematics, and German, for what these graces are worth."[8] There is no evidence, however, that Masterman ever employed Pound for propaganda or intelligence purposes.

Masterman's new chief, John Buchan, was himself soon in hot water. He was singled out for attack by Robert Donald, editor of *The Daily Chronicle*. The major cause of the attack seems to have been Buchan's initial refusal to exploit a sensational but unsubstantiated story. Wellington House did, however, later use it in a short pamphlet, *A Corpse Conversion Factory* (1917). This was the official version of the famous yarn about the discovery of a factory in Liège where the Germans were purportedly melting down corpses to make soap.[9] Donald charged Buchan not only with suppression of news, but also with extravagance. Although Buchan was responsible directly to the prime minister, he did not have ready access to Lloyd George's ear. Donald did, and he managed to get yet another enquiry mounted on the conduct of British propaganda, this time to be made by a committee of the Press Advisory Council, of which Donald was a member.

This committee so harassed Buchan's department that by September 1917 he felt he could no longer continue. He appealed to Lord Milner to suggest to the prime minister that someone be appointed by the cabinet to whom Buchan could have direct access. Lloyd George gave him Sir Edward Carson. Carson incorporated the National War Aims Committee into the Department of Information and conducted yet another enquiry into the operation. From this, Carson concluded that "the attacks on Wellington House appeared to be unjustified."[10]

Soon afterwards, Carson himself was charged with financial irregularity in the conduct of his office. The old fire-eater knew little about propaganda and cared less and less as he turned back towards the vexed affairs of Ireland. Buchan still did not have the access he wanted to cabinet, and he found it impossible to get important decisions made on policy. He finally recommended that the department be made a ministry so that it could have adequate cabinet representation. After Carson resigned from cabinet in January 1918, the way was cleared for a change. No doubt remembering Lord Beaverbrook's success as a propagandist for the Canadians, Lloyd George appointed him the new minister over John Buchan's head. Buchan retained considerable influence in the new structure and was often consulted by Beaverbrook. One of Buchan's jobs was to brief the king on the progress of the war. Later on he reaped the rewards for his propaganda efforts and benefited from his highly placed friends by being created Lord Tweedsmuir and made Governor General of Canada.

As a condition of his consent to becoming chief of propaganda, without salary, Beaverbrook was given cabinet rank as Minister of Information and promised direct access to the prime minister. Before acting, he sought advice on how to streamline the operation. John Buchan freely gave it to him and proposed himself as director of foreign propaganda and chairman of the executive committee consisting of himself, the director of enemy propaganda, the director of home propaganda, and the director of organization.[11] Beaverbrook took some of this advice and appointed Buchan director of intelligence, but, probably wisely, he took no action on the hot potato of home propaganda. Masterman was now well down in the ranks, acting as director of the Literature Department.

The demotion of Masterman and the downplaying of his role have affected his reputation until quite recently when Sanders and Taylor set the record straight in *British Propaganda during the First World War, 1914-1918*. A. J. P. Taylor observes in his biography of Beaverbrook: "When Lloyd George

Plate 32   Lord Beaverbrook, the new Minister of Information, beams at the opening of the Ministry's Press Club, 1918.

became prime minister, he found half a dozen committees dealing haphazardly with British propaganda in foreign countries. There was little to show except for some elegant works on the British way of life."[12] Beaverbrook's own paper, the *Daily Express* disproved this statement. In a leading article that appeared in 1919, the writer referred to Ludendorff's praise of early British propaganda and pointed out that Beaverbrook "only took over and developed an organisation which already existed, and which, though discouraged by Ministers and too often attacked by the Press, was doing the work which had extorted the admiration of the Prussian leader. For the work of the old Department Mr. Masterman and Colonel John Buchan can claim the credit. They laboured diligently to convert the neutrals, of which America was the most important, and according to hostile evidence, they succeeded."[13]

In effect, however, the day of the writer as the maker of propaganda was over. Beaverbrook was essentially a newspaperman; evident in his photograph at the opening of his ministry's press club (plate 32) is the glee and self-satisfaction of a man who has accomplished a masterstroke. Press releases, press relations, the distribution of photographs, the making of war films became much more important functions of the new ministry than the writing of pamphlets and propaganda books, although that activity still went on.

While the function of writers as the creators of propaganda material was considerably diminished, their influence did not cease altogether. In fact, some authors gave way to the more insidious attraction of gaining influence and power within the propaganda machine. One of Beaverbrook's first acts as minister was to invite Rudyard Kipling to join his staff—thus running directly contrary to Masterman's expressed policy of keeping him out of official propaganda. Kipling refused to accept office, but he wrote profusely to the minister about ways to conduct propaganda. Beaverbrook later told C. E. Carrington, "I adopted everything [Kipling] recommended."[14] In a memo dated February 1918, Kipling lectured Lord Beaverbrook about "Morale of Civilians and the Censorship." He was probably thinking about the activities of H. G. Wells when he insisted to Beaverbrook that the civilian was not equipped to understand the army and should be told about his inabilities: "The most fatal attitude of mind the Civilian can take up is that of always thinking: —'Oh, if only a little civilian common sense were applied to the problem.' The problems of War and the handling of men in camp are *not* Civilian problems and in nine cases out of ten civilian methods (excellent where only a few men a [*sic*] concerned) would lead to more delay and perhaps disaster." This is a striking example of how Kipling was willing to leave the entire conduct of military affairs to the professional soldier. In this memo he also lectured Beaverbrook about the Canadian troops' instinctive revolt against the outer signs of discipline—such as saluting. Canadian soldiers tended to be supported in this by their home press, which would often comment on "the rigidity of the British system." Kipling insisted that it was of the first importance to enforce a strict censorship on letters from the Canadian army so that the press could not pick up "letters of a stupid sort" which could be exploited also by "pro-German interests" in the American press.[15] This letter may help explain why censorship of the Canadian press was particularly strong in the latter part of the war.

On 5 March he wrote to Beaverbrook with more recommendations, advising him "for Heaven's sake get at the parsons and priests" and mentioning that he himself is doing a round of speaking engagements for factory hands and cadet corps. Also included in the Kipling file of the Beaverbrook papers are many copies of telegrams requesting Kipling's aid in drafting messages, including this extraordinary request, dated from before Beaverbrook took office, 6 December 1917: "I am so sorry to trouble you again but please may I have fifty to a hundred words message from New Brunswick Battalion in trenches to New Brunswick folks at home asking for reinforcements and for men to take place of war weary who require rest stop Message will be signed by officers."[16] Kipling agreed to this deception and, so far as I can discover, never refused Beaverbrook's other requests.

Beaverbrook also brought Hugh Walpole and Arnold Bennett into his office. Beaverbrook made the acquaintance of Bennett in November 1917, and the two ambitious men soon became fast friends. Bennett was invited to take a seat on the ministry's Imperial War Memorial Committee along with Beaverbrook, Lord Rothermere, and Masterman. On 9 May 1918, Bennett was appointed director of British propaganda in France. He said later of this appointment, "Beaverbrook said that no one could know French psychology better than I do—this conclusion he drew from reading 'The Pretty Lady'!"[17] One might call this a limited sample, but the reason obviously flattered Bennett. He did so well in the job that in August he was made director of propaganda in all friendly countries. Like many of the writers who served in the ministry, Bennett was not paid for his administrative duties, but the post gave him something which he wanted far more—access to the corridors of power and great personalities. He seems to have become quite indispensable to Beaverbrook, whose formidable character brought him into conflict with many officials, especially those of the Treasury and the Foreign Office.

The Foreign Office, in particular, resented the power of this upstart lord and proved an implacable foe. Frequent appeals by Beaverbrook to Lloyd George failed to have any noticeable effect, despite the debt that the prime minister owed Beaverbrook in his own elevation to office. H. G. Wells observed: "The government had created two new ministries for the sake of keeping the inquisitive noses of Northcliffe and his younger competitor, Lord Beaverbrook, out of the ancient mysteries of the Foreign Office. . . . The Ministry of Information was devised to prevent Lord Beaverbrook from becoming too well-informed and the Ministry of Propaganda served a similar purpose in occupying and disordering the always febrile mind of Lord Northcliffe."[18] (There was actually never a Ministry of Propaganda: Northcliffe became Director of Enemy Propaganda at Crewe House.) In *British Propaganda during the First World War*, Sanders and Taylor maintain to the contrary that Northcliffe and Beaverbrook were appointed to undermine the influence of the Foreign Office in propaganda and policy-making.[19] If this is true, the stratagem did not work so far as Beaverbrook was concerned.

Northcliffe appears to have had a somewhat freer hand, and he became an increasingly powerful force in propaganda both in enemy and allied countries. However, he was never "in full charge of government propaganda," as Paul Fussell claims.[20] One of Northcliffe's more astute moves was to persuade Wells to join his department. In May 1918, Wells became responsible for the creation of propaganda literature directed against Germany. In fact, one of Wells's propaganda documents antedates that appointment. In the Public

Record Office there is a private and confidential "Memorandum on the General Principles of Propaganda," dated 21 March 1918. The most interesting and unpleasant aspect of this paper is the section in which Wells suggests deliberate deception in order to induce fear into the German population—such as spreading the rumour through Holland that Britain intended to use "poison bombs of a peculiar malignancy upon the Rhine." He also proposed that Germans be persuaded that the Allies were seeking a reasonable peace on the basis of the overthrow of the German imperialist government and also that the British make clear to the enemy that they were intending to democratize their own empire.[21]

In his autobiography, Wells relates how he soon ran into trouble with the old bureaucracy. He tells how he and his assistant, J. W. Headlam, were invited to the Foreign Office to discuss a further memorandum concerning British war aims with Sir William Tyrrell. Tyrrell proceeded to deliver a discourse on British relations with Germany "that would have done credit to a bright but patriotic schoolboy of eight."[22] He then dismissed them. Wells attributed Tyrrell's blindness to the usual upper-class education by governesses, but he concluded later that it was part of an overall plan to thwart new ideas about foreign policy.

Wells also ran into trouble with his chief over Northcliffe's savage attacks on the German people. The bureaucratic inefficiency, waste, and internal conflicts in the office also enraged him. After only two months as a member of the propaganda organization, he resigned in July 1918.

At the Ministry of Information, Arnold Bennett, as director of propaganda in France, proved to be the most effective of Beaverbrook's associates. He rejoiced in his new-found power and prestige and joined in the battles against the other ministries with gusto. But these battles, detailed at some length by A. J. P. Taylor, finally wore Beaverbrook down. In the ill health that the tensions must have exacerbated, he resigned on 21 October 1918. Two days before that, Bennett had written Beaverbrook announcing that he would resign if Beaverbrook did, since he could not see himself serving under anyone else. He felt that the Ministry of Information had never been given a fair chance and that the hand of every other ministry was against it. The reason for this was the widely held belief that the ministry was brought into being for the sake of the minister, Beaverbrook, and not vice versa.[23] Beaverbrook's response to Bennett's note was to ask him to take over. At the end of October, Bennett became Deputy Minister of Information in sole charge of British propaganda.

He wrote of this dizzy elevation later in an article called "The Greatest Moment": "Imagine a wayward novelist, with no experience of bureaucratic methods, having dominion over hundreds of exalted persons, including Bank Directors, railway directors, historians, K. C.'s, heads of trusts, poets and generals . . . I felt that I was doing something to redress the balance on behalf of all privates, and all officers from Colonels downwards, in all the British armies."[24] The promotion was a triumphant vindication of his defence of the novelist as propagandist, which he had given in the *New Statesman* at the beginning of the war.

It should, however, be pointed out that his role was not always that of redressing the balance. Another light is thrown on his activities by Ford Madox Hueffer in his impressionistic memoirs, *It Was the Nightingale*. Near the end of the war, according to Hueffer, he was summoned from his regiment at the front to the Ministry of Information where he found Mr. Bennett in the presidential chair. Bennett asked him to write an article about the terms of peace which was, in Hueffer's phrase, "to do France in the eye." Bennett's demand was reinforced by Sir William Tyrrell of the Foreign Office, Wells's former opponent. Hueffer, always an ardent francophile, refused to write such an article, and Tyrrell stormed out of the room. But Bennett still wanted him to write something about the terms of peace. Hueffer rejoined his regiment and claimed that he wrote his article on bully-beef cases amidst his other frantic work at the front and sent it off. "The article," Hueffer noted, "advocated giving France a great deal more than Mr. Lloyd George's government desired to give her. A great deal more." The article was reported lost in the post, and a week later he was informed that as a serving officer he was prohibited from writing for the press. This is the reason why, early in 1919, Hueffer avoided Bennett at a party given by the French Embassy for British writers who had furthered the French cause.[25] Hueffer thought enough of this incident to give it further, although somewhat different, treatment in a later book of recollections.

Hueffer was not at the front after March 1917, and the other allegations in the story cannot be checked. It is true, however, that in his articles in the *Daily News* for a year before 11 November 1918, Bennett frequently proposed that the British government should insist on fair peace terms for Germany. He wanted Germany disarmed, but he advocated that she be allowed to take a seat on the League of Nations and given access to world markets on the grounds that vindictive peace terms would lead to yet another war. It may be that this is what Hueffer meant by "doing France in the eye," although this seems unlikely. It is more probable that Bennett suppressed his own francophilia in favour of Lloyd George's desire to veto French territorial claims. Bennett was certainly seeking power at this time. As a minute to Lord Beaverbrook printed in the *Letters* proves, he was planning to consolidate and extend the role of his ministry after the peace was concluded. But the political forces which had ground down so many of his predecessors were at work on him, and repeated applications to the War Cabinet for instructions received no reply. So on 13 November 1918, Bennett concluded his brief reign by resigning and returned to journalism and novel-writing.

He learned later that the future of his ministry had been discussed by cabinet without reference to himself and concluded that he had been treated scandalously. He was fairly sure that John Buchan, the official liquidator of the Ministry of Information, had effectively conspired against him. It is quite typical that the propaganda office which had been a political football from the beginning of the war should have been kicked about so freely at the end. It was wound up summarily and ignominiously, its records either destroyed or scattered.

11

LOST OPPORTUNITIES

I do not want to be self-righteous, because in a national emer-
gency we can be as untruthful as, or more untruthful than,
anybody else. During the war we lied damnably. Let us be clear
about that. . . . I think some of our lies have done us tremen-
dous harm and I should not myself like to see such propaganda
again.

HAROLD NICOLSON
IN THE HOUSE OF COMMONS,
FEBRUARY, 1938

In the latter part of 1916 and throughout 1917, there were several calls for
peace by negotiation among the Allies. These attempts all failed, largely
because of three factors: the alleged military victories manufactured by the
generals and propagandists, the lack of information about the real conditions on the Western Front, and the climate created by the hate and atrocity
propaganda against Germany.

As early as September 1916, the members of Asquith's cabinet were aware
of the deep futility of the war. The historian, Peter Lowe, has observed,
"Within the cabinet great weariness was growing and there were some
indications that a compromise peace was possible."[1] Asquith, griefstricken
by the death in action of his brilliant son, Raymond, asked members of
cabinet to formulate their views on possible terms of peace for later discussion.
Lord Lansdowne, minister without portfolio, drafted a memo in which he
urged the government to begin negotiations with Germany on the terms of
peace immediately.

Discussions of Lansdowne's memo in cabinet brought out sharp divisions
of opinion. Since the public had no knowledge of the issues involved and
Parliament was both ignorant and practically powerless, cabinet members
carried on the discussion in a political vacuum. In this situation the strongest
personality triumphed. Lloyd George came out totally against peace
negotiations. In the end his force and conviction carried the day. The
division in cabinet on the issue contributed to Asquith's fall, Lloyd George's
subsequent rise to power, and the triumph of his hawkish line on the war.

Naturally, Lansdowne was not invited to join the new cabinet, and he retired to the backbenches of the House of Lords. In the spring of 1917, he tried to get the issue of peace negotiations debated in the Lords. Balfour, Minister for Foreign Affairs, refused. In a gesture remarkable in a man so reticent and diplomatic, Lansdowne decided to go public. However, Lord Northcliffe's *Times* refused to publish his letter. Finally, it was published in the *Daily Telegraph* on 29 November 1917, a year after his views had been promulgated in cabinet.

Lord Lansdowne was not only a great landowner, former governor general of Canada, viceroy of India, and secretary of state for war, he was also the father of two sons who had entered the army. One of them was killed in October 1914. His letter was that of a statesman long used to conference tables and of an old man grieving for a lost son. Free of the spirit of hatred and revenge, the letter was a sensible document on the nature of the war and the possible terms for a negotiated peace. Summarizing the enormity of the war, in which a million people had already been killed and which now involved about twenty-four million men, he asserted that prolonging it would be a crime as great as that of starting it. In Allied peace terms, he insisted, there must be reparations for Belgium, but no dismemberment of Germany; the freedom of the seas should be guaranteed to all nations; and Germany should be left free to choose her own government.

After further discussion of reasonable ways and means of settlement, Lansdowne concluded: "We are not going to lose this War, but its prolongation will spell ruin for the civilized world, and an infinite addition to the load of human suffering which already weighs upon it. Security will be invaluable to a world which has the vitality to profit by it, but what will be the value of the blessings of peace to nations so exhausted that they can scarcely stretch out a hand with which to grasp them?"[2]

The letter was greeted with howls of execration in the London press and called up abuse from Lansdowne's colleagues which, according to his biographer, Lord Newton, formerly in charge of propaganda at the Foreign Office, was "marked by violence rare in English political life."[3] The wolf-pack was led by Lord Northcliffe, and running in it were Lord Rothermere and John Hulton. The rest of the London press joined the pack, and Lansdowne was widely reviled as a traitor, coward, and villain. Bonar Law called the letter "a national misfortune." H. G. Wells wrote a blistering attack in a pamphlet which echoed the words of Lansdowne's opening sentence, "In the Fourth Year." This also became the title for his next collection of propaganda pamphlets published in 1918. Lansdowne's peace proposal was merely evidence to Wells of the desires of men of his class to make peace with Germany by promising to retain the House of Hohenzollern in power. Lansdowne's letter to the *Telegraph* was, Wells thought, "but a feeler from the pacifist side of this most un-English, and unhappily most influential, section of our public life. Lord Lansdowne's letter was the letter of a Peer who fears revolution more than national dishonour."[4]

The old Tory peer was an all too easy target for such inaccurate and unjustifiable *ad hominem* attacks, being almost a parody of the hunting and fishing landowning aristocrat who had also resisted the reform of the House of Lords and Irish Home Rule. By attacking the man, his opponents were able to suppress debate on the real merits of his proposals. It seemed that the letter had been torn to pieces by the wolves and dispersed by the winds of patriotism. But in fact all was not lost, and Lansdowne did contribute something to the rising wave of peace feelings in 1918. Many of the English provincial papers had quite different reactions from the London dailies, and the *Saturday Review* printed an editorial on 8 December 1917 which said, in part, "Now that the malice and scurrility of the press and clubs are exhausted, we take leave to say that the publication of Lord Lansdowne's letter has done good."[5] Bernard Shaw praised Lansdowne's letter, but he saw it as a "desperate attempt to capture the ground we should have been the first to occupy" after Germany made some tentative peace proposals.[6]

Bertrand Russell poured ridicule on the press reaction to Lansdowne's letter. He ironically remarked in *The Tribunal* that "One expects to see him mentioned in inverted commas, as Lord 'Lansdowne,' with various aliases in brackets after his name. Before long, it will probably be discovered that his great aunt was born in Kiel, or that his grandfather was an admirer of Goëthe." He went on to praise his "wise and weighty words" and claimed that there was a great body of opinion in the country supporting them, particularly in the Labour Party.[7] President Wilson, influenced by the letter, put forward some peace proposals on 8 January 1918, along lines sketched out by Lansdowne. Lansdowne Committees were formed in Britain to publicize his views, and deputations from them visited Parliament. Lansdowne also received many letters of support from soldiers serving at the front, and he at last managed to force a debate on the question in the Lords on 19 March.

The movement towards peace was gaining momentum when the German army mounted its last great offensive in late March, and all talk of peace died away as the Allied armies fought with their backs to the wall. Lord Newton speculated what might have happened if only Lansdowne's appeal had been made earlier, say in the spring of 1917, when there had been a stalemate, but one not disadvantageous to the Allies. This had been the great opportunity for Lloyd George to do something about negotiations, and he must be held responsible for not seizing it. He considered making peace and, in his memoirs, praised Lansdowne's "great courage and high sense of public duty" in circulating his memorandum in cabinet in 1916. But, he pugnaciously added, "once having started the fight, I felt we must see it right through, until the German military machine was smashed."[8] Yet he, better than anyone else in the government, knew of the overweening optimism and rigidity of Field Marshall Haig and his staff—one of the best-kept secrets of the war. He was aware of the appalling casualties that had already occurred on the Western Front and the continuing wastage of material and money, which few others knew about. For a period he seriously considered sacking Haig, but, he confesses in his memoirs, he could find little support for the action in the cabinet or among the dominion leaders. Most of them, he writes, "were under the spell of the synthetic victories distilled at G.H.Q."[9]—those feats so imaginatively concocted by John Buchan and his cohorts.

In the end, Lloyd George did not act either to make peace or to change generals. He allowed Haig to go through with what he called "the insane egotism of Passchendaele"[10] and then Cambrai, in which defeat was snatched from the jaws of the victory gained by the tanks. Then came the Italian fiasco at Caporetto, Russia's exit from the war, and America's entry, which meant an almost certain eventual Allied victory. The Allies had to go on fighting through 1917 and early 1918 unless they wanted to conclude a peace which might have conceded Alsace-Lorraine to Germany and perhaps some colonies as well. So the propaganda for total victory was stepped up. "Here in England," Lord Newton writes, "every wall was placarded with clenched fists, emblematic of the knock-out blow, and the voice of reason and sanity was drowned in the bellowings of Lord Northcliffe and Mr. Bottomley."[11] Lansdowne was probably too deeply perplexed and hesitant about the ethics of publicizing his views after they had been refused debate in Parliament. He waited too long and lost the opportunity which might have ended the war a year earlier, saved countless lives, and brought about a peace settlement which might have ensured that the world would not be at war again within another generation.

This, of course, is only speculation, since the fact remains that in the spring of 1917, as in November of that year, hatred ran deep in British civilian life. The forces for peace had never been able to reach any accord or establish any goals for united action although, looked at closely, the views of Shaw, Russell, and Lansdowne during 1916 and 1917 were not that far apart. But class, politics, and intellectual styles divided them, as it divided the pacifist members of the Liberal party from those of Labour.

The fact that there was relatively little popular agitation in favour of peace can be blamed on the propagandists who had encouraged what Paul Fussell calls "the mode of gross dichotomy," in which the Hegelian synthesis of a negotiated peace would be anathema.[12] Evasion, hypocrisy, righteousness, vindictiveness, and deference to authority had characterized both official and unofficial propaganda. As a consequence, something intensely fragile and precious had been destroyed, or, as James put it, worn out like a motor tyre: the integrity of language. In the constant blare of lies and hatred, from all sides, the small voice of truth had been drowned out; the vital connection between word and act had been severed.

Although H. G. Wells was one of the loudest voices in the attack on Lansdowne and in support of pursuing the war to the total defeat of Germany, he was at the same time a persistent advocate of a just peace. Wells's essays in *In the Fourth Year: Anticipations of a World Peace* call for, among other things, a League of Free Nations, guarantees to Germany of free trade with the rest of the world, and a democratically elected government for that country. But underneath the essays is a sense of despair that sometimes leaks out onto the page. "Death seems to be feeling always now for those I most love" he writes; "the newspapers that come to my house tell mostly of blood and disaster, of drownings and slaughterings." In spite of these fears, Wells dogmatically reiterates his faith in the nobility and sweetness of the future. There exists at this moment, he believes, all the knowledge necessary for the future happiness of mankind. "We need but the courage to lay our hands upon it," he concludes, "and in a little space of years it can be ours."[13]

In this faith, Wells laboured on until the war dragged to its conclusion. In many of his published writings of the period, he expressed the highest praise for the aims and rhetoric of President Woodrow Wilson, seeing in him something of the new Messiah for whom he was constantly searching in the years of trial. In 1918 he was invited to write a brief to the president on his views about the organization of peace, and he did so at length. Much later, in his *Autobiography*, he expressed doubt that Wilson ever read the brief or, if he did, took any notice of it.

Meanwhile, men were suffering and dying by the hundreds of thousands on the Western Front, their plight almost unknown at home. Siegfried Sassoon was one serving officer who, after a career of legendary heroism, tried to do something about the situation. He went to see Bertrand Russell, who had become the acting chairman of the No-Conscription Fellowship after the chairman, Clifford Allen, had been jailed. Russell helped to edit and publicize the famous statement that Sassoon made protesting the continuation of the war before the whole matter was hushed up through the efforts of Robert Graves. Graves was able to get Sassoon sent to a hospital for shellshocked officers in Scotland, avoiding the court-martial that Sassoon was seeking.[14]

Russell worked in many ways for the cause of peace. He wrote an open letter to President Wilson seeking his intervention as a mediator. It was smuggled out of England and published on the front page of the *New York Times*. In order to get publicity for views that were systematically suppressed by the government, Russell deliberately sought prosecution through his assistance to conscientious objectors. The government, fearing his influence as a philosopher and his standing as the heir to an earldom, avoided the issue. Russell finally brought things to a head when he suggested in an article in *The Tribunal*, the No-Conscription Fellowship newspaper, that American soldiers might be employed as strikebreakers in England as they had been in the United States. He was prosecuted under the Defence of the Realm Act and spent six months in jail. Trinity College deprived him of his fellowship—an action condemned by many liberals in Britain and the United States. D. H. Lawrence observed later that "something seemed to go out of Cambridge when Bertie Russell had to leave."[15] Russell was convinced later that all he had done during the war had been useless. He felt, as many did, that something fragile and precious had been broken in the blind and destructive emotions released by the war. In May 1915, after hearing of the death of his friend Rupert Brooke, he wrote to Ottoline Morrell: "There will be other generations—yet I keep fearing that something of civilization will be lost for good, as something was lost when Greece perished in just this way."[16]

When victory finally came in the west, it was an anticlimax. Many had predicted that the war would go on for much longer since it seemed that German strength had not been substantially diminished, even after the defeats she suffered on the Marne and in the Argonne. Many young Americans, including William Faulkner and F. Scott Fitzgerald, were in training when the Armistice came and were disappointed about missing their chance to play their roles on the stage of world history.

But even though the armistice seemed like another stalemate, there was still hope that the peace treaty would rescue Europe from its eternal troubles. Certainly H. G. Wells thought so. He and other British intellectuals, Gilbert Murray, Leonard Woolf, Wickham Steed, and J. S. Spender, who had been working for years on a plan of reorganization, were waiting in the wings to be consulted. Then Wells's messiah, Wilson, came over for the Peace Conference. "President Wilson," growls Wells in his autobiography, "essentially ill-informed, narrowly limited to an old-fashioned American conception of history, self-confident and profoundly self-righteous, came to Europe and passed us by on the other side. Men of my thinking were left helpless, voiceless, and altogether baffled outside the fiasco of Versailles."[17]

Wells's hopes may have been presumptuous, for there were many forces operating against a just peace treaty at Versailles. One of the strongest was the demand that Germany pay for her alleged crimes against mankind. As James Morgan Read has amply demonstrated, the weakest and most destructive section of the Treaty was Part VII, which called for punishment of those guilty of atrocities. In imposing this section on Germany, the statesmen were prisoners of the monster that they themselves had created through their writers and the press. "Propaganda of atrocities," Read writes, "might be said to have contributed more than any other single factor to the making of a severe peace."[18] Those stories had aroused hatred and fear in the Allied nations; filled with such emotions, people sought vengeance. The German protests against this section went for nothing. There followed that resentment which had much to do with the rise of fascism, the repudiation of the Treaty of Versailles, and, ultimately, the war in which Germany sought its own revenge for these injustices. These were the bitter consequences of Wells's "War That Will End War."

12

DISILLUSIONMENT AND RECONSTRUCTION: WRITERS REFLECT ON THE WAR

So we had failed, had won the fight and lost the prize; the garland of the war was withered before it was gained.
C. E. MONTAGUE, 1922

The best-known literary consequence of the Great War is the literature of disillusion, the work of a generation of young men, most of whom had served in the trenches or in some other branch of front-line service. Indeed, the literature of that war has become almost synonymous with the names of those whose novels and poems were cries of anger, repudiation, anguish, cynicism, or despair: Wilfred Owen, David Jones, Siegfried Sassoon, Robert Graves, Richard Aldington, Ernest Hemingway, e.e. cummings, John Dos Passos, Charles Yale Harrison, Henri Barbusse, and Erich Maria Remarque. Overlooked and almost forgotten in the literature of the Great War, even by such able commentators as Bernard Bergonzi and Paul Fussell, are the works of the older writers: Edith Wharton, Ralph Connor, Beckles Willson, John Galsworthy, Rudyard Kipling, H. G. Wells, and Arnold Bennett. Their work has seemed somehow irrelevant because it does not appear to be in harmony with the prevailing view of "the lost generation," as it came to be called. As a result, some works of considerable value have been forgotten and will have to be summarized before they can be discussed.

It took some time for any literary work of quality to emerge out of war experience. At first those who, as Ezra Pound phrased it, had been "eye-deep in hell" and had emerged with bodies and minds functioning, were silent, shocked, or paralysed with what they knew and could not tell, like Krebs in Hemingway's story "Soldier's Home." People in Krebs's home town did not want to hear the truth, even if he could have told it, because they had "heard too many atrocity stories to be thrilled by actualities."[1]

Then, around 1921, some of them began to find the words for what they had to say, to give form to the inchoate anger which they felt, and to expose the lies to which they had been subjected. The Americans were among the first to speak, perhaps because they had not been so long swallowed up in the nightmare of war and therefore could awake more quickly from it. Dos Passos in *Three Soldiers* (1921), e.e. cummings in *The Enormous Room* (1922), and Hemingway in *In Our Time* (1924) began to break the façade erected in the books of the old men.

Among the first of the books of disillusionment to be written by a British author was C. E. Montague's *Disenchantment*, published in 1922. Montague was forty-seven when the war broke out, and he had been a journalist with the *Manchester Guardian* for sixteen years. He dyed his grey hair, faked his age, and enlisted in the ranks. Having served in the line with the Royal Fusiliers, he was invalided home, but he returned to France as assistant press censor. One of his jobs was to shepherd distinguished visitors around on their trips to the front (plate 33). It was he, for example, who did the honours for Bernard Shaw. He was thus able to see all sides of the war. The ironic narrative in *Disenchantment* tells the whole story, from his enthusiastic rush to the colours in the high days of Kitchener's army, through the gradual cooling down when subjected to the cynical ways of the Old Army, the trauma of front-line service, the squalor of trench-life, the heroism of the troops, to his growing sense of the incredible bungling of the staff. As press censor, he was a party to some of the lies and deceptions invented by the propagandists. He visited one of the sites where the Germans supposedly boiled down corpses for their fat. An Australian sergeant was with Montague. He surveyed the scene and took in the obvious deception. Turning to Montague, he said: " 'Can't believe a word you read, sir, can you?' " —a catch-phrase in the army.[2]

Montague notes that the earliest tactic of the War Office had been to ban all journalists from the front—to treat them as pariah dogs, as he puts it. This changed under Haig's command, and correspondents soon enjoyed the privileges and the confidence of G.H.Q., and they were given the red-carpet treatment, as distinguished writers were. The trouble with that situation was that the journalists were, like the staff, comfortably cushioned from the realities of the front line. "When autumn twilight came down," Montague writes, "on the haggard trench world of which they had caught a quiet noon-day glimpse they would be speeding west in Vauxhall cars to lighted chateaux gleaming white among scatheless woods." The correspondents then unwittingly acquired the views of the gaudy staff: that the troops really enjoyed going over the top, that battle was like a jovial picnic, and that the men's only fear was that the war should end on this side of the Rhine. So, Montague describes the Somme: "The most bloody defeat in the history of Britain, a very world's wonder of valour frustrated by feckless misuse, of

Plate 33   C. E. Montague (2nd from right) in a safe trench with a French officer, a Tommy, and a War Correspondent.

regimental glory and Staff shame, might occur on the Ancre on 1 July 1916, and our Press come out bland and copious and graphic, with nothing to show that we had not had quite a good day—a victory really. Men who lived through the massacre read the stuff open-mouthed."[3] The scepticism about the press, Montague goes on to say, had naturally been carried on into peacetime, whether in respect to the newspapers or government leaders' speeches—"You can't believe a word you read."

Montague was a realist; he recognizes and justifies the necessity of telling lies in wartime as a means of confusing and demoralizing the enemy and protecting Allied forces. The trouble was that the lies were also used to cover up incompetence and waste and old army elitism, while the troops were uselessly slaughtered. And as the war went on, the troops in the line got to know things which were carefully concealed from the public— such as the watering down of the quality of the British army as conscription took effect. The brunt of attack and defence fell increasingly on Canadian and Australian troops, who believed that "only the Guards Division, two kilted divisions and three English ones could be said to know how to fight."[4] Any sense of gallantry and courtesy towards the enemy was felt only in the front lines, as was demonstrated in the Christmas truce of 1914, never to be permitted again. Beyond the lines that spirit died down "westward all the way to London." No wonder cynicism spread among the troops, although they doggedly stuck to their jobs.

At length, the Allies blundered through to victory. "So we had failed"— writes Montague, "had won the fight and lost the prize; the garland of the war was withered before it was gained. The lost years, the broken youth, the dead friends, the women's overshadowed lives at home, the agony and bloody sweat—all had gone to darken the stains which most of us had thought to scour out of the world that our children would live in. Many men felt, and said to each other, that they had been fooled." The politicians and press took over and, in Montague's words, did "the Prussianist goose-step by way of *pas de triomphe*" in the streets of Paris. The troops came back to broken promises and indifference at home. They could not help but say, according to Montague: " 'This is our doing. We cannot wish the war unwon, and yet—if we had shirked, poor old England, for all we know, might not have come to this pass. So we come home draggle-tailed, sick of the mess that we were unwittingly helping to make when we tried to do well.' "5

C. E. Montague's *Disenchantment* is perhaps the bleakest expression of disillusionment: for him the whole war had been a ghastly and costly mistake, a spectacle of useless bravery, endless lies, and profitless sacrifice. It was difficult for most of the writers of his generation to accept this extreme version of the war. When they came to look back on their roles, they had in some measure to justify their reactions and both assume responsibility and assess the meaning of the whole terrible and destructive event.

It is significant that some of the older American and Canadian novelists, even while recognizing the failures and corruptions of the Allies, tried to vindicate and, in some measure, idealize the vast effort. Among others, Edith Wharton, Ralph Connor, and Beckles Willson set down in their fiction means of reconciliation or redemption through a recollection and justification of prewar ideals. In the Adamic or messianic vision of these new-world writers, the Great European War could be seen as part of a larger drama in which the bitter experience and loss of war would yet lead to a paradise partly regained.

The British novelists, on the other hand, found far fewer grounds for hope in the postwar world. Artistic individuality reasserted itself with a vengeance, and in their different ways, John Galsworthy, Ford Madox Ford (he had changed his name from Hueffer in 1919), H. G. Wells, Rudyard Kipling, and Arnold Bennett looked back with irony, bitterness, regret, grief, and wonder at the ordeal the world had suffered and with some dismay at their own complicity in the enterprise. For these men fiction was an attempt to set the record straight for future generations; for some of them it was a warning to others that a writer gets involved in propaganda at the risk of losing his soul as well as his detachment.

Some felt early on that they needed to record their emotions about the war, but they also felt the need for objectivity. In her autobiography, Edith Wharton wrote that she began to think of a war novel in 1917. She believed, however, that she could not deal with the emotions aroused by the war until time had taken her far enough away from the experience. She began the novel in 1922 and wrote it, she said, "in a white heat of emotion."[6] It was published in 1923.

A Son at the Front is told from the point of view of a middle-aged painter, John Campton, who manages to survive the war with his ideals battered but not destroyed. He is an American painter, long resident in Paris, who has a son, born in France, who is called up to fight in the French army. His mother, divorced from Campton and remarried to a rich American businessman, pulls every string to keep her son out of the fighting zone. Campton goes along with her schemes since he is not convinced that an American's son has any business fighting for this European cause. Unknown to both his parents, the son, George, wangles his way into a combat regiment, is badly wounded, and dies in a Parisian hospital just as the United States enters the war.

At its most important level of meaning, *A Son at the Front* is a dramatization of the twists and turns of the mind and conscience of an artist who had given himself up for many years to his work and to sensuous enjoyment. Wharton represents the difficult and often bitter battle that Campton fights before he realizes that the war is necessary, despite all the loss and suffering, and that love can include the values of sacrifice and memory as well as those of possession and enjoyment. On another level, the novel is the record of the troubled growth of a typical American consciousness into an awareness of responsibility—from the personal to the national and finally to the international. This apparently mirrors the progress of American opinion between 1914 and 1917 as the nation moved from isolation to confusion and finally to participation.

At its most acute, *A Son at the Front* shows Wharton's awareness that the war would make what Campton calls "an unbridgeable abyss" between the generations—for George's experience in the trenches remains a closed book to his father. She documents the corruption and inefficiency behind the lines and does not gloss over the carnage at the front. Moreover, she realizes how the nature of language has been changed by the war. "I was considering how the meaning had evaporated out of lots of our old words," a friend of John Campton remarks, "as if the general smash-up had broken their stoppers."[7] All these realizations do not, however, lead to Campton's disillusionment after his son's death. As the novel ends, he is preparing to make a monument for his son's grave. In George's experience, he reflects, "there ran the life-giving power of a reality embraced and accepted. George had been; George was; as long as his father's consciousness lasted, George would be as much a part of it as the closest, most actual of his immediate sensations."[8] In spite of its over-reliance on coincidence, *A Son at the Front* is a strongly argued justification of the war and, incidentally, of America's role in the conflict.

Another who reacted to disaster at the front with confirmed idealism was a Presbyterian minister, Charles W. Gordon, better known as Ralph Connor, author of the enormously successful romances, *The Man From Glengarry* and *The Sky Pilot*. At the age of fifty-four he was appointed chaplain to the 79th Cameron Highlanders of Winnipeg. He accompanied his battalion to the Somme, but he was at the base hospital when the Camerons went in to take Regina Trench in October 1916. Two hundred and fifty-seven men returned of the original eleven hundred. In his autobiography, *Postscript to Adventure*, Connor blames staff bungling for the massacre. The battalion was assured that the wire in front of the trench had been cut and that a strong point which could enfilade an attack had been blown up. Neither report was true.

Returning to Canada in 1917, he made such an effective speech about his experiences with the battalion to parliamentarians and churchmen in Ottawa that he was asked by the prime minister to make a propaganda tour of the United States. He spoke in halls and churches about the sacred cause of the Allies, and he was addressing a meeting of the Yale Alumni Association in New York when the message came that the president had asked Congress to declare war on Germany.

It is hardly surprising, then, that Connor's war fiction should be unstintingly patriotic and idealistic. *The Major*, published in 1917, was written to expose pro-German sentiment in Canada and to encourage recruiting. It established the formula by which many novels of this genre were to be written: either the hero or one of the central figures is a pacifist or indifferent to the war. He is converted by atrocity stories or by a woman, or both, enlists and goes off to fight, and either dies or emerges with an aesthetically acceptable wound.

The Sky Pilot in No Man's Land (1919) follows this formula. The hero is a young and quite priggish preacher, Barry Dunbar, who joins up as padre at the outbreak of war and spends most of his time upbraiding his soldier-charges for their swearing and drinking. His universal unpopularity is redeemed after his father, mortally wounded while serving as a sergeant in the first Canadian contingent, tells him he should not act as a censor but go with his men as a friend and tell them about God. He does so and performs extraordinary feats of heroism and sacrifice. Many of the incidents of the novel are based on Gordon's own experience at the front, including the slaughter of his battalion on the Somme. Instead of going to base hospital as Gordon did, however, Barry insists on going up to the front with his men and is killed while helping to carry back a wounded man from an advanced trench. Before that, in the approved sentimental tradition, he has married a nurse in the Volunteer Aid Detachment who is to bear his child. The padre's dying words provide the cliché on which the book ends, " 'Major—tell—the boys—that—God—is good—Never—to be—afraid—but to—carry on—' "

In *The Sky Pilot in No Man's Land* there is no recrimination about the bungled staff work that led to the slaughter of the battalion. Barry thinks: "The thing in which they were engaged was vastly more important than the fate of any individual or of any battalion. Victory was necessary, was guaranteed, and was demanding its price."[9] These sentiments are reminiscent of Hay's and Kipling's belief in the necessity of joyful sacrifice to the battalion.

But other writers who followed Connor's successful and sentimental formula were not so willing to continue the cover up. One of these was Beckles Willson, who spent the war years travelling around just behind the front lines collecting trophies for the British and Canadian war museums after he left Beaverbrook's propaganda office. In 1924, he published *Redemption*, in which he attempts to assess the meaning of the war for himself and for Canada and incidentally to pay off his old score against Beaverbrook.

He follows the basic formula of Ralph Connor's war novels, but he is far more critical of Allied propaganda and of the conduct of the war. The novel includes an attack on atrocity propaganda and chronicles its deadly effect on some German-speaking Canadians. It follows the fortunes of a Nova Scotian, Gregory Vant, who enlists, goes to France, is wounded, and then serves as an Intelligence Officer at Corps Headquarters. There he sees "the intrigues and vacillation of purpose, the jealousies, the political interference against which some of the bravest officers struggled in vain. He learned for the first time of the deadly toadyism towards insufferable opportunists who were turning the war to their own advantage and that of their own miserable clique."

Vant is transferred later to Army headquarters, where more incompetence and intrigue are revealed to him. He works on the plans for a new advance—apparently, the Somme offensive. "It was only a vast and costly diversion," Vant thinks, "It would not ultimately shorten the war by a single day or assist in the ultimate victory. And events proved him right."

Vant turns then to attack the war-correspondents, whom he calls "simple agents of official propaganda . . . retailers of gossip, concocters of agreeable and often exciting anecdote." One of them complains that they cannot tell the truth—and if they did, "the whole rotten house of cards would topple down." They had to be loyal, not to England, or the Empire or the King, "but to this system and these brass-hatted popinjays."[10]

Even though Vant continues to be shocked and outraged both in France and on the home front by the blunders, waste, and corruption, the convention in which the novel is written demands that the hero perform brave deeds and be decorated and wounded. Sickened by base duties, Vant goes back to front-line service and is wounded again. He finds himself after the armistice in a hospital bed next to an old friend, a French-Canadian whose reluctance to join up had been overcome by patriotism and who has been blinded in battle. The novel ends with a conversation between them. It is not, as one might expect, a conversation full of cynicism even though they both confess to disillusionment. Instead, the men discuss how Canada has redeemed itself in the war, "Somehow," Vant says, referring to the two solitudes of French and English Canada, "back again in our own land, we will find the way to unity—and the beautiful things we have lost."

Vant thus glosses over not only his own devastating attack on the conduct of the war but also the damage that the war had done to French-English relations through the conscription crisis, increased racial hatred, and the divisive election of 1917. He concludes the novel with an optimism worthy of its source—the philosopher, Pangloss. " 'It will all come right in the end,' " Vant tells his French-Canadian friend, " 'but in the meantime we must abandon quixotism and cultivate our garden.' "[11]

The novel's title, *Redemption*, presumably referred both to the personal redemption that Vant and his fellow Canadians have found in battle and also to the redemption of Canada as a nation made by the collective experience of war. This is, ironically, a development of Beaverbrook's idea that the trenches of Flanders were the baptismal font of the new nation. Other Canadian novelists such as Beverly Baxter and Robert J. C. Stead shared this view.[12] Like Edith Wharton, they maintained that the war, in spite of everything, was necessary and morally justifiable. These novelists were in effect writing a new version of the old story of the new world coming in to redress the balance of the old and bringing a vision of a better future rising from the ashes of a strife-torn Europe.

Most of the older British writers, Galsworthy, Ford, Wells, Kipling, and Bennett among them, did not have such visionary ideas, and they had to look elsewhere for reasons and solace. Evidently Galsworthy's experience with propaganda rankled in his mind. After the war he sought to satirize the whole business in *The Burning Spear*, published in 1919 under a pseudonym and reprinted in 1925 under his own name. The novel is a rather weak adaptation of *Don Quixote*. Chivalric romance had driven the Don mad; war and propaganda literature have done the same to the fifty-eight-year-old Mr. Lavender. He has a Sancho Panza in Joe Petty, his chauffeur, and a Dulcinante in Isobel, a pretty V.A.D. nurse who lives next door.

Lavender goes down to what Galsworthy calls the Ministry of Propagation to volunteer his services. The minister takes him on, without pay, and promises him material for his speeches. He tells Lavender: " 'If you want any atrocities we can give you them. No facts and no figures; just general pat.' "[13] Lavender goes off to find an audience, which he does in a farcical episode. He makes a speech about the importance of manpower and how women must have many babies, is pelted with stones, pushed into a pond, and called pro-German. Undeterred, Lavender continues his pilgrimage about the country. He abuses a conscientious objector, plans to trap a suspected enemy alien, and continuously spouts the rhetoric that readers of this book will be familiar with. For example: " 'Not . . . by physical weight and force shall we win this war, for it is at bottom a question of morale. Right is ever victorious in the end, and though we have infinitely greater material resources than our foes, we should still triumph were we reduced to the last ounce, because of the inherent nobility of our cause.' "

He is invited to lunch with Isobel's father, Major Scarlet, who heartily agrees with his views about the need for total victory and adds, " 'Yes . . . we must just go on killing Germans and collaring every bit of their property we can.' "[14] Scarlet asserts that all the submarine and Zeppelin crews ought to be hanged, their towns bombed out of existence, and the people treated like vermin. But this is too much for the gentle Mr. Lavender, who loses his temper and calls Major Scarlet a Prussian in his jackboot.

The common sense about the war is expressed by the Sancho Panza figure, Joe Petty, who tells his master " 'I've got no opinions on anything, except that I want to live a quiet life— just enough beer and 'baccy, short hours, and no worry.' " Petty blames the press, Parliament, and the mayors for dreaming up aspirations such as Imperialism, Liberty in Europe, and the sacrifice of the last man and the last dollar to the Cause. It is his opinion that: " 'The 'ole point of an aspiration is the sacrifice of someone else.' "[15]

After some more misadventures in public speaking, Lavender appears to be convinced of the truth of Joe's observations. He decides that he is not cut out to be a propagandist. His reflections on the point seem to echo those of Galsworthy himself. " 'I am two men,' " Lavender says, " 'one of whom is me and one not me. . . . The one which is me loves these pigeons, and desires to live quietly with my dog, not considering public affairs, which, indeed, seem to be suited to persons of another sort. . . . Ought I not, rather, to be true to my private self and leave the course of public affairs to those who have louder voices and no private selves?' "[16] Deciding that he has made a fool of himself, Lavender resolves upon his own sacrifice. He erects a great pile of propaganda books, pamphlets, periodicals, and newspapers in his garden on which to immolate himself.

He sits down to compose a last interview with himself to convey the meaning of his act to the world. " 'I feel . . . that extravagance of word and conduct is fatal to my country, and having so profoundly experienced its effects upon myself, I am now endeavouring by a shining example to supply a remedy for a disease which is corroding the vitals and impairing the sanity of my countrymen and making them a race of second-hand spiritual drunkards.' "

He places four volumes of the history of the war as stepping stones to the top, lights the pyre, and climbs up. He fixes his eye on the bedroom of his Dulcinante, Isobel, and waits for the end. At that moment, the flame dies at the words in a newspaper: " 'The Stage is now set for the last act of this colossal world drama.' "[17] He relights it, blows up the flame, and reascends. At the last moment, however, Isobel awakes, sees Lavender, and rescues him from the flames.

The Burning Spear is only moderately successful as a satire and only moderately funny. Unfortunately, Galsworthy did not have the talents of Cervantes or of Jonathan Swift, and he could not deal with the gross subject of propaganda with the savagery and wit that it so richly deserved. It was an opportunity missed. *The Burning Spear* shows, however, that there was at least one British writer who was honest enough to admit that he had been duped and used, that "spiritual conversion" had made of him a "spiritual drunkard." It was a confession that the whole attempt to lift the British cause to a higher plane with the rhetoric of moral superiority and purity had been a betrayal of the very virtues that Galsworthy himself had aired in such articles as "Diagnosis of the Englishman." The novel was an acknowledgement that what he, and his fellow writers had turned out in quantity had had about as much truth as those medieval romances that had sent Don Quixote mad. The trouble was that such literature had helped derange the whole nation. British writers, Galsworthy is saying in *The Burning Spear*, in his cool and ironic way, could not disclaim their responsibility for this madness.

For the one propaganda writer who felt his responsibility— in his words, duty—so strongly that he joined up, fictionalizing his experiences became a way to regain sanity. When Ford Madox Hueffer abandoned his career as writer and propagandist and joined the army, he faced physical and psychological hardships scarcely imaginable to the other writers of his generation who stayed at home and wrote or made the occasional tour of the front to get material for propaganda. Army discipline and training came hard, and he was often in trouble with his superiors. In his subsequent autobiographies, his military career was the subject of a certain amount of fantasy and exaggeration. He was never wounded or gassed, as he claimed, never even served in the trenches. On the other hand, he was subjected to a good deal of shelling and the other stresses of service at or near the front.

After training, he went out to France in July 1916 as a junior officer in the 9th Welch Battalion, a unit of the 58th Infantry Brigade. During the Battle of the Somme, he was in the front-line transport and saw the consequences of that military disaster. A number of companies of the 9th Welch were in the ghastly battle of Mametz Wood and suffered heavy casualties. According to his biographer, Arthur Mizener, after ten days on the Somme, the hut in which Ford was working sustained a near miss from a shell, and he was knocked down, suffering concussion and damage to his teeth. He was sent to hospital and there lost his memory for thirty-six hours. His memory did not function properly until 1923.[18] The wards in the military hospital, filled with wounded and dying men, also gave him terrible nightmares which plagued him for years.

The rest of his military career was inglorious. It was punctuated by spells in military hospitals, where he sometimes felt he was losing his mind. He often ran afoul of superior officers and was given unpleasant jobs, such as guard duty over German prisoners of war. The only bright spot in this career was its interruption by an invitation from the French government to proceed to Paris. There he was formally congratulated for his propaganda book *Between St. Dennis and St. George*, which had been translated into French. In March 1918, he was invalided home. He was released from the army in January 1919. The experience of front-line duty, the boring, deadly work of a junior officer, and the petty bureaucracy of army life gave him the material for his great tetralogy, *Parade's End*.

Over and above the normal stresses of an ordinary soldier's life, Ford's ever-active imagination bred fears and hallucinations against which he had constantly to struggle. Moreover, his near bankruptcy at the time and his tempestuous relationship with Violet Hunt, whom Henry James used to call "purple patch," led to endless anxieties. More than most soldiers, too, Ford was concerned about the conduct of the home government after the fall of Asquith and what he perceived to be the decay of morality in Britain.

Many of these anxieties are reflected in *No Enemy: A Tale of Reconstruction*, a novel which he published in 1929, but which was mainly written just after the war. The autobiographical narrator says: "I don't think that many of those who were one's comrades *in illo die* did not at times feel a certain hopelessness. . . . And so they would sit in the chairs of the lost and forgotten amidst a world where the ideals which sent all those millions to destruction were lost too . . . and forgotten. You will say this is bitter. It is. It was bitter to have seen the 38th Division murdered in Mametz Wood—and to guess what underlay that!"[19] The author had good reason for bitterness about this episode. General Rawlinson inexplicably failed to follow up the initial success of the attack on this wood on 1 July 1916. Instead of consolidating the success, the troops were withdrawn. When the attack was renewed, Martin Middlebrook writes, "the casualties incurred were enormous and might have been avoided by bold action on that day."[20]

Like many another demobilized soldiers, Ford also suffered the pangs of disillusionment at the indifference and callousness of the civilian population. That disillusionment is treated at length in the autobiography, *It Was the Nightingale* (1933). Ford felt like a ghost in London after the war. Nobody seemed to remember him or his work.

With his new mistress, Stella Bowen, he moved down into a small dilapidated cottage in Sussex and started raising pigs and vegetables, just like so many other returned warriors who took refuge on the land. There he had an encounter which sounds even more fanciful than many he recalled in his several autobiographies. It is worth repeating because, even if it is an imaginative vision, it gives the clue to the germ and central motif of what is probably the greatest English novel written about the Great War, *Parade's End*. Moreover, the incident shows how Ford was able to bring order out of the chaos of his war experience and shape it into fiction.

Ford was feeding his pigs, covered in mud and dressed in an old pair of khaki shorts and shirt, when a voice came over the hedge:

"Didn't I once meet you at Henry James'?"
Standing above me on the bank was the comfortable and distinguished figure of Sir Edward Elgar. I did not remember having met him at Henry James' but I knew him for the great local man—and of course as the composer of the *Dream of Gerontion*—and *Land of Hope and Glory*.

There came into my mind suddenly the words: "The band will play: *Land of Hope and Glory*" . . . The adjutant will say: "There will be no more parades. . . . "

It worried me slightly that I could no longer be certain of all the phrases of that ceremonial for the disbanding of a battalion. . . . Nothing in the world was further from my thoughts than writing about the late war. But I suppose the idea was somewhere in my own subconscious, for I said to myself: "If I do not do something about it soon it is possible I shall forget about the details. . . . " And I wondered how the common friend of myself and Sir Edward would have treated that intractable subject. I imagined the tortuous mind getting to work, the New England scrupulousness, the terrific involutions . . . and for the rest of the day and for several days more I lost myself in working out an imaginary war-novel on the lines of "What Maisie Knew."[21]

Later in the book, Ford takes up the thread again: "I found I knew still every 'detail' of Infantry Drill. . . . I found I still had by heart all the paragraphs of King's Regulations and Military Law that a regimental officer could be required to know. I went over in my mind every contour of the road from Vailleul to Locre, Locre-Pont de Nieppe, Nieppe down to Armentières—and of all the by-roads from Nieppe to Ploegsteert, Westoutre, Dramoutre.

And I found I could remember with astonishing vividness every house left, in September 1916, along the whole road, and almost every tree—and hundreds of shell holes!"[22]

These passages are of the first importance because they give a microcosm of *Parade's End*'s macrocosm, the essence of the vision Ford was later to portray at length and in detail. The comfortable, distinguished figure of Elgar represented that secure Edwardian world—also a kind of Gerontion's dream of betrayal—that preceded the Great War, a world of ranks, titles, parades, hope, and glory. The mud-covered khaki figure whom Elgar addressed had emerged from the mud and khaki of Flanders, that pig-sty of destruction that decimated the younger generation.

The image that came into Ford's mind at that moment became central to the tetralogy and gave the title to *No More Parades*. At the beginning of the war, Tietjens came across a fellow in the War Office devising the ceremonial for disbanding a Kitchener battalion. He points out the implication of this absurd activity to McKechnie, the shell-shocked officer working in his hut:
" 'Don't you see how symbolical it was: the band playing *Land of Hope and Glory*, and then the adjutant saying *There will be no more parades*? . . . For there won't, there damn well won't. . . . No more Hope, no more Glory, no more parades for you and me any more. Not for the country . . . Nor for the world, I dare say . . . None . . . Gone . . . Na poo, finny! No . . . more . . . parades!' "[23]

Ford's memory, in which he took an immense pride, had not returned to normal by 1922, and yet it seems clear that the idea of writing a book on this theme about the war suddenly brought things back. The writing was for him a therapeutic act, as writing *A Farewell to Arms* was for Hemingway. How to do it? The example of Henry James, with his total dedication to dramatizing and rendering life, was for Ford the obvious one to follow. *What Maisie Knew* was the one book that Ford said he kept constantly with him throughout his war service. As he wrote in *No Enemy*, *What Maisie Knew* represented for him at the front exactly the atmosphere of what was going on in England—"a tenuous, misty struggle of schemes."[24] Such a struggle, in a different form, also went on behind the front, among the gaudy staff, as Tietjens called it. Moreover *Maisie*, by its scenic, impressionistic method, its indirectness, its technique of telling the tale mainly through what James called "the ironic centre" of the consciousness of the major character,[25] often mazed in bewilderment and confusion, was just what he wanted for *Parade's End*.

For Ford, writing the book was something more than showing the reality of war. *Parade's End* also shows the tenuous nature of man's grasp on reality. When the solid world itself is constantly being shattered by high explosives, a man's very belief in reality is brought into question. Surely one of the strongest illusions of the artists of Ford's generation was of the permanency of things, on which, one could argue, was also based the idea of the permanence of institutions and ideas. "You may say," Ford wrote in *It Was the Nightingale*, "that everyone who had taken physical part in the war was then mad. No one could have come through that shattering experience and still view life and mankind with any normal vision. In those days you saw objects that the earlier mind labelled as *houses*. They had been used to seem cubic and solid permanences. But we had seen Ploegsteert where it had been revealed that man's dwellings were thin shells that could be crushed as walnuts are crushed. Man and even Beast . . . all things that lived and moved and had volition and life might at any moment be resolved into a scarlet viscosity seeping into the earth of torn fields. . . . It had been revealed to you that beneath ordered Life itself was stretched the merest film with, beneath it, the abysses of Chaos."[26]

Here was the central distinction between those who had been in the war and those who had stayed at home or sat safely in staff chateaux behind the lines. There, clean clothes or shining boots and spurs, like those worn by Colonel Levin from the gaudy staff in *No More Parades*, could still be worn; parades could still take place. At the front, however, men went to their death or maiming without a parade, like cattle to the abattoir. It was Ford's achievement to have dramatized that disparity, to have sounded that abyss, and eventually to have crossed to the other side.[27]

Ford sang not only of arms and the men who carried them, but also of the peace which preceded the war and was the last of the England in which he had grown up. The pre-1914 England of legend as shown in Part 1 of *Some Do Not . . .* is the traditional one of leisure, privilege, order, glamour, and style, but it is by no means the secure haven of that legend. The almost omniscient Tory Tietjens demonstrates to his own satisfaction, if not to that of anyone else, the certainty of a general war in Europe and sees evidence of deep strains in English society itself. In fact the novel confirms George Dangerfield's analysis of the hysteria widespread in that society.[28] The violence in the public and private life in *Some Do Not . . .* , particularly in the treatment of the suffragettes, shows these deep strains. Even the mildly obscene conversation in the club house of the Rye golf links overheard by General Campion, Tietjens, and Macmaster is, according to the latter, "the last of England."[29]

The novel's central concern, however, is to show what happens to the Tory gentleman at war. The title of volume 1 is from a poem by Ford himself which is misquoted by MacMaster:

> 'The Gods to each ascribe a differing lot:
> Some enter at the portal. Some do Not!'[30]

Owing to his birth, education, and brains, Tietjens could enter every portal, whereas Macmaster, the son of a Scots tradesman, has to batter at the doors. But the title also refers to all the taboos and conventions that Tietjens bears around with him. As Sylvia says of her husband, " 'He's so formal he can't do without all the conventions there are and so truthful he can't use half of them.' "[31] The code of the English gentleman, as it survived up to 1914, was an impressive list of commandments that had its roots in the public school tradition of reticence, understatement, and not "peaching."

Around the ambiguity of the title then circles all the ambiguities of the first part of the tetralogy. Tietjens is through every portal that matters in English society, but given his intelligence and passion and his personal situation, in which his wife is constantly and blatantly unfaithful, he is subjected to an intolerable strain that is many times multiplied by his conduct as a gentleman and later as an officer. Public school conventions, though admirable in many ways in the administration of a civilized society, are sometimes absurd and against nature. The mask of the gentleman is sufficient so long as it fits over the features of a nullity, but when it is placed over the face of a man of strong passions and needs, of vital intelligence and critical faculty, then it can produce a strain bordering on madness.

Tietjens joins the army partly because he cannot bear to go on doing what is expected of him in his government office in the Department of Statistics. He tells Valentine Wannop that he was supposed to fake figures to the detriment of the French. He also says: " 'It was probably impolitic to fake—to overstate!—a case against enemy nations. The chickens would come home to roost in one way or another, probably.' " He is also totally disillusioned with the civilian direction of the war. " 'I seem to see these fellows with clouds of blood over their heads . . . And then. . . . I'm to carry out their orders because they're my superiors. . . . But helping them means unnumbered deaths.' "[32]

Tietjens's army service does not alleviate his worry about that particular problem. In the second volume, *No More Parades*, Tietjens is organizing drafts to be sent to the front from a base which is being continuously raided by German planes. It is December 1917. The depression over his personal situation and the stress of his work are deepened by his distrust of the home cabinet. "These immense sacrifices," he reflects, "this ocean of mental sufferings, were all undergone to further the private vanities of men who amidst these hugenesses of landscapes and forces appeared pygmies! It was the worries of these wet millions in mud-brown that worried him. They would die, they could be massacred, by the quarter-million, in shambles. But that they should be massacred without jauntiness, without confidence, with depressed brows; without parade. . . . "[33]

There will be no more parades not only because the conditions of modern war make them impossible, but also because, as Tietjens points out, the element in society that went in for parades has suffered most heavily in the regular and volunteer regiments during the first two years of the war. As commissioned ranks are cut down, the demand for officers from among the other ranks grows so that the old class distinctions between commissioned and non-commissioned ranks gradually blurs. The snobbish deplore this, but Tietjens, whatever else may be said against him, is not a social snob. Even though it means that he loses his most experienced and efficient N.C.O., he welcomes into the officers' mess the newly commissioned ex-Sergeant Major Cowley, who is sentimentally expansive and drops his aitches.

It is in this part of the novel that the most memorable and ghastly incident occurs, the killing of O-Nine Morgan by a fragment of a German bomb. He dies in a great pool of blood in Tietjens's arms, a scene which constantly returns to haunt him. Indeed the whole impressionistic, chaotic treatment of the war in this part and the next, *A Man Could Stand Up*, has not been surpassed in vividness and reality in any war novel.

In the latter part of *Some Do Not . . .* and in *Parade's End* and *A Man Could Stand Up*, Ford deliberately abandons the realistic mode in which he had represented the Edwardian peacetime world of England. He moves into an impressionistic, non-linear style in order to represent the deranged world of the Great War. Robert Green has contended: "Christopher's inability to perceive his situation in November, 1917 'realistically,' and his adoption, instead, of the 'impressionism' of the paragraphs quoted shows the impotence of his old code."[34] But this change of style was not so much an "adoption" as an imperative for Ford: the only way he could create the stressed consciousness of Tietjens with authenticity. *A Man Could Stand Up* in fact moves into post-impressionist modes of cubism and surrealism in order to portray a world in which at any moment its creatures can be blown apart by high explosives. Green alludes to this in his discussion of a scene in a dugout in which: "Soldier's 'brown limbs,' as in a Picasso or a Braque, have been separated from their trunks. Man's humanity, even his organicism, is perpetually threatened."[35] The novel moves towards total disintegration in consciousness and prose style as the incessant noise, confusion, bloodshed, fear, fatigue, waiting, and depression send Tietjens to the brink of madness. In fact, after he has been blown up by a shell—an incident brilliantly portrayed by Ford "like a slowed down movie"—and has lost his memory, he is mad for a time.[36] He touches the bottom of the abyss. But Ford recognizes that *in extremis* a man's soul is tested, and he can emerge stronger and saner than before. Ford's insight has been lent empirical validation by the clinical work of the psychologist, R. D. Laing.

The other main centre of consciousness in the first three volumes of *Parade's End* is Valentine Wannop, as intense and intelligent in her own way as Tietjens is in his. Ford uses her to dramatize the tensions of the home front, to show the changes in the roles of women in wartime and the agonies of separation for those with men at the front. Overworked, overtired, confused, misinformed, Valentine too has to keep a tight hold on her sanity through plunging herself into even more work; she too is given an impressionistically disconnected consciousness, as she struggles, almost without hope, towards the belief that she will in the end be reunited with Christopher.

Through a massive doggedness and devotion to duty, Tietjens survives. The title of *A Man Could Stand Up* points towards peace. The phrase occurs to Tietjens as he awaits a dawn attack in the trenches. He thinks of the dawn also "wetly revealing" George Herbert's parish of Bemerton, and he imagines himself, like Herbert, standing up on a hill looking down to Salisbury spire.[37] It is an image of rest and dignity after the prolonged discomfort and indignity of the shoulder-hunching and ducking of the trenches. It means peace and the coming reunion with Valentine. It also means that Teitjens has found himself at last as a man through the war. No longer the eternal second-in-command, no longer a sort of "Hamlet of the Trenches," as he has called himself, he is now, through the unfitness of his colonel, a commander of a battalion.[38] Standing up reasserts man's inherent dignity in the face of wars and social cataclysms, suffering and death. He realizes that there will be no more automatic respect, because the England which Tietjens had represented is as dead as the 18th century to which he had partly belonged. He is now coarser and harder and can ignore the conventions and prohibitions that once seemed inexorably part of his personality as an English public school gentleman.

The fourth part of the tetralogy, *Last Post*, is less successful than the rest because it loses much of the tension of the earlier three. The point of view is divided among several characters, the main one being Christopher's elder brother, Mark, who is lying fatally ill and speechless in bed. The novel traces the destiny of Christopher as he settles down with Valentine in a country cottage after having renounced his claim to the family estate. Sylvia has at last consented to a divorce, and Tietjens takes up his new occupation selling old furniture. Robert Green makes the point that *Last Post* shows Ford's commitment to man's ecological need "to locate his life within natural rhythms which he had attempted to destroy between 1914 and 1918 . . . to introduce some meaning into a demented world."[39] Malcolm Bradbury also points out that the novel "is attempting to reach towards the limits of language . . . the extreme of the aesthetic order beyond time and history."[40] In moving away from the controlling consciousness of Christopher Tietjens, however, Ford sacrifices the focus that had made of the other three novels of the tetralogy such a revealing document about a man and his times. The reader does not know how that powerful and critical intelligence is reacting to the events that take place in the circumstances of his life in the postwar world.

The more appropriate conclusion to *Parade's End* is in the joy and hysteria of the Armistice celebrations at the end of *A Man Could Stand Up*. Then, in a confusion that mirrors the confusion in which the war itself has been fought, the lovers, Christopher and Valentine, are finally reunited. But the conclusion emphasizes that, although the fighting is over, the legacy of the war remains. As the Old Pals gather in Tietjens's chambers in the Inns of Court, from which Sylvia has removed all the furniture, they display the physical and psychic wounds that they all suffer. One is missing an eye, one a leg, one has almost completely lost his mind. Tietjens himself will recover, but he will always remain scarred by the experience. Valentine reflects as she looks on at the wild party: "Hitherto, she had thought of the War as physical suffering only; now she saw it only as mental torture. Immense miles and miles of anguish in darkened minds. That remained. Men might stand up on hills, but the mental torture could not be expelled."[41]

Ford's major achievement was to make his readers see that too and to make them understand the nature of the Great War as no other writer has succeeded in doing. He was able to do that through his successful forging of new techniques. He understood that the old realism was no longer adequate to represent a world of war in which reality as men had known it literally dissolved. Impressionist and post-impressionist techniques created new landscapes of mind in *Parade's End*. The memory of what the Great War was really like will not fade so long as the tetralogy is read.

For H. G. Wells, on the other hand, disillusionment with the conduct of the war led him for a time into an intense religiosity, which produced the curious book, *God the Invisible King* (1917). He then turned towards education as a way out of the chaos that previous generations had made of the world. *Joan and Peter* (1918), a long and unsuccessful novel, is a *bildungsroman* about two young people of the leisure class coming of age in the war. It contains a series of lectures by Peter's uncle, Oswald, Wells's surrogate, on the general mismanagement of the war. The novel passed quickly over the period covered by *Mr. Britling Sees It Through*, which Wells calls "the spectator phase," and moves into the next phase, which corresponds to the rise to power of Lloyd George. That phase marks an end to a period of "chaotic freedom" and "the rediscovery of the State as a necessary form into which the individual life must fit."[42]

That chilling formula guides Peter's change of consciousness as he serves on the front, is badly wounded, and begins to formulate his ideas about the coming peace. Through Peter, Wells attacks what he called the Anglican, amateurish, old guard, who continue to make a parade about the honour and glory of war. The change in that attitude is indicated by the change from the poetry of Rupert Brooke to that of Siegfried Sassoon. "His song," Wells writes, "is no longer of picturesque nobilities and death in a glorious cause; it is a cry of anger at the old men who have led the world to destruction."[43]

Peter's experience at the front leads him to condemn the "incredible incompetence in both the political and military leadership of the country," which had led Britain to go through the war "blundering, talking and thinking confusedly, suffering enormously."[44] Such waste, Oswald tells his nephew, is the consequence of the neglect of higher education during the past fifty years. Only the stout heart and good sense of the common people have saved the country.

To make his point clear, Oswald drafts a lecture to Peter and Joan, who have married, about how his and preceding generations had so let things go that no real leadership had emerged from the war—no Nelson, no Wellington. In military and civil affairs, the Anglican ideal had been merely to blockade. Consequently, millions had died at the fronts, "not in stateliness and splendour but in a vast uproar, amidst mud, confusion, bickering, and incoherence indescribable."[45] Even so, the war had been an affair of honour, fought necessarily. It is up to Joan and Peter's generation to put aside "that England of the Victorian old men,"[46] of privilege and Empire and precedence, and build a new world based on good education and a world community.

The lecture remains undelivered, just as the letter at the end of *Mr. Britling* does. Peter is too impatient to start creating the new world through technology and science. He dreams of studying medicine and then going into research. Joan, who has spent the war as a chauffeur for various ministries, wants to become a builder, designing good cheap houses for the multitudes. They are impatient to leave the old leisured world of 1914 far behind.

The novel fails because of its constant hectoring; it is a piece of propaganda aimed at exposing the kind of propaganda that Wellington House had espoused throughout the war. At the same time, there is in the figure of Oswald Wells's increasing awareness of his own irrelevance to the emerging generation who had fought the war. Arnold Bennett recalls in his journal a conversation that he had with Wells at his club on 10 October 1917. "My boom is over," Wells concluded. "I've had my boom. I'm yesterday."[47] In *Joan and Peter* he still felt compelled to try to influence his unheeding successors. Aware that the younger generation is not listening, he delivers the lecture anyway.

Wells's apparent failure to get through led to a later curious book called *The Bulpington of Blup, Adventures, Poses, Stresses, Conflicts and Disasters in a Contemporary Brain* (1933). By that time, Wells had seen his dreams of salvation through God and through education die, the re-emergence of political chaos at home and abroad, and the onset of the Depression. He had also seen the rise of a new literary generation. Through *The Bulpington of*

Blup he sought to lay some of the blame. The hero is modelled closely on Ford Madox Ford. Bulpington's career is in effect a parody of Ford's wartime activities and postwar pursuits in France. In Ford, Wells saw a representative of all the social, literary, and political tendencies which he abominated. Moreover, Ford was the inheritor of the mantle of Henry James, so *The Bulpington of Blup* is an updating of *Boon*, in which Wells had attacked James's theories of art. Most galling of all to Wells was the fact that Ford was looked upon by many of the young writers of the period as their leader and master.

Bulpington, scion of an upper-class family with literary pretensions, shirks joining up until he is handed a white feather by a woman in the underground train. Although for a time an influential uncle is able to wangle him a staff job, he soon winds up as a junior officer in the trenches. He runs away in panic when the Germans attack under cover of gas and, though unwounded, finds himself in hospital. He is lucky enough to meet there a sympathetic medical officer who has him sent home as a shellshock case. Bulpington spends the rest of the war in a pleasant rest home until his release from the army in April 1919.

His influential uncle is now a leader of the Reconstruction movement that is supposed to compensate for every sacrifice the war had exacted. The vision "glowed very brilliantly for a time, led to some complex speculation in building materials, and faded out delicately and completely in a year or two."[48] Bulpington tries a reconciliation with his former girlfriend Margaret, whom he had let slip after starting a career of casual amours, but his pretensions about his war service are exposed by her new boyfriend, the doctor who had sent him home from France.

Bulpington also tells Margaret about his dreams of a new beginning in literature. "There would have to be new forms," he says, "new men, new schools. The old reputations stood up over us now like great empty hulls that had served their purpose, Hardy, Barrie, Conrad, Kipling, Galsworthy, Bennett, Wells, Shaw, Maugham, and so forth; they had all said what they had to say; they were finished. . . . They were pre-war. They ought to have gone on to the bonfires of Armistice Day. . . . There would be new conceptions of life, new conceptions of happiness and sex, expressed in a new language, a language richer and more subtle, reforged for new needs."[49] Wells seeks to make Bulpington's literary pretensions seem as absurd as his amorous ones.

Exposed as a fraud, Bulpington leaves England for France, joins the avant garde in Paris, and turns high Catholic and Tory. He becomes the editor of a magazine, *The Feet of the Young Men*, an absurd parody of Ford's *Transatlantic Review*. When this fails, he returns to an inherited cottage in Devon, where he becomes a local personage and a great defender of high Anglicanism and

T. S. Eliot, whom he calls "one of the Master Minds of our age. . . . The Young adore him."[50] The book culminates at a dinner party at which the drunken Bulpington relates glorious and fantastic stories about his war career and staggers home shouting at the stars: "I am a liar in a world of lies. Lies? Dreams. . . . I shape my life as I like, past and future, just as I please. . . . Love me, love my lie. . . . Uncertainties. Convulsions. Disasters. But against it all—*Romance.*"[51] With this culminating jibe at the novel that Ford wrote in collaboration with Conrad, Wells sends Bulpington to bed, dead drunk, after he has smashed a portrait of the Delphic Oracle, representing the Future.

There was enough factual material in this portrait of Bulpington to make Ford look ridiculous, especially in respect to his sentimental Toryism, his endless fabrications about himself, and his obsessive devotion to art and the avant garde. Nevertheless, *The Bulpington of Blup* is an unfair and vindictive attack on a man who had worked unceasingly in the cause of good writing and had been most generous to his friends, including H. G. Wells.

The animus in *The Bulpington of Blup* stems from the fact that Wells did not really believe in the role of the imagination in fiction. His novels are transmuted autobiography, his heroes usually projected versions of his various selves, and his characters are less important than his ideas. Consequently, he must have believed *Parade's End* to be an elaborate attempt by Ford to justify and render heroic his own inglorious career as a soldier. And Tietjens represents many of the things that Wells had attacked during the war: the leisured, Anglican or Anglo-Catholic landed gentry wedded to the land and an England older than the one represented by the new scientific minds and aggressive businessmen. The artistic method of *Parade's End* also must have been an affront to everything that Wells believed in; its rich artifice would have seemed to him like an elaborate tissue of lies and deception.

If this is the case, then Wells missed the point of *Parade's End*, which, in the final analysis, is an examination of the way in which Tietjens' Tory values proved inadequate to the world at war and have changed to meet the realities of postwar life, just as the techniques of the novel have changed to encompass the realities of war itself. Like Wells, Ford was interested in seeing what might emerge from such a crucible and endure, but his methods of representing human experience are infinitely subtler than any Wells could imagine. The Methodist preacher in Wells had dreamed of a land "fit for heroes" emerging from the nightmare of war, and he had supplied a blueprint for reform in *Joan and Peter*. He had supposed that all the changes forced on Britain by the war, all that blood spilt in a just cause, all that suffering for the sake of democratic evolution had to bring about massive improvements in British life and in international affairs.

Wells had apparently really believed in all the hyperbole of his own propaganda, swallowed whole the idea of moral regeneration through this last of all wars. It had seemed inconceivable that this golden opportunity to reshape the world and guide its progress towards an ideal international community could be missed. When British life slipped back into many of its old grooves, demobbed soldiers returned to old routines, the dream of an international order gave way to the Treaty of Versailles, the United States withdrew from the League of Nations, and the economic depression set in, Wells felt as disillusioned as any idealistic soldier returning from the trenches to the malaise of the postwar period. Wells ironically reveals in *The Bulpington of Blup* what he came to feel about his own wartime effusions. A science professor spouts words very similar to those of Wells about a "War to End War" and "a world in travail with the World State." His sceptical son—who becomes a conscientious objector—listens to this lecture and his face "expressed a stoical endurance of the irrational."[52]

Ford had been there, and he knew that he could adequately portray the changes wrought by the Great War only through exploring the tormented and confused consciousness of one man. Wells had looked on a new generation and, not recognizing until much later his own part in the betrayal, was surprised and bitterly disappointed when he found that that generation could not share his vision of a scientific and perfect future. Partly to assuage his anger and frustration, he attacked a man whom he thought represented all that was retrogressive and ineffectual in the postwar world and modern art forms. He thus unwittingly revealed his own limitations.

Of all the men of this generation, the one who underwent the deepest and subtlest change was Rudyard Kipling. His son John was reported wounded and missing after the Battle of Loos in September 1915. Through the influence of Kipling's old friend, Lord Roberts, John had been commissioned in the Irish Guards, went out to France with his regiment, and was killed after three weeks of service. Kipling, aided by Sir Max Aitken, spent many fruitless weeks trying to find out if John was a prisoner, and months passed before another friend, Rider Haggard, found a man who had been a witness of the action in which John was killed. Haggard learned that John was last seen crying from the agony of a mouth wound. He did not pass this information on to the Kiplings. As Angus Wilson notes, it is grimly ironic to place this fact against Kipling's epitaph for his son:

> My son was killed while laughing at some jest.
>   I would I knew
> What it was, and it might serve me in a time
>   when jests are few.[53]

Rudyard Kipling was never able to talk about his loss, but he endeavoured in some measure to commemorate the death in accepting the commission to write *The Irish Guards in the Great War*. Although there is plenty of glory in this history, there is also a great deal of sombre fact. Typically, Kipling's son receives only one mention in the book, in the second half of a compound sentence in which Kipling describes how the second battalion was under fire near Lens: "Here 2nd Lieutenant Clifford was shot and wounded or killed — the body was found later — and 2nd Lieutenant Kipling was wounded and missing."[54] The suppression behind this laconic statement is indicated by a few words in the introduction to the history: "There were, too, many, almost children, of whom no record remains. They came out from Warley with the constantly renewed drafts, lived the span of a Second Lieutenant's life, and were spent. In most instances, the compiler has let the mere facts suffice; since, to his mind, it did not seem fit to heap words on the doomed."

Kipling found another outlet for his powers of commemoration when he became one of the Imperial War Graves Commissioners, which he remained for the last eighteen years of his life. The commission faced an enormous job for, as Charles Carrington has remarked, "a million British dead were found, exhumed, identified, and reburied in permanent cemeteries with headstones, inscriptions, gardens, and memorial crosses."[55] Kipling wrote most of the inscriptions, including the most famous one, "Their Name Liveth For Evermore," the words cut into the Stone of Sacrifice in each cemetery. Those phrases, proud and sonorous, are the rhetoric that screens the realities of trench warfare, just as those neat and ordered gardens of death remain a façade over the indescribable physical conditions in which most men fought and died on the Western Front.

There were other "Epitaphs of War," however, which did not appear on gravestones, but which did express Kipling's mounting, if hidden, disillusion with the leadership of the country and the trade unions. These are a few specimens of that verse:

Batteries Out of Ammunition

If any mourn us in the workshop, say
We died because the shift kept holiday.

Common Form

If any question why we died
Tell them, because our fathers lied.

This next one probably refers to Lloyd George, whom Kipling detested with a passion:

A Dead Statesman

I could not dig; I dare not rob;
Therefore I lied to please the mob.
Now all my lies are proved untrue
And I must face the men I slew.
What tale shall serve me here among
Mine angry and defrauded young?[56]

In writing *The Irish Guards in the Great War*, for which he interviewed many officers and men, Kipling found out in detail about the brutal realities of trench warfare that his propaganda had concealed. Consequently, the fiction that Kipling wrote in the later years and after the war is informed with a different spirit. Through it all can be traced the enduring sorrow for his son and his sympathy for all those similarly sorrowing as well as pity for those killed, maimed, and psychologically crippled by the war. The stories were the means by which he could order his inchoate sense of grief and loss. He called on several institutions and ideals to do so, including Christianity, art, love, and masonic ritual.

The first of these tales of reconciliation, "On the Gate, a Tale of '16," was published a year after John's death. It is a sentimental story of the emergency caused at Heaven's Gate by the crowds of Allied soldiers who suddenly arrive after being killed in a great battle. St. Peter, in his infinite wisdom, lets the fighting sinners through. Unlike Barrie, however, Kipling does not admit German soldiers to his heaven.

Until 1926, Kipling could not bring himself to write more directly about his son. In that year he published "The Gardener." Although flawed, the story provides a fascinating glimpse of Kipling's psychology. It enabled him to use his experience as a war graves commissioner since it is set in a military graveyard under construction. It opens with a woman searching for the grave of her nephew among "a merciless sea of black crosses." The "nephew" is actually her illegitimate son, whom she had never acknowledged. "The Gardener" thus resembles "Mary Postgate" in its study of unfulfilled motherhood. It is somewhat spoiled by the sentimental way in which Kipling uses the Christ figure as the gardener who leads the woman to the right grave and relieves her of the burden of her concealment: " 'Come with me . . . and I will show you where your son lies.' "[57]

Kipling closely identifies himself with the mother, Helen. She has served on various war committees and holds strong views about the proposed village war memorial. Like Kipling, she has spent many months making enquiries about her missing son. Unlike Kipling, however, she has the satisfaction of finding the place where her son's body rested; for her, as for many others, "there was an altar upon earth where they might lay their love." Kipling had no such altar, and he was no doubt projecting upon Helen both the grief he felt for his son, which as a father he could not properly express, and the wish fulfillment of the finding of the grave.

"The Gardener" is quite harrowing in its evocation of loss and grief, but it is consoling in the emotion that is at last acknowledged and expressed. The story also allowed Kipling to retract some of his propaganda literature. Helen's son, Michael, did his training in a camp on Salisbury Plain like the one that Kipling had celebrated in his recruiting pamphlet *The New Army*. In "The Gardener," however, there is nothing about beautifully fit and joyous trainees. Here half the men "were breeding meningitis through living overcrowdedly in damp tents."[58] There is an oblique reference to the senseless battle in which John was killed. Michael is hurled out to France "to help make good the wastage at Loos." "While the Somme was being manufactured," as Kipling grimly puts it, Michael is sent into a quiet sector. There he is killed by a stray shell splinter. Like so many deaths in the Great War, his death is random and inglorious.

The most important framework for Kipling's postwar stories of reconciliation and reconstruction was provided by the Order of Masons. Masonic ritual supplied a deep-felt need for Kipling at this time; he appears to have derived solace from its arcane practices and mystical overtones. He was one of many of his generation to turn to such forms of consolation when the war shattered their orderly world. " 'All Ritual is fortifying,' " says Brother Burges, the tobacconist who runs Lodge 5837. " 'Ritual's a natural necessity for mankind. The more things are upset, the more they fly to it.' "[59]

Burges has established his quasi-legal lodge as place where Mason-soldiers from all over Britain and the Empire could drop in. In the story "In the Interests of the Brethren," first published in December 1918, Kipling describes one evening in the life of the luxuriously appointed lodge, where instruction for wounded and shell-shocked men is carried out by the brothers. According to the narrator, the lodge is fulfilling an essential function that has been ignored not only by other lodges, but also by the church.

Another Masonic story is "A Madonna of the Trenches," in which for the first time in his fiction Kipling describes the real conditions of trench warfare. These conditions are confessed by a former platoon-runner, Strangwick, who is in a traumatic condition. Strangwick reveals to the sympathetically listening narrator and another lodge-brother, a doctor, an incident that took place in Butcher's Row, a trench made up of the corpses of French *poilus*. The bodies on the floor of the trench creak when stepped on. But the cause of Strangwick's trauma is not so much the trench but, as he eventually confesses in a manner reminiscent of a Freudian analysis, the sight of an apparition. The apparition, he is convinced, was that of his Aunt

Armine, who appeared to him and to her illicit lover, his platoon sergeant, on the night of her death. Strangwick is convinced that the apparition was not an hallucination, as the Angels of Mons might have been, but a real spirit. The incident has driven him half-insane: " 'You see,' " he explains to his listeners, " 'there wasn't a single god-dam thing left abidin' for me to take hold of, here or hereafter. If the dead *do* rise—and I saw 'em—why—why *anything* can 'appen. Don't you understand?' "[60]

To add to Strangwick's trauma, his platoon sergeant, known to him as Uncle John, commits suicide after seeing the apparition of Armine by sealing himself inside a dugout with two charcoal-burning braziers. However, the comfort afforded by the Lodge and his confession to two sympathetic listeners seems to ease the burden from Strangwick's mind, and he falls into a deep sleep, heralding psychic recovery.

The device of the apparition allows Kipling partly to evade the more obvious source of trauma among soldiers—prolonged service under fire. Nevertheless, "A Madonna of the Future" provides a convincing picture of life in the trenches. Kipling's wartime rhetoric about "the Boche" and "the Hun" and fighting "wild beasts" is finished. The enemy is simply "Jerry"— doing a rotten job, just as the British soldiers are. There is no glory here, only mud and cold, darkness and fear and duty, against which are placed the grateful heat of the charcoal brazier— ironically also an effective instrument of suicide—the comfort of tobacco, and the hope of home leave.

Another effective story dealing with the neurosis of the trenches is "The Janeites," which is also told within the framework of Lodge 5837. As some of the masonic brothers clean and polish the lodge on a Saturday afternoon after the war, an almost illiterate ex-gunner called Humberstall tells his story. He had been invalided home with shellshock, but unable to stand the home front, he illegally rejoins his old unit, where he is made steward. The particular attraction of the mess is that all the members are devotees of Jane Austen. Humberstall is initiated into the cult. All members sustain their sanity amidst the madness of trench warfare by trading inside jokes and literary criticism of her work. The mess is blown up during the German advance of March 1918. Humberstall is the only survivor. Jane Austen's works sustain him through this second trauma, just as Masonic ritual sustains the brothers.

And so the war, which had begun for Kipling in a gust of exultation and relief and continued in a barrage of revenge propaganda, fiction, and verse, concluded for him in artistic versions of emotions too deep for tears. A profound psychological change took place in Kipling in that time. The old patriotism, based on dreams of Britain's imperial greatness and the collective soul of the unit—whether it be the school, the ship, or the regiment— gave way under the impact of personal grief to a recognition of the subtler and deeper bonds of love, of religion, of art, of fellowship. In particular, the male bonding organization, the Masons, provided him with a means of confessing and thus exorcising the obscure traumas of war in complex narratives that rivalled the complexities of Masonic rite. These stories allowed him to express his knowledge of the realities of trench warfare and to come to terms with the death of his son. What he had—perhaps for the sake of his own sanity— to believe was the certainty of life after death and the reality of consolation afforded by elaborate funeral inscriptions and repeated ceremonials.

Although many of the older writers, particularly Galsworthy, Wells, and Bennett, strove to demythologize the war, Kipling is an exemplum of Paul Fussell's contention that the movement of Great War literature was "towards myth, towards a revival of the cultic, the mystical, the sacrificial, the prophetic, the sacramental, and the universally significant."[61] " 'I can just stand 'Last Post.' It's 'Tipperary' breaks me,' " says one of the brothers in another Masonic story "A Friend of the Family."[62] Those terrible memories could be alleviated and ordered, at least, by the nightly "Last Post" at the Menin Gate and the flame at the grave of the Unknown Soldier—both of which were Kipling's ideas. These were ways of dignifying the finally monstrous fact of the death of all the young men, so many of whom, like John Kipling, could never be identified and placed in a marked grave.

And finally, there is Arnold Bennett, who stayed in propaganda and wound up in charge at the end. Bennett wished to carry on Lord Beaverbrook's ambitious plan to centralize propaganda and consolidate this "mushroom ministry" in the government. He immensely enjoyed his new-found power. All this is echoed in the fictional Lord Raingo's reflections as minister: "He loved his work; he had developed a passion for it. He smacked his lips over conferences, press-audiences, press-lunches, minutes, finance, cables, broadcasting, films, intimate banquets for foreign nobs. And all these were nothing compared with the large comprehensive scheme for unifying every kind of propaganda under one roof and his own headship."[63]

When the Armistice came, Bennett's fall from office was as rapid as his rise. In part, *Lord Raingo*, published in 1926, was revenge for the treatment accorded Lord Beaverbrook and himself by Lloyd George's government, just as Willson's *Redemption* was revenge against Lord Beaverbrook for the treatment that Willson had received.

In writing *Lord Raingo*, Bennett had the active co-operation of Beaverbrook, and the portrait of the hero is a kind of composite of the press lord, the novelist, and Lord Rhondda, the food controller in 1917 and 1918. Beaverbrook told Bennett about Rhondda's concern for his mistress, who was a suicide, his hypochondria, and his much publicized death, all of which are incorporated into the novel.[64]

As James G. Kennedy has suggested, "Arnold Bennett is one of several novelists whose practice suggests that an artistic effect is not the less for its referring to historical or biographical facts."[65] Indeed, the novel achieves much of its intensity from melding the personal warp of the hero's life with the solidly public weft of national political life. It has important things to say about the war, about how propaganda was organized, and about the realities of administrative power. There seems to have been nothing quite like it until C. P. Snow began his study of political life in *Strangers and Brothers*.

The hero, Samuel Raingo, is an aging millionaire, with a country house near the coast where he keeps his wife and a flat in town where he keeps his mistress, Delphine. He has a heart condition and is depressed and hypochondriacal. Since his business does not occupy all his time, he is at a loss to know what to do with himself. The time is 1917, but he feels completely cut off from the war. His only son is in limbo as a prisoner of war in Germany.

Then Raingo receives a summons from the prime minister, an old friend, and is asked to take on the Ministry of Records—an undisguised version of the Ministry of Information. Sam skilfully uses his heart condition as a counter in the game and exacts a peerage from the prime minister as his price for taking the post. He claims that even running for a safe seat in the Commons would be too much for him. The prime minister, Andy Clyth, is a fairly close copy of Lloyd George. A canny politician, he has come up from obscurity to power by displacing an easy-going predecessor. Raingo, though playing it close to his chest, is delighted with the prospect of office, and his sentiments were those which Bennett himself expressed: "There was no finance in it at all—there was only glory, prestige, power; chiefly power."[66]

He sets about his business with relish. First, he successfully "nobbles" the Paris press, which has been bitterly criticizing the British conduct of the war. Then he "nobbles" the London paper most opposed to the government. The methods are not disclosed, but bribery seems to play no small role in the matter. Then Lord Raingo begins to centralize propaganda—spread around among the Foreign Office, the War Office, the Admiralty, and the Ministry of Munitions—into the Ministry of Records. His great weapon—and one which was continually mentioned in the numerous secret parliamentary enquiries into propaganda—is the secret service money, which is largely controlled by his ministry. Raingo soon becomes a power to be reckoned with.

At this point in the novel, Raingo's alienated wife kills herself by driving her car off the road. Shortly afterwards, his son returns to England, having escaped from a German prison camp. Geoffrey blames his father for letting his mother drive the car and curses him for entering the government. He tells him " 'I'm surprised that you should be working for that scoundrel Clyth.

Responsible for all the mismanagement of the war! He only got where he is because he happened to have someone over him who wouldn't stand up to him. All the best men thrown out, one after another. And look at the new lot. Good God! What a crew of circus-performers, liars, whoremongers and millionaires!' "[67]

Raingo is shocked by his son's outburst. He believes that he has been completely broken down by his war experience and his captivity. "Yesterday a boy," he reflects; "to-day an old, damaged, disillusioned man." It is true that Geoffrey's nerves have been upset by his recent experience and that he is frequently depressed and suffers from claustrophobia. At the same time, he is perceptive and intelligent. Bennett uses him throughout the rest of the novel as an effective critical viewpoint against the essentially corrupt world of power and politics into which Raingo has slipped with ease and complacency. But even the self-centered Raingo is shaken hard by his son's charges. His secretary watches the stricken Sam and thinks: "Politics! Titles! Propaganda! What odious, contemptible tinsel and mockery."[68]

But Raingo soon resumes his engrossing work and returns to the favours of his mistress, which he can now enjoy unhampered by an inconvenient wife. As the head of a "mushroom ministry," he gets particular joy from his battles with the heads of the older departments. His strongest opponents are the red-tabbed and spurred men at the War Office, who are humiliated by having to go cap-in-hand to him for their share of the secret service money. For the first time in his life, Raingo has realized something that all his millions made in finance had not brought him—the prestige and real power of office. Only one thing is denied him in that respect—a thing for which he intensely envies the prime minister—the power to move men by rhetoric. He does not speak in the House of Lords because he is a boring orator. This failing reflects with some accuracy Bennett's own speech impediment as well as Beaverbrook's nervous reluctance to speak in the House.

Much of the book describes the day-to-day running of the Ministry and the complicated politics associated with relations with other ministries and the cabinet. Bennett's charting of these complex waterways of power gives a fascinating insight into the British political process in wartime as well as into the effect on an individual of a sudden climb to power. It looks for a time as if Raingo will succeed. He has complete success with the press, gained through his previous manipulation of newspaper opinion in support of his financial schemes. Failure only comes when he loses the support of the prime minister, who has always envied Raingo his wealth. With Clyth's support, Raingo could have triumphed over all the machinations of the other ministries; without it, in the end, he is almost powerless. Having to juggle the elements of his coalition cabinet constantly, Clyth decides that his easiest course lies in sacrificing his old friend and new colleague. Ultimately, he is a man without loyalty, save to his own power. By that he is seen to be totally corrupted.

Apparently at the peak of his power, Raingo is feted at a dinner he has arranged for the overseas press corps. But Fate steps in and strikes him down with pneumonia. He has tried to do too much, and his bad health, which has brought him his title, has ironically also brought about his downfall.

Most critics agree that Sam's dying is needlessly prolonged and throws the novel off balance. Probably Bennett wanted Raingo to represent an older generation of ruthless, hard businessmen who had moved in on the government establishment during the war. Raingo fights death as he has fought every other adversary. His passing is symbolic of the passing of that generation, while the burden is handed on to the new generation as represented by his son, Geoffrey. At the end of the novel, it appears that he will carry on his father's businesses and marry the younger sister of Raingo's mistress, thus symbolizing a union of two widely separated classes.

But the real interest of *Lord Raingo* does not rest in these symbolic overtones, which are clumsy at best, but in the prolonged study of men and power that it contains. Anyone with a knowledge of the history of the period will recognize not only Lord Beaverbrook and Lloyd George but also General Smuts, Bonar Law, and Lord Milner. Winston Churchill appears as the pugnacious Tom Hogarth, who has been captured in a colonial war and escaped, "had reigned in seven departments of State, fought, written and fought; he was the most brilliant advocate in the House, and one of the finest polemical and descriptive writers in the country; he had every gift except common sense, and he could rise victorious even from the disasters imposed on him by an incurable foolishness."[69]

Churchill was great enough to overlook the last part of this thumbnail sketch, for, according to Bennett's biographer Reginald Pound, he commended Bennett on the accuracy with which he had portrayed cabinet meetings. "You must have been a fly on the wall," he said. As Pound adds, this is more in the nature of a tribute to Bennett's chief adviser on the novel, Lord Beaverbrook.[70]

What many of the critics of the novel appear to have missed, however, is the strong vein of irony that runs throughout. Like Wells, Bennett went through his own disillusionment, particularly after his fall from power as propaganda minister. That disillusionment manifested itself in *Lord Raingo* in a subtle attack on the conduct of those in charge of the nation's war effort. All the politicians are more or less venal and self-centred, all devoted first to the cult of their own power and only secondly to the conduct of the war. Among all the political infighting and manoeuvring, the realities of the war are ignored and barely mentioned. Bennett shows, too, the shoddy nature of propaganda work. The first rule of the game is impressing the men who count. After that, the truth has to be suppressed. By corruption, flattery, and persiflage the press at home and abroad is "nobbled" and the grim facts concealed.

All this is brilliantly summed up by Bennett at the beginning of the "Apotheosis" chapter. Here Raingo reaches the summit of his power and figures as the star of the party which he gives for the overseas press corps, attended also by the prime minister and half the cabinet. "Towards the end of the evening it had been established and many times ratified by libation that the English-speaking peoples—that was to say, Britain and her far-flung broods, including, of course, the people of the United States, whose representatives there present duly admitted, while not exulting in, their parentage— were God's chosen and the possessors of all fine qualities, and the sole salvation of the world (excepting, of course, the Continental Allies, who were also the possessors of all fine qualities and the salvation of the world); whereas Germany, with her misguided friends, existed only to prove the principle of evil and to be smashed to pieces by the righteous. Even war had become glorious,—and the men in the trenches were not forgotten."[71] There is a savage irony in this sustained flow of clichés and the devastating anticlimax. And yet the fact remains that Arnold Bennett himself played a large part in propagating all the rhetoric and falsity that he was pillorying here so effectively.

Moreover, he had succumbed to a temptation surely felt by many writers, whose trade tends to keep them on the sidelines of great affairs. This was the temptation to wield power, to affect events, to control the destinies of others, often at the expense of personal life and artistic detachment. It was a temptation to which Sir Gilbert Parker, John Buchan, H. G. Wells, and even, to a degree, Rudyard Kipling had all succumbed—to accept power achieved through their gifts as writers to use as administrators or policymakers. Seldom had mere novelists achieved this degree of influence in the affairs of state. It was heady and corrupting: so heady that it was fatally easy for them to believe that the ends could justify the means—that a victory by the Allies was worth the duplicities of propaganda.

Bennett in particular was divided between his work as a propagandist and his responsibility as a novelist. In the propagandist and deputy minister, the patriot, the time-server, the powerseeker, and the sycophant all emerged; in the novelist, the realist, the suppressed ironic self, the irreverent outsider from the provinces asserted himself to knock the props out from under the pretence and to explore the rottenness at the core of the system. His solitary surviving representative of the new order and of the suffering at the root of the war is Raingo's son, Geoffrey, recently escaped from prison camp, emaciated, shellshocked, cynical, disillusioned, bitter, yet ruthlessly honest. He is a symbol of what was to come out of the world that men like Lord Raingo had both built and helped to destroy.

Epilogue

CONSEQUENCES

*"I hope," [the division-commander] concludes, "that you will
conduct yourselves to the greater glory of Canadian arms. . . . "
To us this business of military glory and arms means carrying
parties, wiring fatigues, wet clothes and cowering in a trench
under shell-fire. We stand rigid and listen to the harangue.*

CHARLES YALE HARRISON, 1930

The generation of the trenches, disillusioned and often cynical, rapidly
discounted the propaganda myth that the older authors had generated with
such flourish and zeal. The abyss between the schoolboy version of war, the
imagery of knights and angels, and the reality of Flanders was unbridgeable.
Some, like Wilfred Owen, detected the self-serving pride of that myth, as is
shown in that withering poem, "The Parable of the Old Man and the Young":

> Then Abram bound the youth with belts and straps,
> And builded parapets and trenches there,
> And stretched forth the knife to slay his son.
> When lo! an angel called him out of heaven,
> Saying, Lay not thy hand upon the lad,
> Neither do anything to him. Behold,
> A ram, caught in a thicket by its horns;
> Offer the ram of pride instead of him.
> But the old man would not so, but slew his son,
> And half the seed of Europe, one by one.[1]

That "ram of pride" which sustained the older writers in their vision of the
glory of the war and made them pour scorn on the notion of a negotiated
peace was in its turn offered up for sacrifice by the younger writers. The list
of authors condemned to the scrap-heap by Bulpington in Wells's *The
Bulpington of Blup* — "Hardy, Barrie, Conrad, Kipling, Galsworthy, Bennett,

Wells, Shaw, Maugham and so forth"—turned out not to be as ironic as Wells intended. It is probably significant that those who have best survived the test of time, Hardy, Conrad, and Shaw, were those who subscribed least to the propaganda myth of the Great War. Certainly the prestige that had clung to the names of all great writers before the war substantially diminished after it. Even H. G. Wells, who continued to be consulted by heads of state, felt himself to be increasingly irrelevant. Their opinions on public questions were no longer listened to with the same degree of attention or sought by newspaper publishers.

The debasement of the word in the Great War, as described so presciently by Henry James, had a great deal to do with the decline of the prestige of the author and perhaps also something to do with the widely shared sense of the loss of decency and the diminution of civilized values in postwar England. D. H. Lawrence expressed it bluntly in his description of the fall of Prime Minister Asquith: "He is too much the old, stable, measured *decent* England. Alas and alack, that such an England must collapse and be trodden under the feet of swine and dogs."[2] Ezra Pound also gave eloquent expression to this decline in *Hugh Selwyn Mauberly*:

> There died a myriad,
> And of the best, among them,
> For an old bitch gone in the teeth,
> For a botched civilization.[3]

Wilfred Owen, one of the myriad who died, also alluded to this loss in "Strange Meeting":

> Now men will go content with what we spoiled,
> Or, discontent, boil bloody, and be spilled.
> They will be swift with swiftness of the tigress.
> None will break ranks, though nations trek from progress.[4]

Paul Fussell has ascribed the mass migration of writers out of England after the war to their confinement in the trenches and to their sense of despair and frustration in postwar England or America. The ex-warriors, Robert Graves, Ford Madox Ford, Osbert Sitwell, Edmund Blunden, and among the civilians D. H. Lawrence, Aldous Huxley, Ezra Pound, Bertrand Russell, and Katherine Mansfield all left for extended travel or residence abroad, while many Americans, including Hemingway, Malcolm Cowley, Harold Stearns, and Fitzgerald fled to Paris.[5]

After the war, writers resumed their traditional roles as outsiders and critics of the existing order. Satire was one of the most successful literary genres of the 1920s. Causes of all kinds were ridiculed; earnestness, moralism, romance, and sentimentalism were discounted. At the end of the twenties, some of the most powerful and influential war novels were published, including Hemingway's *A Farewell to Arms*, Sassoon's *Memoirs of an Infantry Officer*, and Charles Yale Harrison's *Generals Die in Bed*. In these novels, in reaction to the inflated rhetoric of wartime propaganda, language has been stripped back to its essentials, the prose is concrete, the syntax is simple, and the direct speech is colloquial, with frequent obscenities. Many of these obscenities, however, had to bowdlerized for contemporary publication. War is seen to be a largely futile occupation in which men are sent out to meaningless deaths by incompetent senior officers for the sake of empty ideals. Writers revert frequently to the naturalist mode—which had been largely superseded by the wave of prewar romanticism. To the postwar writers, naturalism, with its emphasis on characters deprived of free will and dominated by their blood and nerves, was an almost inevitable mode and one which has remained influential in war fiction.

Given such pervasive and negative images of war in literature and the public mind, it is not surprising that the politicians of the western democracies swung to the extreme in rejecting war as an instrument of national policy. The consequences were soon to be seen in the failure of the League of Nations in the face of the aggression of the European dictators, the triumph of appeasement, and, later, the unwillingness of the United States to become involved in the Second World War.

When some writers tried to organize a protest against their governments' refusal to intervene against the fascists in the Spanish Civil War, the whole issue of the writer and propaganda surfaced again. T. S. Eliot and Ezra Pound refused to become involved and reiterated Yeats's declaration of independence from causes. Similarly, when some American writers tried to organize their brethren to protest against American intervention in Vietnam, Tom Wolfe and William Styron, among others, refused to get on the bandwagon.[6]

The hard question remains: is the writer's first duty to his detachment, to isolation, to a devotion to art so strong that it puts him apart from all propaganda, whether for the state or against, or are there occasions when that isolation has to be sacrificed in order to join a cause? The question by its very nature can never be settled. Even George Orwell, that uncompromising defender of the writer's freedom, felt obligated to work as a propagandist for the BBC Indian Service during the Second World War. New evidence reveals, however, that he resigned largely because he could not endure the censorship of his work by the Ministry of Information, to which the BBC was responsible in wartime.[7]

Certainly the lessons taught by the propaganda efforts of the Allies in the Great War have been salutary. Ever since then, writers have been far more aware of the nature of the modern state and of their responsibility towards truth. A healthy scepticism about group effort in support of a cause is usually to be found in any community of writers. It is hard to believe that any government in Britain, the United States, or Canada could secretly assemble round a table twenty-five of its most important writers and persuade them to dedicate their efforts to writing in support of a war.

NOTES

NOTES TO CHAPTER ONE

1. Harold Innis, *The Bias of Communication*, ed. Marshall McLuhan (Toronto: University of Toronto Press, 1951), p. 78.
2. Quoted by Alan Sandison, *The Wheel of Empire* (London: Macmillan, 1967), pp. 6-7.
3. See Sandison's treatment of these four authors in *The Wheel of Empire*.
4. Christopher Martin, *The Edwardians* (London: Wayland, 1974), p. 11.
5. C. F. G. Masterman, *The Condition of England* (London: Methuen, 1909), p. 249.
6. *The Times*, 18 July 1914.
7. Bernard Bergonzi, "Before 1914: Writers and the Threat of War," *Critical Quarterly* 6 (Summer 1964): 126.
8. I. F. Clarke, *Voices Prophesying War, 1763-1984* (Oxford: Oxford University Press, 1966), pp. 144-52.
9. Arthur Conan Doyle, *The German War* (London: Hodder and Stoughton, 1914), pp. 143-52.
10. H. G. Wells, *The Country of the Blind and Other Stories* (London: Nelson, 1911), p. 415.
11. George Dangerfield, *The Strange Death of Liberal England* (London: McGibbon and Kee, 1961), p. 371.

NOTES TO CHAPTER TWO

1. William Wordsworth, *Poems*, vol. 2 (London: Longman, Hurst, Rees, Orne, and Brown, 1815), pp. 238, 241.
2. A. Conan Doyle, *The War in South Africa: Its Causes and Conduct* (London: Smith, Elder, 1902), p. 107.
3. S. K. Ratcliffe, "English Intellectuals in War-Time," *Century Magazine* 94 (October 1917): 826-27.
4. Edith Wharton, *A Backward Glance* (New York: Appleton-Century, 1934), pp. 336-38.
5. *The Letters of Henry James*, ed. Percy Lubbock (New York: Scribner's, 1920), 2:286.
6. *The Selected Letters of Henry James*, ed. with an introduction by Leon Edel (New York: Anchor, 1960), p. 213.
7. Quoted by Norman and Jean Mackenzie in *H. G. Wells: A Biography* (New York: Simon and Schuster, 1973), p. 297.
8. *New York Times*, 5 August 1914, 3:1. The article was actually printed the day Britain declared war on Germany.
9. Eric J. Leed, *No Man's Land: Conflict & Identity in World War I* (Cambridge: Cambridge University Press, 1979), chapter 2.
10. L. C. F. Turner, *Origins of the First World War* (London: Arnold, 1970), p. 112.
11. Richard Harding Davis, *With the Allies* (London: Duckworth, 1915), pp. 22-28.
12. In Emmet Crozier, *American Reporters on the Western Front, 1914-1918* (New York: Oxford University Press, 1959), pp. 41-42. This is a comprehensive account of the work of American correspondents and of the immense difficulties they faced, and sometimes overcame, with the censors.
13. Ironically, Lord Haldane was later forced to resign from the Cabinet for his alleged German sympathies.
14. Lucy Masterman, *C. F. G. Masterman* (London: Cassells, 1939), p. 272.
15. In *British Propaganda during the First World War, 1914-1918* (London: Macmillan, 1982), chapter 1, M. L. Sanders and Philip M. Taylor speculate that Wellington House was chosen because it had organized a successful publicity campaign to explain

the benefits of the National Insurance Act.

16. The list appears in Lucy Masterman's biography of her husband, p. 272.

17. Charles Mallett, *Anthony Hope and His Books* (London: Hutchinson, 1930), p. 243.

18. *The Journals of Arnold Bennett*, ed. Frank Swinnerton (Harmondsworth: Penguin, 1971), p. 379.

19. Hardy did write a few patriotic poems, including "A Call to National Service," but his only really abusive remarks about the Germans are the last lines of "The Pity of It":

Sinister, ugly, lurid be their fame;
May their familiars grow to shun
    their name
And their breed perish everlastingly.
(*Moments of Vision* |London: Macmillan, 1917|, p. 230).

20. Ivor Nicholson, "An Aspect of British Official Wartime Propaganda," *Cornhill Magazine* (May 1931): 593-606.

21. The most complete record of the organization, methods, content of British propaganda in the Great War is Sanders and Taylor's *British Propaganda during the First World War, 1914-18.*

22. Public Record Office, London (PRO), Ministry of Information, Files 4/4a.

23. PRO, Inf, 4/11.

24. Cate Haste, *Keep the Home Fires Burning* (London: Lane, 1977), p. 94.

25. Parker's activities in this period are documented in J. C. Adams's *Seated with the Mighty: A Biography of Sir Gilbert Parker* (Ottawa: Borealis, 1979), chapter 14.

26. PRO, Inf., 4/5.

27. PRO, Inf., 4/11.

28. PRO, Inf., 4/5.

29. PRO, Inf., 4/5.

NOTES TO CHAPTER THREE

1. Paul Fussell, *The Great War and Modern Memory* (New York and London: Oxford University Press), pp. 8-35.

2. *The Letters of Arnold Bennett*, ed. James Hepburn (London: Oxford University Press, 1968), 2:349.

3. Sir Arthur Conan Doyle, *To Arms!* (London: Hodder and Stoughton, 1914), p. 13.

4. There is considerable confusion about Kipling's activities and commitments as a propagandist. His biographer, C. E. Carrington, asserts that while he was repeatedly asked to write propaganda for the government, he refused to do so (*Rudyard Kipling: His Life and Work* |London: Macmillan, 1955|, p. 429). Masterman, on the other hand, wrote in a cabinet memorandum to Sir Edward Grey that his whole activity had been devoted to preventing the Kiplings from writing propaganda, but his only hope in stopping them would be to get them locked up "as a danger to the State" (Lucy Masterman, *C. F. G. Masterman*, p. 277). Kipling himself, in a letter to Lord Beaverbrook of 5 March 1918, recommending a literary agent who had worked for Wellington House, stated that Watt had written to him |Kipling| many times in the past few years "saying that Wellington House wanted to do so and so, and would like to include such and such a

bit of my work" (copy of holograph letter from Kipling to Beaverbrook, Lord Beaverbrook Papers, House of Lords Record Office, File c/199). The evidence suggests that Kipling did write propaganda quite often at the request of various government departments.

5. Rudyard Kipling, *The New Army* (New York: Doubleday and Page, 1914), 4, "Canadians in Camp," 5, 11. These pamphlets were also collected and published the following year in London under the title *The New Army in Training* (Macmillan).

6. Ibid., 5, "Indian Troops," p. 7.

7. Ibid., 6, "A Territorial Battalion and a Conclusion," p. 9.

8. H. C. Peterson, *Propaganda for War: The Campaign against American Neutrality* (Norman: University of Oklahoma Press, 1939), p. 58.

9. See also Sanders and Taylor for the Wellington House exploitation of the Lusitania medal incident, pp. 130-31.

10. Sir Gilbert Parker, *What Is the Matter with England?* (London: Darling, 1915), p. 10.

11. Sir Gilbert Parker, *Is England Apathetic? A Reply* (London: Darling, 1915), p. 11.

12. Sir Gilbert Parker, *The World in the Crucible: An Account of the Origins and*

Conduct of the Great War (London: Murray, 1915), p. 76.

13. PRO, Inf. 4/11.

14. Anthony Hope Hawkins, *The New (German) Testament: Some Texts and a Commentary* (London: Methuen, 1914), p. 59.

15. Gerhard Ritter, *The Sword and the Sceptre*, trans. Heinz Norden (Coral Gables, FL: University of Miami Press, 1972), p. 113.

16. Quoted by Stanley Weintraub in *Journey to Heartbreak: The Crucible Years of Bernard Shaw, 1914-1918* (New York: Weybright

and Talley, 1971), p. 29.

17. George Bernard Shaw, *Common Sense about the War*, *The New Statesman*, Special War Supplement, 14 November 1914, p. 5.

18. *New York Times*, 18 November 1914, p. 3.

19. Quoted by Weintraub in *Journey to Heartbreak*, p. 138.

20. *New York Times*, 9 July 1916, 5:2.

21. *Journey to Heartbreak*, p. 229.

NOTES TO CHAPTER FOUR

1. G. K. Chesterton, *The Crimes of England* (London: Palmer and Hayward, 1915), p. 126.

2. Hilaire Belloc, *The Two Maps of Europe* (London: Pearson, 1915), p. 102.

3. Robert Speaight, *The Life of Hilaire Belloc* (London: Hollis and Carter, 1957), pp. 355-56.

4. *The Letters of Arnold Bennett*, ed. James Hepburn (London: Oxford University Press, 1968), 2:351.

5. Arnold Bennett, *Liberty: A Statement of the British Case* (London: Hodder and Stoughton, 1914), pp. 28-29.

6. Ibid., pp. 42, 46, 47, 58.

7. *The Letters of Arnold Bennett*, 1:237.

8. "English Intellectuals in War-Time," p. 828.

9. John Galsworthy, *A Sheaf* (London: Heinemann, 1916), p. 173.

10. Ford Madox Ford, *Return to Yesterday: Reminiscences 1884-1914* (London: Gollancz, 1931), pp. 423-44.

11. Lucy Masterman, *C. F. G. Masterman*, pp. 259-60.

12. *The Outlook*, 34, 8 August 1914, pp. 174-75.

13. Ibid., 24 August 1914, pp. 270-76.

14. Ford Madox Hueffer, *When Blood Is Their Argument: An Analysis of Prussian Culture* (London: Hodder and Stoughton, 1915), p. 23.

15. Ford Madox Hueffer, *Between St. Dennis and St. George: A Sketch of Three Civilizations* (London: Hodder and Stoughton, 1915), p. 206.

16. Ibid., p. 66.

17. Ibid., p. 193.

18. Ibid., pp. 202-3.

19. *When Blood Is Their Argument*, pp. x-xi.

20. Thomas Moser, *The Life in Fiction of*

Ford Madox Ford (Princeton, NJ: Princeton University Press, 1980), p. 199.

21. Gilbert Murray, *Faith, War, and Policy* (London: Oxford University Press, 1918), p. 7.

22. Gilbert Murray, *The Foreign Policy of Sir Edward Grey, 1906-1915* (Oxford: Clarendon Press, 1915), pp. 9-10.

23. Murray, *Faith, War, and Policy*, p. 45.

24. Ibid., p. 81.

25. Ibid., pp. 91-92.

26. Letter by John Buchan to Gilbert Murray, 19 February 1918, Buchan Papers, Queen's University Library, Kingston, Ontario.

27. *The Autobiography of Bertrand Russell, 1914-1944* (London: Allen and Unwin, 1967), pp. 11, 16-17.

28. Ibid., pp. 42-43.

29. Lawrence's tortured wartime career is chronicled in Paul Delany's *D. H. Lawrence's Nightmare: The Writer and His Circle in the Years of the Great War* (New York: Basic Books, 1978).

30. Bertrand Russell, *Justice in War-Time* (London: Allen and Unwin, 1916), p. 1.

31. Ibid., p. 3.

32. Ibid., pp. 13-14.

33. Edmund Gosse, *Inter Arma, Being Essays Written in Time of War* (London: Heinemann, 1916), p. iv.

34. Ibid., p. 3.

35. Ibid., p. 4.

36. Ibid., p. 31.

37. Ibid., p. 35.

38. Ibid., pp. 37-38.

NOTES TO CHAPTER FIVE

1. Denis Mackail, *The Story of J. M. B.: A Biography* (London: Davies, 1941), pp. 473-74.
2. C. Hartley Grattan, *Why We Fought* (New York: Vanguard, 1929), p. 54.
3. Roger Lancelyn Green, *A.E.W. Mason* (London: Parrish, 1952), p. 136.
4. *New York Times*, 19 September 1914, p. 5.
5. *Sixty American Opinions on the War*, ed. by S. R. H. and J. F. M. (London: T. Fisher Unwin, 1915), p. 93. The editors, Samuel Robertson Honey and James Fullerton Muirhead, were American citizens. Muirhead was born in Scotland, lived in London and the United States, and was the publisher of *The Blue Guides* to Europe. Honey was born in England, fought in the American Civil War, and then became a lawyer in Rhode Island. He served for a term as lieutenant-governor of the state.
6. *The Letters of Theodore Roosevelt*, ed. E. E. Morrison, *et al.* (Cambridge, MA: Harvard University Press, 1954), 8:884.
7. Theodore Roosevelt, *America and the World War* (Toronto: McLeod and Allen, 1915), p. xv.
8. Ibid., p. 2.
9. *The Letters of Theodore Roosevelt*, 7:922n.
10. Mrs. Humphry Ward, *England's Effort: Six Letters to an American Friend* (London: Smith, Elder, 1916), p. vii.
11. Ibid., p. 151.
12. Janet Penross Trevelyan, *The Life of Mrs. Humphry Ward* (New York: Dodd, Mead, 1923), p. 281.
13. Mrs. Humphry Ward, *Towards the Goal* (London: Murray, 1917), p. 57.
14. Henry James, *Within the Rim and Other Essays, 1914-1915* (London: Collins, 1918), p. 14.
15. Ibid., p. 35.
16. Ibid., p. 45.
17. Ibid., p. 77.
18. Ibid., pp. 89-91.
19. Ibid., p. 30.
20. Quoted from Hunt's *The Flurried Years* in Simon Nowell Smith's *The Legend of The Master: Henry James* (New York:

Scribner's, 1948), p. 163.
21. *New York Times*, 21 March 1915, 5:3-4.
22. Michael S. Reynolds, *Hemingway's First War: The Making of "A Farewell to Arms"* (Princeton, NJ: Princeton University Press, 1976), pp. 60-62.
23. Ernest Hemingway, *A Farewell to Arms* (New York: Scribner's, 1929), p. 191.
24. For details of her heroic efforts, see R.W.B. Lewis, *Edith Wharton, A Biography* (New York: Harper and Row, 1975), pp. 365-71, and her own account in *A Backward Glance* (New York: Appleton-Century, 1934).
25. Edith Wharton, *Fighting France, From Dunkerque to Belfort* (New York: Appleton-Century, 1915), p. 234.
26. For a brief account of Conrad's propaganda activities, see Avrom Fleischman, *Conrad's Politics* (Baltimore, MD: Johns Hopkins University Press, 1967), pp. 44-45.
27. *The Book of the Homeless*, ed. Edith Wharton (Boston and London: Macmillan, 1916), p. 31.
28. Ibid., p. 45.
29. *The Letters of Henry James*, ed. Percy Lubbock (London: Macmillan, 1920), 2:393.
30. Typescript holograph letter, Henry James to Owen Wister, Wister Papers, Manuscript Division, Library of Congress, Washington, DC.
31. Owen Wister, *The Pentecost of Calamity* (London: Macmillan, 1915), p. 74.
32. Owen Wister, *Roosevelt: The Story of a Friendship, 1880-1919* (New York: Macmillan, 1930), pp. 351-52.
33. Holograph letter, Wister Papers.
34. Holograph letter, Parker to Wister, 21 September 1915, Wister Papers.
35. *Voices From the Great War*, ed. Peter Vansittart (London: Cape, 1981), p. 513.
36. Stanley Cooperman, *World War I and the American Novel* (Baltimore, MD: Johns Hopkins University Press, 1967), p. 34.
37. H. L. Mencken, *Prejudices: A Selection*, ed. James T. Farrell (New York: Vintage, 1958), p. 105.

NOTES TO CHAPTER SIX

1. James R. Mock and Cedric Larson, *Words That Won the War* (Princeton, NJ:

Princeton University Press, 1939), p. 4.
2. Harold Lasswell, *Propaganda Techniques*

in the World War (1927, repr. New York: Garland, 1972), p. 118.

3. George Creel, *How We Advertised America* (New York: Arno, 1922), p. 60.
4. Ibid., p. 262.
5. PRO, Inf. 4/11.
6. Buchan to Creel, 1 February 1918, CPI Files, 1A1, National Archives, Washington, DC.
7. CPI Files, 1A1.
8. *Words That Won the War*, pp. 66-74.
9. CPI Files, 3A1.
10. Floyd Dell, *Upton Sinclair: A Study in Social Protest* (New York: Doran, 1927), p. 144.
11. This whole exchange of letters is in the George Creel Papers, Manuscript Division, Library of Congress.
12. I have treated the whole question at greater length in my article "Upton Sinclair and the Socialist Response to World War I," *Canadian Review of American Studies* (Summer 1983): 121-30.
13. *New York Times Current History*, June 1916, p. 461.
14. Quoted by James Woodress in *Booth Tarkington: Gentleman from Indiana* (Philadelphia: Lippincott, 1955), p. 200.
15. Ibid., p. 201.
16. *New York Times*, 27 August 1916, 5:6.
17. *New York Times*, 18 August 1918, 4:2.
18. Gertrude Atherton, *Adventures of a Novelist* (London: Cape, 1932), p. 513.
19. Creel to Wilson, 24 May 1920, Creel Papers, Library of Congress.

NOTES TO CHAPTER SEVEN

1. *The Letters of Arnold Bennett*, 2:364n.
2. Kinley E. Roby, *A Writer at War: Arnold Bennett 1914-1918* (Baton Rouge, LA: Louisiana State University Press, 1972), p. 140.
3. Ibid., p. 139.
4. *The Journals of Arnold Bennett*, p. 392.
5. Arnold Bennett, *Over There, War Scenes on the Western Front* (London: Methuen, 1915), p. 128.
6. Ibid., p. 76.
7. Ibid., pp. 96-97.
8. Ibid., pp. 183, 257.
9. *A Writer at War*, p. 126.
10. Rudyard Kipling, *France at War* (London: Macmillan, 1915), p. 4.
11. Richard Harding Davis, *With the French in France & Salonika* (New York: Scribner's, 1916), pp. 59-60.
12. *France at War*, pp. 25-28.
13. Ibid., pp. 48-50.
14. Ibid., p. 51.
15. Ibid., p. 64.
16. Ibid., pp. 20-21.
17. Rudyard Kipling, *The Fringes of the Fleet* (New York: Doubleday and Page, 1915), 6, "Patrols," pp. 8-9.
18. Rudyard Kipling, *The War in the Mountains* (New York: Scribner's, 1917), 1, "The Roads of an Army," p. 7.
19. Ibid., 5, "The Trentino Front," p. 6.
20. Ibid., 6, "Podgorno," p. 5.
21. Ibid., 6:4.
22. Sir Arthur Conan Doyle, *The German War* (London: Hodder and Stoughton, 1914), p. 78.
23. Sir Arthur Conan Doyle, *Memories and Adventures* (Boston: Little Brown, 1924), p. 349.
24. Sir Arthur Conan Doyle, *A Visit to Three Fronts* (London: Hodder and Stoughton, 1916), p. 14.
25. Ibid., p. 10.
26. Ibid., pp. 48-49.
27. Ibid., p. 72.
28. Ibid., pp. 77-78.
29. For details of this period, see Constance Babington Smith's *John Masefield, A Life* (Oxford: Oxford University Press, 1978), part 3.
30. John Masefield, *Gallipoli* (London: Heinemann, 1916), p. 3.
31. Of the many accounts of the campaign, *Gallipoli* by Robert Rhodes James (New York: Macmillan, 1965) is the best so far.
32. Masefield, *Gallipoli*, p. 33.
33. John Masefield, *The Old Front Line* (New York: Macmillan, 1917), p. 29.
34. Ibid., p. 9.
35. John Buchan, *Nelson's History of the War* (London: Nelson, 1915-19), 5:30-31.
36. Ibid., 5:32.
37. John Buchan, *The Future of the War* (London: Hodder and Stoughton, 1916), pp. 13-14.
38. MS Letter, John Buchan to Susan Buchan, 27 June 1916. Buchan Archive, Queen's University Library.
39. John Buchan, *The Battle of the Somme:*

First Phase (London: Nelson, 1916), p. 16.
40. Ibid., p. 31.
41. The Great War and Modern Memory, p. 178.
42. The Battle of the Somme: First Phase, p. 83.
43. Ibid., p. 58.
44. Basil Liddell Hart, A History of the World War 1914-1918 (London: Faber and Faber, 1934), p. 315.
45. In Col. Howard Green's introduction to John Masefield's, The Old Front Line, (Bourne End, Bucks.: Sparbooks, 1972), p. 50.
46. Martin Middlebrook, The First Day on the Somme, 1 July 1916 (London: Lane, 1971), p. 264.
47. Buchan, The Battle of the Somme: First Phase, p. 35.
48. John Buchan to Susan Buchan, 1 July 1916, Buchan Archive, Queen's University Library.
49. Buchan, The Battle of the Somme: First Phase, pp. 63-66.
50. Hart, A History of the World War, pp. 324-25.
51. Buchan, The Battle of the Somme: First Phase, pp. 98-105.
52. Ibid., p. 71.
53. Hart, A History of the World War, p. 326.
54. John Buchan, The Battle of the Somme: Second Phase (London: Nelson, 1917), p. 21.
55. Ibid., pp. 27-28.
56. Ibid., pp. 75-76.
57. Middlebrook, The First Day on the Somme, p. 295.
58. A. J. P. Taylor, The First World War: An

Illustrated History (Harmondsworth: Penguin, 1966), p. 140.
59. Hart, A History of the World War, p. 327.
60. Arthur Marder, From Dreadnought to Scapa Flow (London: Oxford University Press, 1966), 3:177.
61. The First Day on the Somme, p. 282.
62. John Buchan, Memory Hold-the-Door (London: Hodder and Stoughton, 1940), p. 177.
63. A full account of Sir Max Aitken's wartime activities can be found in A. J. P. Taylor's Beaverbrook: A Biography (New York: Simon and Schuster, 1972), chapter 5. My account owes a good deal to the "Report on the Joint Establishment of the Canadian War Records," submitted by Max Aitken, the officer in charge, to Sir Robert Borden, 16 March 1916, Public Archives of Canada, Borden Papers, MG 26, H, vol. 64.
64. Hart, A History of the World War, 1914-1918, p. 253.
65. Sir Max Aitken, Canada in Flanders (London, New York, Toronto: Hodder and Stoughton, 1916), 1:78-81.
66. Borden papers, PAC, vol. 75, File C4318.
67. Charles G. D. Roberts, Canada in Flanders, 3:121.
68. This imbroglio is reported in two confidential letters, Beckles Willson to Sir Sam Hughes, 21 August 1916, and Sir Max Aitken to Sir Robert Borden, 25 September 1916. Borden Papers, PAC, vol. 64, File C4311.
69. Beckles Willson, In the Ypres Salient: The Story of a Fortnight's Fighting, June 2-16 (London: Simpkin, Marshall, Hamilton, Kent, n.d.), pp. 11-13.

NOTES TO CHAPTER EIGHT

1. Arthur Machen, The Bowmen and Other Legends of the War (London: Simpkin, Marshall, 1915), pp. 35-38.
2. Ibid., p. 11.
3. Ibid., p. 15.
4. Ibid., pp. 83-84.
5. Harold Begbie, On the Side of the Angels (London: Hodder and Stoughton, 1915), p. 9.
6. Ibid., p. 57.
7. Phyllis Campbell, Back of the Front (London: Newnes, n.d. [1915]), p. 114.
8. A. J. P. Taylor, The First World War, p. 29.

9. Rudyard Kipling, A Diversity of Creatures (New York: Scribner's, 1917), pp. 485-86.
10. J. M. S. Tompkins, The Art of Rudyard Kipling (London: Methuen, 1959), p. 135.
11. A Diversity of Creatures, p. 511.
12. Ibid., pp. 512-13.
13. The Strange Ride of Rudyard Kipling, p. 302.
14. A Diversity of Creatures, p. 514.
15. Rudyard Kipling, Debits and Credits (London: Macmillan, 1927), p. 27.
16. Ibid., p. 47.
17. Letter to the author from C.E. Carrington,

30 March 1973.

18. Material for this section is drawn in part from Janet Adam Smith's *John Buchan: A Biography* (London: Hart-Davis, 1968).

19. John Buchan, *The Thirty-Nine Steps and the Power House* (London: Nelson, 1945), p. 16.

20. Ibid., p. 51.

21. For a discussion of this scheme and other motifs in Buchan's wartime thrillers, see *The Interpreter's House: A Critical Assessment of John Buchan*, by David Daniell (London: Hodder and Stoughton, 1975), pp. 118-43.

22. John Buchan, *Greenmantle* (London, 1916), p. 15.

23. Ibid., pp. 107-8.

24. Sir Arthur Conan Doyle, *His Last Bow: Some Reminiscences of Sherlock Holmes* (London: Murray, 1917), pp. 299-300.

25. James M. Barrie, *Der Tag* (London: Hodder and Stoughton, 1915), pp. 20-42.

26. Denis Mackail, *The Story of J. M. B.: A Biography*, pp. 437-44.

27. James M. Barrie, *Echoes of the War* (London: Hodder and Stoughton, 1918), pp. 76-77.

28. *The Great War and Modern Memory*, p. 28.

29. Ian Hay, *The First Hundred Thousand, Being the Unofficial Chronicle of a Unit of "K(1)"* (Edinburgh and London: Blackwood, 1916), pp. 120-21.

30. Ibid., p. 199.

31. Ibid., p. 338.

32. *The First World War*, 99.

33. *The First Hundred Thousand*, 341.

34. Ian Hay, *Carrying On—After the First Hundred Thousand*, (Edinburgh and London: Wm. Blackwood, 1917), p. 5.

35. Ibid., p. 173.

36. Ibid., p. 183.

37. Ibid., p. 184.

NOTES TO CHAPTER NINE

1. Viola Hunt and Ford Madox Hueffer, *Zeppelin Nights: A London Entertainment* (London: Lane, 1916), p. 1.

2. Ibid., p. 7.

3. Ibid., pp. 169-70.

4. Ibid., p. 245.

5. Ibid., p. 283.

6. Ibid., p. 307.

7. *Return to Yesterday*, p. 220.

8. G. K. Chesterton, *Autobiography* (London: Hutchinson, 1936), p. 247.

9. H. G. Wells, *The War That Will End War* (London: Palmer, 1914), p. 91.

10. Ibid., p. 99.

11. *Experiment in Autobiography*, 2:670-71.

12. Lovat Dickson, *H. G. Wells: His Turbulent Life and Times* (London: Macmillan, 1969), p. 261.

13. H.G. Wells, *Mr. Britling Sees It Through* (New York: Macmillan, 1916), pp. 46-47.

14. Ibid., p. 163.

15. Ibid., p. 283.

16. Ibid., p. 405.

17. Lovat Dickson, *H. G. Wells*, p. 267.

18. *Mr. Britling Sees It Through*, p. 437.

19. Robert Graves, *Goodbye to All That* (New York: Anchor Books, 1957), p. 250.

20. *Arnold Bennett in Love*, ed. George and Jean Beardmore (London: David Bruce and Watson, 1972), pp. 92-93.

21. "Arnold Bennett," in *Columbia Essays on Modern Writers*, no. 23, ed. by William York Tindall (New York: Columbia University Press, 1967), pp. 34-35.

22. Arnold Bennett, *The Pretty Lady* (London: Cassell, 1918), p. 217.

23. Ibid., p. 90.

24. Ibid., p. 160.

25. James G. Kennedy, "Reassuring Facts in *The Pretty Lady* and *Lord Raingo* and Modern Novels," *English Literature in Transition: 1880-1920* 7 (1964): 133-35.

26. *The Pretty Lady*, pp. 165-66.

27. Ibid., p. 350.

28. Ibid., p. 351.

29. Ibid., p. 171.

30. John Galsworthy, *Saint's Progress* (London: Heinemann, 1918), p. 176.

31. Ibid., pp. 177-79.

32. Ibid., pp. 236-37.

33. Ibid., p. 403.

NOTES TO CHAPTER TEN

1. Nicholson, "Official Wartime Propaganda," p. 603.
2. *Autobiography*, p. 251.
3. Frances Stevenson, *Lloyd George: A Diary*, ed. by A. J. P. Taylor (New York: Harper and Row, 1971), p. 25.
4. Ibid., p. 120.
5. In *Art at the Service at War, Canada, Art and the Great War* (Toronto: Univ. of Toronto Press, 1984), Maria Tippett also discusses some of the British propaganda department's use of artists to depict the war.
6. Janet Adam Smith, *John Buchan*, p. 200.
7. MS letter, F. S. Oliver to John Buchan, 8 February 1917, Buchan Archive, Queen's University Library.
8. Ezra Pound to C. F. G. Masterman, *Agenda*, vol. 23, nos. 3-4 (Autumn-Winter 1985/86) p. 136.
9. *British Propaganda during the First World War, 1914-1918*, p. 147.
10. Nicholson, "Official Wartime Propaganda," p. 604.
11. MS letter, Buchan to Beaverbrook, 14 February 1918, House of Lords Record Office, Westminster, File c/134.
12. *Beaverbrook*, pp. 137-38.
13. Quoted by Nicholson, "Official Wartime Propaganda," pp. 605-6.
14. Copy of a letter by Lord Beaverbrook to C. E. Carrington, 8 December 1954, Beaverbrook Papers, House of Lords, General Correspondence.
15. Memo by Kipling to Beaverbrook, Beaverbrook Papers, House of Lords, c/199.
16. Telegram, Beaverbrook to Kipling, c/199.
17. *The Letters of Arnold Bennett*, 1:263.
18. *Experiment in Autobiography*, 2:697.
19. *British Propaganda during the First World War*, p. 82.
20. *The Great War and Modern Memory*, p. 87.
21. PRO, Inf. 4/9. This memorandum is quite different from the one by Wells printed in Sir Campbell Stuart's *Secrets of Crewe House* (London: Hodder and Stoughton, 1920), pp. 61-81.
22. *Autobiography*, 2:266.
23. MS copy of a letter, Bennett to Beaverbrook, 19 October 1918, Beaverbrook Papers, c/31.
24. *The Letters of Arnold Bennett*, 1:266.
25. Ford Madox Ford, *It Was the Nightingale*, pp. 18-20.

NOTES TO CHAPTER ELEVEN

1. Peter Lowe, "The Rise to the Premiership, 1914-1916," in *Lloyd George, Twelve Essays*, ed. A.J.P. Taylor (London: Hamilton, 1971), p. 121.
2. Lord Newton, *Lord Lansdowne, A Biography*, (London: Macmillan, 1929), p. 467.
3. Ibid., pp. 468-69.
4. H. G. Wells, *In the Fourth Year: Anticipations of a World Peace* (London: Chatto and Windus, 1918), p. 76.
5. *Lord Lansdowne, A Biography*, p. 470.
6. *The New York Times Current History*, March 1918, p. 452.
7. *The Tribunal*, 6 December 1917, p. 2.
8. David Lloyd George, *War Memoirs*, (London: Odham's, 1937), 2:1205-6.
9. Ibid., 2:1315.
10. Ibid., 2:1329.
11. *Lord Lansdowne, A Biography*, p. 478.
12. *The Great War and Modern Memory*, p. 79.
13. *In the Fourth Year*, pp. 155-56.
14. *The Life of Bertrand Russell*, pp. 321-24. Sassoon's ironic and self-mocking treatment of this episode in *Memoirs of an Infantry Officer* is accepted at its face value by Paul Fussell. At the time, it was an important gesture for Sassoon. If it had not been so cleverly hushed up, it might well have been an effective protest against the war.
15. *The Life of Bertrand Russell*, p. 290.
16. Russell, *Autobiography*, p. 52.
17. *Experiment in Autobiography*, 2:707.
18. James Morgan Read, *Atrocity Propaganda* (New Haven, CT: Yale University Press, 1941), p. viii.

NOTES TO CHAPTER TWELVE

1. *The Short Stories of Ernest Hemingway* (New York: Scribner's, 1938), p. 243.
2. C. E. Montague, *Disenchantment* (London: McGibbon and Kee, 1922, repr. 1968), p. 74.
3. Ibid., pp. 76-77.
4. Ibid., p. 96.
5. Ibid., p. 136.
6. Wharton, *A Backward Glance*, p. 369.
7. Edith Wharton, *A Son at the Front* (New York: Scribner's, 1923), pp. 187-88.
8. Ibid., p. 423.
9. Ralph Connor, *The Sky Pilot in No Man's Land* (Toronto: McClelland and Stewart, 1919), p. 303.
10. Beckles Willson, *Redemption* (London and New York: Putman's, 1924), pp. 388-94.
11. Ibid., p. 396.
12. The fiction of the period is discussed in Crawford Kilian's unpublished MA thesis, "The Great War and the Canadian Novel, 1915-1926," Simon Fraser University, 1972.
13. John Galsworthy, *The Burning Spear* (London: Heinemann, 1925), p. 176.
14. Ibid., pp. 176-79.
15. Ibid., p. 187.
16. Ibid., pp. 225-26.
17. Ibid., pp. 242-43.
18. Arthur Mizener, *The Saddest Story: A Biography of Ford Madox Ford* (Cleveland: World, 1971), p. 288. My account of Ford's military career is largely based on Mizener's study.
19. Ford Madox Ford, *No Enemy: A Tale of Reconstruction* (New York: Macaulay, 1929), pp. 203-4.
20. *The First Day on the Somme*, p. 289.
21. *It Was the Nightingale* pp. 161-62.
22. Ibid., pp. 224-25.
23. Ford Madox Ford, *No More Parades* in *The Bodley Head Ford Madox Ford*, ed. Graham Greene (London: Bodley Head, 1963), 4:28.
24. *No Enemy*, p. 203.
25. *The Novels and Tales of Henry James* (New York: Scribner's, 1907), 11:xi.
26. *It Was the Nightingale*, pp. 63-64.
27. This is not the place for an extended analysis of *Parade's End*. In any case a good deal of excellent criticism of the tetralogy appears in the following studies: Paul L. Wiley's *Novelist of Three Worlds: Ford Madox Ford* (Syracuse, NY: Syracuse University Press, 1962); Carol Ohman's

Ford Madox Ford: From Apprenticeship to Craftsman (Middletown, CT: Wesleyan University Press, 1964); Ambrose Gordon's *The Invisible Tent: The War Novels of Ford Madox Ford* (Austin: The University of Texas Press, 1964); Thomas C. Moser's *The Life in the Fiction of Ford Madox Ford* (Princeton: Princeton University Press, 1980); and Robert Green's *Ford Madox Ford: Prose and Politics* (Cambridge: Cambridge University Press, 1981).
28. See above, pp. 7-8.
29. *Some Do Not . . .* , in *The Bodley Head Ford Madox Ford*, 3:78.
30. Ibid., 34. The line in Ford's original poem reads: "Some rest on snowy bosoms! Some do not!" ("Mr. Bosporus and the Muses," 1922).
31. Ibid., p. 46.
32. Ibid., pp. 293-94.
33. *No More Parades*, in *The Bodley Head Ford Madox Ford*, 4:16-17.
34. Robert Green, *Ford Madox Ford: Prose and Politics*, p. 157.
35. Ibid., p. 156.
36. *A Man Could Stand Up*, in *The Bodley Head Ford Madox Ford*, 4:452.
37. Ibid., p. 340.
38. Ibid., p. 415.
39. *Ford Madox Ford: Prose and Politics*, p. 166.
40. Quoted by Green, ibid., p. 166.
41. *A Man Could Stand Up*, p. 452.
42. H. G. Wells, *Joan and Peter: the Story of an Education* (London: Cassell, 1918), p. 579.
43. Ibid., p. 582.
44. Ibid., pp. 685-86.
45. Ibid., pp. 693-94.
46. Ibid., p. 718.
47. Bennett, *Journals*, 2:206.
48. H. G. Wells, *The Bulpington of Blup: Adventures, Poses, Stresses, Conflicts, and Disasters in a Contemporary Mind* (Toronto: Macmillan, 1933), p. 315.
49. Ibid., p. 348.
50. Ibid., p. 408.
51. Ibid., p. 412.
52. Ibid., p. 209.
53. *The Strange Ride of Rudyard Kipling*, 304-5.
54. Rudyard Kipling, *The Irish Guards in the Great War. Collected Works* (New York:

Macmillan, 1941), 22:14.
55. *Rudyard Kipling*, p. 442.
56. *Rudyard Kipling, Verse*, definitive edition (London: Hodder and Stoughton, 1940), pp. 387-88.
57. Rudyard Kipling, *Debits and Credits* (London: Macmillan, 1927), p. 414.
58. Ibid., p. 403.
59. Ibid., p. 61.
60. Ibid., pp. 153-54.
61. *The Great War and Modern Memory*, p. 131.
62. *Debits and Credits*, p. 305.

63. Arnold Bennett, *Lord Raingo* (London: Cassell, 1926), p. 228.
64. See James G. Kennedy, "Reassuring Facts in *The Pretty Lady* and *Lord Raingo* and Modern Novels," *English Literature in Transition, 1880-1920* 7 (1964): 133-35.
65. Ibid., p. 136.
66. *Lord Raingo*, p. 34.
67. Ibid., p. 185.
68. Ibid., p. 190.
69. Ibid., p. 61.
70. Reginald Pound, *Arnold Bennett* (London: Heinemann, 1952), p. 313.
71. *Lord Raingo*, p. 266.

NOTES TO EPILOGUE

1. *The Collected Poems of Wilfred Owen*, ed. with an introduction by C. Day Lewis (London: Chatto and Windus, 1963), p. 42.
2. In Bernard Bergonzi, *Heroes' Twilight: A Study of the Literature of the Great War* (London: Constable, 1965), p. 143.
3. Ezra Pound, *Personae* (London: Faber and Faber, 1952), p. 200.
4. *The Collected Poems of Wilfred Owen*, p. 35.

5. Paul Fussell, *Abroad: British Literary Traveling Between the Wars* (Oxford: Oxford University Press, 1980), pp. 4-15.
6. See *Authors Take Side on Vietnam*, ed. Cecil Woolf and John Bagguley (London: Owen), 1967. The Spanish War questionnaire is reprinted in this book on p. vii, and Eliot's and Pound's answers are reprinted on p. 227.
7. *Orwell: The War Broadcasts*, ed. by W.J. West (London: Duckworth, 1985), pp. 54-57.

BIBLIOGRAPHICAL NOTE

Propaganda and propaganda techniques have been extensively studied since the 1930s. I shall list here only the books and articles that I have found particularly useful. A pioneering but still essential study is Harold Lasswell's *Propaganda Techniques in the World War* (1938. Reprint. New York: Garland, 1972). The most complete study of the organization and distribution of propaganda by the Allied nations is in the Hoover War Library Publications: George Bruntz's *Allied Propaganda and the Collapse of the German Empire in 1918* (Stanford, CA: Stanford University Press, 1938). The book contains a thorough bibliography of work done in the field up to that time. A recent study by Cate Haste called *Keep the Home Fires Burning: Propaganda in the First World War* (London: Lane, 1977) broadly surveys the whole field of British propaganda in the Great War. Miss Haste, however, made only passing references to the role played by writers in this effort. The pioneering study that partially revealed the writers' contribution to the war was made by J. D. Squires in *British Propaganda at Home and in the United States from 1914 to 1917* (Cambridge, MA: Harvard University Press, 1935). Two subsequent books amplify Squires's researches: H. C. Peterson's *Propaganda for War: the Campaign against American Neutrality, 1914-1917* (Norman: University of Oklahoma Press, 1935), and James Morgan Read's *Atrocity Propaganda: 1914-1919* (New Haven, CT: Yale University Press, 1941). Since the publication of these three books, more material about British propaganda in the Great War has become available in the Public Record Office. A book making use of some of this material has recently been published by M. L. Sanders and Philip M. Taylor, *British Propaganda during the First World War, 1914-1918* (London: Macmillan, 1982). The book deals with the organization of propaganda and chronicles some of the struggles and intrigues over its direction between the Foreign Office, the Home Office, and the service departments.

Although many of the archives concerning British propaganda during the Great War appear not to have survived, there is a copy of the catalogue of British propaganda publications in the library of the Imperial War Museum in London: *Schedule of Wellington House Literature*, marked *Confidential*. It is not dated but, with additions, is brought up to the completion date of

26 November 1918. The *Schedule* contains 1162 items in the form of books, pamphlets, and miscellaneous publications. This, so far as I have been able to discover, is the only extant copy.

On the American side, James R. Mock and Cedric Larson made a good study of the Committee for Public Information in *Words That Won the War: The Story of the Committee on Public Information* (Princeton, NJ: Princeton University Press, 1939). Stephen Vaughn has had access to subsequently released material in writing *Holding Fast the Inner Lines: Democracy, Nationalism, and the Committee for Public Information* (Chapel Hill: University of North Carolina Press, 1980). This is a richly documented but rather uncritical account of the CPI and its role in helping create "the imperial presidency." The role of American journalists has been studied by Emmet Crozier in *American Reporters on the Western Front, 1914-1918* (New York: Oxford University Press, 1959), and Philip Knightley has written trenchantly of reporters, British and American, in *The First Casualty: From the Crimea to Vietnam: The War Correspondent as Hero, Propagandist and Myth Maker* (New York: Harcourt Brace Jovanovich, 1975).

There has been no dearth of studies of the younger writers of the Great War. Notable for their broad view of the subject are Stanley Cooperman in *World War I and the American Novel* (Baltimore, MD: Johns Hopkins Press, 1967); and Paul Fussell in *The Great War and Modern Memory* (New York: Oxford University Press, 1975). A German perspective can be found in *The First World War in German Narrative Prose: Essays in Honour of George Wallis Field*, ed. C. N. Genno and H. Wetzel (Toronto: University of Toronto Press, 1980). An international account of writers and the war can be found in *The First World War in Fiction: A Collection of Critical Essays,* ed. Holger Klein (London: Macmillan, 1976).

A substantial historical reassessment of the Great War has been taking place in recent years. Marc Ferro's book *The Great War, 1914-1918* (London: Routledge and Kegan Paul, 1969, translated 1973) led the way. It is a clear and objective account of the beginnings of the war, its nature, and its tragic conclusion. The psychology of the war has preoccupied many writers. In *The Generation of 1914* (Cambridge, MA: Harvard University Press, 1979), Robert Wohl has poignantly described in a "collective biography" the ideals, illusions, and fate of that generation. Finally, Eric J. Leed has brought the new dimension of psychohistory to bear on the question in his study, *No Man's Land: Combat and Identity in World War I* (Cambridge: Cambridge University Press, 1979). It is an uneven but fascinating analysis of the structure of the experience of war, its psychology, its myths, and its neuroses.

INDEX